The Problem of Poetry in the Romantic Period

Also by Mark Storey

CLARE: The Critical Heritage (*editor*)

THE POETRY OF JOHN CLARE: A Critical Introduction

POETRY AND HUMOUR FROM COWPER TO CLOUGH

THE LETTERS OF JOHN CLARE (*editor*)

BYRON AND THE EYE OF APPETITE

THE PRIVATE PAPERS OF HENRY RYECROFT (Gissing) (*editor*)

POETRY AND IRELAND SINCE 1800 (*editor*)

ROBERT SOUTHEY: A Life

The Problem of Poetry in the Romantic Period

Mark Storey

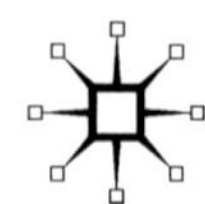

Published by PALGRAVE
Houndmills, Basingstoke, Hampshire RG21 6XS and
175 Fifth Avenue, New York, N. Y. 10010
Companies and representatives throughout the world

PALGRAVE is the new global academic imprint of
St. Martin's Press LLC Scholarly and Reference Division and
Palgrave Publishers Ltd (formerly Macmillan Press Ltd).

Outside North America
ISBN 0–333–73890–X

In North America
ISBN 0–312–23044–3

This book is printed on paper suitable for recycling and made from fully managed and sustained forest sources.

A catalogue record for this book is available from the British Library.

Library of Congress Catalog Card Number: 99–048510

10 9 8 7 6 5 4 3 2
09 08 07 06 05 04 03 02 01

Printed and bound in Great Britain by
Antony Rowe Ltd, Eastbourne

For Tom, Jonny, Hetty, and Hannah

Contents

Preface

> We Poets in our youth begin in gladness;
> But thereof comes in the end despondency and madness.
> (Wordsworth, 'Resolution and Independence')

One of the central curiosities of what we now call Romantic poetry is the variety of claims made on behalf of the Muse, whilst at the same time the Muse's servants doubt the validity of their function. Whereas it could be said that the mid-eighteenth-century poets had a confidence and certainty about what they were doing, the Romantics, for all their fine noises, frequently question the very basis of their faith. To discuss these poets in terms of questioning is not in itself new: L.J. Swingle's book *The Obstinate Questionings of English Romanticism* (1988) sums up in its title the Romantics' search for the right questions, as much as for the right answers; Tilottama Rajan, in *Dark Interpreter* (1980), has set out persuasively the Romantics' doubts about language as a stable medium. Edward Bostetter, as early as 1963, was addressing similar issues in his *Romantic Ventriloquists*, only to earn the severe rebuke of M.H. Abrams in his affirmative *Natural Supernaturalism* (1973). My concern here is something rather different: as the Romantic writers attempt to formulate an idea, or ideas, of what it means to be a poet, they seldom arrive at any kind of consensus. Each poet jumps from one mode to another, hoping, in Wordsworth's phrase, to create 'the taste by which they would be enjoyed'; but many of them fail this very test, for the reason that there is so much uncertainty about the nature of that taste and that enjoyment. There are obviously large aesthetic questions at stake here, and this study aims neither to resolve them nor to give a full account of each and every theoretical statement. Where I hope to be offering a new perspective is in an examination of the ways in which the poets' own aesthetic questionings get entangled in the poetry.

The question of identity is crucial, in that a poetry that tends to define itself in terms of the poet redefines itself in terms of who the poet actually is. Recent work has raised some related issues, particularly from a psychological and phenomenological point of view; some of this is very abstruse, and not to my mind very helpful for a reading of the poetry. I am certainly not trying to duplicate Charles Rzepka's work in *The Self as Mind* (1986), nor Andrea Henderson's more recent book, *Romantic Identities: Varieties of Subjectivity* (1996). I am, of course, only too conscious of such major books as Susan Wolfson's *The Questioning Presence* (1987), Thomas Weiskel's *The Romantic Sublime* (1976), and Andrew Cooper's *Doubt and Identity in Romantic Poetry* (1988). The present study concentrates much more centrally on the nature of the poet, on how each poet struggles with a definition of poetry that involves a definition of the self as poet, and on how this struggle manifests itself in the poetry. I should say here that some of the more obvious poems – Keats's Odes, say, or Wordsworth's 'Immortality Ode' and Coleridge's 'Dejection', let alone 'The Ancient Mariner' – are mentioned only in passing. Michael O'Neill's very recent and valuable book, *Romanticism and the Self-Conscious Poem* (1997), confirmed me in my belief that I need not – indeed, could not – address all the major poems. I have quite often dwelt on apparently less important poems, where the struggles can be seen in greater clarity.

There are clearly many interrelated issues, not all of which can be pursued here: the gradual professionalisation of literature, a phenomenon abhorred by many, including Coleridge; the frequent desire for anonymity (and its connection with the current vogue for the 'authentic'), ranging from the first edition of *Lyrical Ballads* in 1798 to Robert Southey's playing with the reader of his *Doctor* (1837–8, in seven volumes) as to who might have written it. Even Byron considered anonymous publication; many writers toyed with pseudonyms, the funniest being Coleridge's Silas Tomkyns Comberbache (merely to get into, before hurriedly getting out of, the army); John Clare, following as did others in Chatterton's footsteps, was so unsure of his abilities that he occasionally passed himself off as Marvell, Davenant, and even fictitious characters he thought he might get away with, not to mention his later identification with Byron. There is the large question of the language of poetry, which becomes a debate about the nature of language itself. Several recent studies have focused on the gendering of Romantic writing: here again, I am conscious of the fact that all the writers discussed here are male, just as they themselves are often inhibitedly aware of this very fact. But if I do not mention women writers, nor do I have room, alas, for Blake, Landor, Crabbe, Southey, Rogers, Moore, Scott, or Campbell. Every now and then I have wanted to pursue the connections with the prose writers of the period, particularly the Mary Shelley of *Frankenstein*, which brings us up so sharply against the very dangers of the Promethean act of creativity.

Wordsworth's whole poetic life can be seen as a wrestling with the question he puts in the Preface to *Lyrical Ballads*: *The Prelude* becomes an exploration of the contest between private and public, as he peers into the abyss of 'despondency and madness' so central to 'Resolution and Independence': much of the impetus of this study derives from the repeated sense of shock delivered by those famous lines. If *The Excursion* seems to have solved the problem, it could be argued that this is at the expense of the poetry. Coleridge's doubts about his poetic abilities are mirrored in an almost crazy variety of styles and voices, as he presents us with the challenge of so much Romantic poetry: is its task to address the major political upheavals of the age, or is it to nurture the soul in solitude? (Robert Southey can be seen as a voice of the age, in that he writes public poems whilst declaring that he is 'unfit to mingle with the world'; 'the world beyond', he says, 'is not for me'. I regret that in a study about loss and absence I have had to countenance this particular sad loss.) Keats, all of whose poems are about poetry, and therefore about themselves and about the self of the creator, is obviously a central figure in the argument, as is Shelley, the 'unacknowledged legislator' for whom the poet is also one who sings like the nightingale 'to cheer its own solitude'. Byron, the 'pampered egoist' in Hazlitt's telling phrase, is perhaps the most teasing of all the Romantic poets, taking himself the more seriously the more he denies it. Because I have discussed his poetry in detail elsewhere, in the context of the tradition of humour as one means of coping with the vagaries of the self, I have steered my discussion here in a rather different direction. There are fascinating links between Byron and John Clare. Rather like George Darley, who wants to remain unseen and unheard, Clare is the poet on the margins of Romantic discourse; and yet he has, for personal reasons, the best cause to question the nature of his identity. In so doing, he unwittingly demonstrates the central conundrum of Romantic poetics.

There are a few personal points to be made. My own experience has been that any particular piece of work grows out of what has gone before, and that is certainly the case here. Some articles I wrote on aspects of Darley, Byron, and Clare (in, respectively, the *Keats–Shelley Review*, the *Swansea Review*, and the *John Clare Society Journal*, and on which I have drawn here) allowed me to begin speculating on the question of literary identity; to have spent many hours with John Clare is to have been in constant contemplation of the problem; my more recent engagement with Robert Southey was, apart from anything else, an exploration of one particular literary identity, the more interesting for me because Southey has so often been in danger of disappearing from view altogether. Even that odd hero George Gissing has a part to play, in that in *The Private Papers of Henry Ryecroft* he explores the paradox of the writer who 'ought never to have taken to professional authorship at all'.

I have had the inestimable benefit of many cohorts of enthusiastic, questioning students, on whom I have tried out some of the preoccupations that emerge in this book. Generous colleagues and friends have had a role, often unwittingly, in the book's genesis: to spare their blushes at any association they might regret, I do not name them; I hope they know who they are. But I have no hesitation in naming, in the Dedication, the most important people in the whole wide 'unintelligible world'.

Mark Storey
February 1999

1
Lyrical Ballads: 'The burden of the mystery'

Wordsworth and Coleridge are perhaps the two most elusive writers of this period, in terms of the claims they would like to make for poetry. Whereas we can always excuse Keats on the grounds that any 'theoretical' remarks about poetry are thrown out in the midst of letters, Wordsworth and Coleridge both give the impression that they are working to an agenda: advertisements, prefaces, essays, all seem calculated to lend weight to a project they cannot quite define. But that weight can in fact become part of the 'burden of the mystery', and we are left, as with Keats, with the sense of that puzzled and puzzling darkness, rather than with any hoped-for lifting of the burden. I would want to argue that Keats's sense of self-identification with the Wordsworth of 'Tintern Abbey' was in fact healthy, a reminder of the similarities between two poets who are often seen as poles apart. Of course, both Wordsworth and Coleridge were happy to work towards conclusions and solutions (it was one of Coleridge's characteristics that Keats found least congenial): in Wordsworth's case, he presents for us, as early as 1814, in his Prospectus to *The Excursion*, his whole life's work, both what he has done and what he plans to do, as part of a grand scheme. But the famous image of the Gothic cathedral – with *The Prelude* as the mere portico – so grand, religious and affirmative, should not blind us to the fact that he cannot, in the end, get much further than the beginning.

Only those who would value arrival over the journey itself would berate Wordsworth for not completing *The Recluse*: as many have pointed out, the fragment as form is more than just a generic aspect of Romantic poetry, it is a reflection of the desire *not* to finish, a compulsive need on the part of most of the poets to repudiate completion.[1] Different poets confront this in different ways: whereas Coleridge presents 'Kubla Khan' as a fragment, and secondarily as a 'psychological curiosity' (letting himself, he hopes, off the critical hook), Keats acknowledges that he can finish neither version of *Hyperion* (whether we accept his stylistic excuses is another matter); Byron's death put an end to *Don Juan*, but there is a strong sense that, but for his fatal fever at Missolonghi, the itch to write would have kept the poem going for as long as he was interested. Wordsworth's own solution was to return, again and again, to his portico, to *The Prelude*, working at it for most of his creative life. In the process (and that is the important word), he presented himself with several different versions of his own life, even if he was hoping to leave one single version for posterity: it is this organic nature of the poetry of the period ('The Growth of a Poet's Mind') that lends such a tentative air to so much of the writing. For to define poetry – let alone redefine it – requires a definition of the poet.

As early as *Lyrical Ballads* (1798), problems of definition, of expectations (and therefore of the relation between writer and audience) emerge in ways that are crucial, and yet hard to unravel. In this chapter I want to address some of the implications of the volume(s) as a whole: literary history has, after all, and with good reason, often taken 1798 as an absolutely key moment. At the same time, I do not believe it is possible to abstract from *Lyrical Ballads* some kind of coherent theory of poetry: what interests me here is precisely the contradictions in the argument, the frequent clashes between what is postulated in the Preface and what happens in the poems themselves. Sarah Hutchinson wrote, soon after the publication of the first edition, that the *Lyrical Ballads* 'have been universally laughed at, with very few exceptions'; famous scoffers included Charles Burney and (more woundingly for Wordsworth) Robert Southey.[2] Much recent criticism and many modern readers have found it difficult to take the poems seriously. I would prefer to take my cue from Hazlitt: 'fools have laughed at, wise men scarcely understand them.'[3]

The 1798 Advertisement throws out several challenges to the unsuspecting reader. Wordsworth, as so often, wants to have things both ways: whilst appealing to tradition, he asserts the experimental nature of the volume; whilst offering his poems as strange and new, he resorts to the idea of taste, espoused not only by Reynolds (mentioned by name), but by so many writers of the eighteenth century, which depends on a sense of literary history and continuity. But if this sounds rather drily theoretical, there is an equally strong sense of the very nature of 'poetry' being taken by the scruff of the neck and vigorously shaken. Such apparent contradictions might be seen as indicative of his own confusions; but there is an element of the rhetorician at work here, which is worth dwelling on for that very reason, in that so much Romantic theorising can be seen as varieties of rhetoric. The opening paragraph, for example, with its distant echo of Terence's embrace, in very different circumstances, of all things human:

> It is the honourable characteristic of poetry that its materials are to be found in every subject which can interest the human mind. The evidence of this fact is to be sought, not in the writings of critics, but in those of poets themselves.

Harmless as this might seem to us, it was certainly not a tenet of all readers and writers, let alone the poets to whom Wordsworth appeals for sanction. He presents it as fact, as though it provides the basis on which the whole volume is structured; and by so doing, with a cunning sleight of hand he hopes to have his audience on his side when he goes on to admit that most of these poems are 'experiments'. Rather surprisingly, the nature of the experiment turns out to be linguistic, which in turn leads into a brief discussion of the nature not only of poetry, but of 'poetic pleasure'. The poems

> were written chiefly with a view to ascertain how far the language of conversation in the middle and lower classes of society is adapted to the purposes of poetic pleasure. Readers accustomed to the gaudiness and inane phraseology of many modern writers, if they persist in reading this book to its conclusion, will perhaps frequently have to struggle with feelings of strangeness and awkwardness: they will look round for poetry, and will be induced to enquire by what species of courtesy these attempts can be permitted to assume that title. It is desirable that such readers, for their own sakes, should not suffer the solitary word *poetry* (a word of very disputed meaning) to stand in the way of their gratification; but that while they are perusing this book they should ask themselves if it contains a natural delineation of human passions, human characters and human incidents; and if the answer be favourable to the author's wishes, that they should consent to be pleased in spite of that most dreadful enemy to our pleasures, our own pre-established codes of decision.

It is quite clear that we are being offered much more than the usual humble author's *apologia* for what is to follow (humble, none the less, in that the volume is published anonymously in 1798); it becomes clear, as we move through the second part of this Advertisement, just how much Wordsworth wants to attack the current state of literary taste, and how much he wants to claim for his (and Coleridge's) own 'experiments'. The reader is urged to refrain from any 'rashness of decision' when it comes to responding to these poems: it almost amounts to his saying that a failure to respond favourably will be a failure of reading, not of writing.

There is much here that is contentious: the relationship between reader and writer (looking ahead to the Preface, but to other pronouncements too on the need for the poet to be several steps ahead when it comes to 'taste'); the current mode of reading literature; a reluctance to use the word 'poetry' if that is going to mislead people; the implications, not spelt out here, of the language of poetry, and the relation between that and aesthetic 'pleasure' (by using the word 'poetic', Wordsworth begs the question even more, especially since he himself goes on to question the very idea of poetry). Perhaps the central contradiction is that between the claims of a 'natural delineation' of human passions, and the recognition that strangeness and awkwardness will be the dominant emotions of most readers: in other words we are both getting poetry and not getting it, being offered what is natural, but in such a way that it will seem anything but. It is hard to imagine many of Wordsworth's contemporary readers finding much help here, when it comes to reading the actual poems.

Whatever the holes in the argument of the Advertisement, Wordsworth pronounced himself sufficiently pleased with the response to the first edition: those who would like his poems, he had predicted, would like them greatly, those affronted would be so with equal force. But he was still not satisfied, for the good reason that in terms of the usual contract between poet and audience he felt he might not have kept his side of the bargain. There was a nicely articulated cause for this, in that he was not sure of 'the exact import of the promise which, by the act of writing in verse, an author in the present day makes to his reader, but I am certain that it will appear to many persons that I have not fulfilled the terms of an engagement thus voluntarily contracted.' The nature of this contract lies at the centre of much of the theoretical discussion of poetry of this period, amongst poets and critics. It is important to note that Wordsworth had, even in the Advertisement, felt the need to touch on this, whilst at the same time not quite giving his readers enough to make sense of: as it emerges in the argument of the Preface, the vexed relationship of writer to reader is linked to the definition of poetry, but also to the definition of success. Furthermore, Wordsworth here uses the word 'theory' when he talks of those who 'have advised me to prefix a systematic defence of the theory upon which the poems were written.' In other words, in spite of his hesitation and reluctance (not wanting to 'be suspected of having been principally influenced by the selfish and foolish hope of *reasoning* him into an approbation of these poems'), Wordsworth is acutely conscious that the *Lyrical Ballads* (swollen, by 1800, into two volumes) represents rather more than the 'experiment' of 1798. It is, now, much more of a clarion call for a new type of poetry, 'well adapted to interest mankind permanently, and not unimportant in the multiplicity and in the quality of its moral relations'. We might well think that a poet more sure of his success would be less inclined to proceed with the defence that constitutes the Preface; he himself provides one answer to this, when he says that to provide a coherent rationale would be far too ambitious an enterprise (and of course he was right about this, which is itself suggestive of the central problem). None the less, in place of any 'systematic' defence, he feels obliged to write something of an introductory nature, to poems 'so materially different from those upon which general approbation is at present bestowed'. Not only is he aware, then, of the contract between himself and the reader, he is fully aware of just how much he will seem to have violated that contract. Once again, the contradiction: he wants to reassure his readers even as he tells them that there can, beyond a certain point, be no reassurance.

Both the Preface and the poems that follow are difficult; what is more, they can seem to be built on shallow foundations. So many assumptions are made, so many half-truths presented as fact, that modern readers of a theoretical or vexatious bent react against the whole enterprise. Wordsworth can be seen to be forcing us into the approbation he had hoped would come naturally; his loftiness of tone – more noticeable when set against the 'naturalness' or 'simplicity' of much of the language of the poems themselves – can make him seem, not the 'man speaking to men', but a forerunner of the prophetic Shelley, the 'unacknowledged legislator', but content if his fit audience though few should reach the magic number of six (or, for that matter, an echo of the Blake whose whole method of working ensured nothing more than a small handful of readers). Wordsworth can sound like Matthew Arnold, confident of his own rightness:

I do not know how, without being culpably particular, I can give my

> reader a more exact notion of the style in which I wished these poems to be written, than by informing him that I have at all times endeavoured to look steadily at my subject: consequently I hope that there is in these poems little falsehood of description, and that my ideas are expressed in language fitted to their respective importance. Something I must have gained by this practice, as it is friendly to one property of all good poetry, namely good sense ...

'Good sense' does not, nowadays, make us feel as confident as Wordsworth would have us: looking 'steadily at the subject' is not as simple as he implies, any more than Arnold's desire to 'see things whole' can be quite as easily satisfied as he would like us to think: for ideas to be expressed in language 'fitted to their respective importance' is not as obviously consequent upon looking steadily at his subject as he casually asserts.

There are many such moments scattered throughout the Preface, and it is partly for this reason that Wordsworth has been ridiculed. The problem is compounded by the fact that he is not merely trying to explain his own 'theory', which means, in part of course, his own practice; he is also trying to answer the question that he himself poses: 'What is a poet?' He would like to think that the one involves the other, and of course this should be true: but to write about your own approach to poetry is not necessarily to write about poetry in general, especially if you have in the first place questioned the very term 'poetry', and in the second place you are saying that what you are doing distinguishes you from other poets. The general and the particular might be seen, not so much to support each other, as to cancel each other out. I am inclined to think that Wordsworth is more aware of this than he allows, and that the volume as a whole has never the homogeneity he would have liked for it.

Since Wordsworth himself refers so prominently to the language and the style of these poems – it seems the main thrust of the Advertisement – it is easy to regard this as the central point of his argument. He had referred in 1798 to the 'conversation of the middle and lower classes of society': in the first paragraph of the Preface this has become 'an experiment, which I hoped might be of some use to ascertain how far, fitting to metrical arrangement a selection of the real language of men in a state of vivid sensation, that sort of pleasure and that quantity of pleasure may be imparted which a poet may rationally endeavour to impart'. There are deep, almost impenetrable philosophical and aesthetic issues behind this second statement, issues which

Wordsworth, far more so than Coleridge, was ill-equipped to pursue. The most we can do is try to follow his general progress, and discern the underlying pattern of the argument: the idea of language *qua* language leads us – and at times himself – away from the central point, which is social and moral. It is perfectly true that Coleridge devoted much of his attack on Wordsworth, in the *Biographia Literaria* (1817), to the matter of language, in particular what the 'language of men' might be; but this was really a reflection of Coleridge's sometimes arcane interest in the relation between language and matter, language and idea.[4] It is in fact far more typical of those Romantic writers who theorise about poetry to remove it altogether from a discussion of language: for Blake, for Shelley, for Hazlitt, for John Stuart Mill, poetry is an attitude of mind, a concept that often ends up being equivalent to the 'Imagination'. Significantly, in a note to the Preface, Wordsworth acknowledges the irksomeness of the customary distinction between poetry and prose, as opposed to his preference, that between poetry and fact (or science).

Wordsworth's major literary point about language can be seen in his discussion of 'poetic diction' – for which, typically, he requires an Appendix – and it is no accident that Gray is the figure he uses as his Aunt Sally. For it had been Gray who had averred that the language of poetry should be as far removed as possible from that of the everyday, whereas for Wordsworth that resort to 'poetic diction' became anathema. There are several reasons for this: Coleridge, as we shall see, was made all too aware, as a young aspiring writer, of the dangers of the Parnassian style, and he too was part of the move, at the end of the century, away from lofty Miltonics or quasi-Spenserianisms (notwithstanding 'The Ancient Mariner') towards a language that was spoken, more direct, less self-consciously literary. Whilst the Della Cruscans might have congratulated themselves on their precious versifying, and whilst a whole range of writers explored the pleasures of sensibility, we need to remember that Coleridge admired Cowper particularly for his 'divine chit-chat', for that semi-conversational blank verse that grew out of Thomson's *Seasons*, and was to lead into Coleridge's own conversation poems, and then curiously into Wordsworth's 'Tintern Abbey' and a more exalted form of Miltonic ruminative verse in *The Prelude*.

Just as important was a general shift towards 'simplicity', allowing Coleridge to poke fun at it, before the century was out, in his mock-simplistic sonnets under the name of Nehemiah Higginbottom (not far removed from Southey's 'Abel Shufflebottom', though Coleridge denied the connection);[5] by 1808 a mock epic, *The Simpliciad*, was guaranteed an understanding audience. The role played in all this by the ballad form cannot be overestimated: Percy's *Reliques* (1765) had an extraordinary popularity, encouraging in turn further collections of old poems. *Lyrical Ballads* would not have appeared but for the trend that had started in the 1780s.[6] Wordsworth's own involvement owed much to his knowledge of Coleridge, and therefore of Robert Southey. He could, in fact, have spared himself all the trouble and confusion he got into in his discussion of language and metre; it had already been demonstrated that the ballad could, to use his own words, 'follow the fluxes and refluxes of the mind when agitated by the great and simple affections of our nature.' It is true, and importantly so, that his ballads were 'lyrical', by which he meant that it was the emotion, rather than the action, that was important: he would cast over the things of every-day reality the glow of the imagination (whereas Coleridge would attend to the supernatural – hence the difference beween, say, 'The Ancient Mariner' , and 'Peter Bell' or 'The Idiot Boy'). But the ballad, with its directness of utterance, its lack of clutter, allows the very appeal to permanence and continuity of which he speaks elsewhere: in the face of the evils of the present age, the 'almost savage torpor' that craves 'for extraordinary incident' and is rewarded with 'frantic novels, sickly and stupid German tragedies, and deluges of idle and extrava-gant stories in verse', he clings on to a 'deep impression of certain inherent and indestructible qualities of the human mind, and likewise of certain powers in the great and permanent objects that act upon it which are equally inherent and indestructible.' Hence the importance of his surprising anticipation of T.S. Eliot that 'not only the language of a large portion of every good poem, even of the most elevated char-acter, must necessarily ... in no respect differ from that of good prose, but likewise that some of the most interesting parts of the best poems will be strictly the language of prose, when prose is well written.'

In explaining his reluctance to give a full 'defence' of his 'theory', Wordsworth almost passes over one of the most important points of the whole volume: he says that it would be an impossible task, 'without pointing out in what manner language and the human mind act and react on each other, and without retracing the revolutions, not of literature alone, but likewise of society itself'. He tackles, as we have seen, language and mind; there is a sense in which he shows his alert-ness to the changes of literature, and the need for further changes; but the revolutions 'of society itself' (apart from that general sense of things getting out of kilter, upon which he does not elaborate) do not get explored. And yet the point is both simple and obvious: the word 'revolution', so soon after the American and French Revolutions, could not fail to have particular reverberations. The careers of all the first generation of Romantic writers were intimately involved in those gigantic upheavals: Blake works backwards from the French Revolution, to America, to Europe, and then on to Asia and Africa; Coleridge's early poems reflect his own anxieties about France, after the initial jubilation; Southey understood and embraced, initially, the significance of the French Revolution, and in fact sustained his enthusiasm longer than either Coleridge or Wordsworth. But we must not forget that however exultant Wordsworth had been (as opposed to his distressed Bristol friends)[7] at the overthrow of Robespierre, he too had prayed for the defeat of England at France's hands: furthermore, he had actually been in France when things erupted. On one level he was the most involved of them all.

The atmosphere of Britain in the 1790s was frenetic; the treason trials of 1794 summed up for many the reality of the dangers. It is easy to see how the grand scheme of Pantisocracy could be seen either as a gesture of defiance, with its own Revolutionary, egalitarian, anti-property logic, or as an escape. But whatever those confusions, there can be little doubt about the thrust of Wordsworth's argument at this point, this early, in the Preface: his whole theory of poetry depends upon the events of the last decade. The significance of those events could be put, in terms of poetry, quite simply: literature, given the claims he was to go on to make for it, had to confront its responsibilities. It was part and parcel of the social upheaval of the time; to write poetry was, for better or worse, a political act; most of the poems in *Lyrical Ballads* are social poems. Wordsworth is extending the subject matter of poetry, but also the audience. He is in effect saying to the Cumberland Beggar, the Female Vagrant, the Mad Mother, the Forsaken Indian Woman – these poems are about you; but they are also for you. Whether or not this pious hope could be, or was, realised, has been a vexed question of Wordsworth criticism.

The argument is made more difficult by the frequent recourse to the countryside, and its inhabitants, as the ideal model(s) for his case. Modern readers have to make something of an imaginative and historical leap at this point, in that we are no longer quite so ready to accept the country/city dichotomy without questioning its basic assumptions. For present purposes, there are two points to be emphasised: on the one hand the whole literary and philosophical tradition that leads up to the end of the eighteenth century, and which can embrace the apparent simplicities of Cowper and the complexities of Rousseau; on the other hand, Wordsworth's personal investment in the natural world (explained, of course, much more fully in *The Prelude,* the whole of which has, in one important sense, to be read back into the *Lyrical Ballads,* since it is the experiences described in *The Prelude* that allow him to write the *Lyrical Ballads*). Wordsworth talks of the 'primary laws of our nature', and later in the same passage of the 'beautiful and permanent forms of nature'; it is his task to make the connection between the two kinds of nature. This central passage demands quotation: we might question its terms (it is easy to see why words like 'condescension' and 'sentimentality' become part of the Wordsworth charge-sheet), but it is out of the beliefs and affirmations of this passage that the thrust of the Preface's argument grows.

> The principal object, then, which I proposed to myself in these poems was to choose incidents and situations from common life, and to relate or describe them throughout, as far as was possible, in a selection of language really used by men; and at the same time to throw over them a certain colouring of imagination, whereby ordinary things should be presented to the mind in an unusual way; and further, and above all, to make these incidents and situations interesting by tracing in them, truly though not ostentatiously, the primary laws of our nature: chiefly as far as regards the manner in which we associate ideas in a state of excitement. Low and rustic life was generally chosen, because in that condition the essential passions of the heart find a better soil in which they can attain their maturity, are less under restraint, and speak a plainer and more emphatic language; because in that condition of life our elementary feelings co-exist in a state of greater simplicity, and consequently may be more accurately contemplated and more forcibly communicated; because the manners of rural life germinate from those elementary feelings, and from the necessary character of rural occupations are more easily comprehended, and are more durable; and lastly, because in that condition the passions of men are incorporated with the beautiful and permanent forms of nature.

We are also brought back to the linguistic ideal, well and repeatedly stated by the mid-eighteenth-century writers on whom so much of Wordsworth's argument is based, and from whom he seeks his authority. The importance of the language of the inhabitants of this landscape is this, that they

> hourly communicate with the best objects from which the best part of language is originally derived; and because ... they convey their feelings and notions in simple and unelaborated expressions. Accordingly such a language, arising out of repeated experience and regular feelings, is a more permanent and a far more philosophical language than that which is frequently substituted for it by poets who think they are conferring honour upon themselves and their art in proportion as they separate themselves from the sympathies of men.

Behind the apparently most simple of ballad poems – 'Simon Lee', 'The Last of the Flock' – lies this complex web of belief, which is both a moral cry against the degeneracy of the age – and therefore a cry for the necessity of each poem's having a 'worthy purpose' – and a cry for the importance of poetry and of the poet.

Wordsworth's claims for the status of the poet are often quoted; but the 'man speaking to men' turns out to be far less one of the people than we might have supposed. He possesses qualities available to few.

> He is a man speaking to men; a man, it is true, endued with more lively sensibility, more enthusiasm and tenderness, who has a greater knowledge of human nature, and a more comprehensive soul, than are supposed to be common among mankind; a man pleased with his own passions and volitions, and who rejoices more than other men in the spirit of life that is in him; delighting to contemplate similar volitions and passions as manifested in the goings-on of the universe, and habitually impelled to create them where he does not find them.

Poetry's object, it transpires, is 'truth, not individual and local, but general and operative ... [it is] the language of man and nature ...'. As Wordsworth moves towards his peroration, the claims for the poet become more far-reaching: once again, no paraphrase will compensate for his own proud formulations.

> Poetry is the breath and finer spirit of all knowledge; it is the impassioned expression which is in the countenance of all science. Emphatically may it be said of the poet, as Shakespeare hath said of man, 'that he looks before and after.' He is the rock of defence of human nature, an upholder and preserver, carrying everywhere with him relationship and love ... Poetry is the first and last of all knowledge: it is as immortal as the heart of man.

But because such claims are so daunting, we begin to hear that undercurrent of anxiety that imbues so much of the poetry. For, if the poet is indeed all these things, then how can he communicate such knowledge and wisdom? The linguistic problem raises its head again: whereas he had hoped that the simplicity and directness of everyday speech would effect this communication, Wordsworth is reminded of the gap between himself and his audience – made worse by his belief that no literary language can in fact recreate the 'liveliness and truth ... of that which is uttered by men in real life under the actual pressure of those passions'. For all his talk of one thing being 'fitted' to another, Wordsworth confronts the dilemma of the poet who has almost to deny himself the claims of language; as others have pointed out, sufficiently tellingly, he faces something of the awfulness of this realisation in other places, most notably in one of his *Essays on Epitaphs*, where, as Coleridge puts it, he ponders this very contradiction, 'a poem which affects not to be poetry'.[8] Words are 'too awful an instrument for good and evil to be trifled with; they hold above all other external powers a dominion over thoughts.' But the corollary of this is too terrible to contemplate: 'language, if it do not uphold, and feed, and leave in quiet, like the power of gravitation or the air we breathe, is a counter-spirit, unremittingly and noiselessly at work to derange, to subvert, to lay waste, to vitiate, and to dissolve.' [9] This talk of loss, of derangement, should remind us of two things: the frightening and frightful move from 'love and gladness' to 'despondency and madness' in 'Resolution and Independence'; and the point Wordsworth makes in the Preface, almost in passing, about the poet's 'disposition to be affected more than other men by absent things as if they were present.' Wordsworth's is very much the poetry of absence and loss. Typically, having extolled the virtues of nakedness and simplicity, he finds himself, almost like Harry Gill, chilled by the self-imposed exposure, the poet cursed (like Coleridge's Ancient Mariner) precisely because he is a poet.

Any close reading of the Preface should leave us in little doubt as to Wordsworth's own doubts and difficulties: as he himself is ready to acknowledge, the very existence of the Preface (whether placed at the front of the first volume, or, as in later editions, at the back of the second) indicates the need to explain. It verges, not so much on an outright admission of failure in the poems, as on an acceptance that these matters are both too complex, and too important, to be left to speak for themselves. He knows that, in his poems, he has taken risks, that he has left himself open to ridicule, for the simple reason that both readers and writers can make 'arbitrary connections of feelings and ideas with particular words and phrases, from which no man can altogether protect himself. Hence I have no doubt that in some instances feelings even of the ludicrous may be given to my readers by expressions which appeared to me tender and pathetic.' Part of his defence is that it is the reader who is more likely to be wrong than the writer, because the writer has given such matters more thought. Behind his frequent claims for what his poetry, if read rightly, might achieve – 'in its nature well adapted to interest mankind permanently, and likewise important in the multiplicity and quality of its relations' – stalks that less comforting idea of the poet as a supremely solitary figure. Hence the insistence of those questions: 'What is a poet? To whom does he address himself? And what language is to be expected from him?' Wordsworth attempts, as honestly as he can, some answers, but they rarely have the ring of total conviction. As Lakeland gossip repeatedly asserted, the 'natives' seldom identified themselves with the audience Wordsworth declared he was addressing: far from his ideal image of common ground between poet and audience, he leaves too often a very different image, one of complete isolation. Poetry might be 'the image of man and nature'; but, as he declares in his peroration, 'the power of any art is limited.' We might recollect, at this point, his talk of the poet's dealing in the 'infinite complexity of pain and pleasure'; or the 'tendency of metre to divest language in a certain degree of its reality, and thus to throw a sort of half-consciousness of unsubstantiated existence over the whole composition'. These are far more than mere hints of unease at the whole project in which he is engaged: they are reflections of the disturbance that ripples along the surface of so many of his poems, echoes of himself as man and poet, caught in that terrifying awareness of solitude that colours so much of *The Prelude*. The fact that he appears to need solitude, even to the extent of inventing it (as in 'I wandered lonely as a cloud'), does not mean, necessarily, that it brings him comfort: Wordsworth, at his best, looks neither to life nor to art for that.

As I have suggested, the main debate about poetry in the 1790s had centred on the need to give poetry a social dimension, and in particular the recognition that this had altered radically and dramatically very largely because of revolutionary politics. Blake had been the major, but largely unrecognised, figure to demonstrate such imperatives, to such an extent that poems like 'London' and 'The Tyger' have to be read, at least in part, as historical documents.[10] Wordsworth and Coleridge both knew the *Songs*, and there can be little doubt about their influence. Many would argue that Wordsworth, with his 'wise passiveness', never matches the sheer ferocity of Blake's wholesale assault on the political *status quo*; but that is merely to say that they are, for all their similarities, very different kinds of poet. It is the 'tygers of wrath' that are Blake's instructors, the paths of excess his road to wisdom. The result is that Blake is a much easier poet to read and absorb, on his own terms, than the Wordsworth of *Lyrical Ballads*: he does not need to write a Preface to the *Songs of Innocence and of Experience*. He certainly relishes the subversive uses of humour, whether gentle or savage; but we would scarcely ever mistake his style for that of Wordsworth (very occasionally, as in 'Poor Susan', Wordsworth catches the tone and rhythm of Blake, but that merely serves to underline the general stylistic and emotional differences between them). It is as though Blake had established, very early on in his career (and *Poetical Sketches* bears this out) what he thought poetry was, and what a poet was: the Piper of Innocence is all too soon replaced by the Bard, the prophetic figure who sees past, present and future.

It could be argued that Wordsworth, certainly in *The Prelude*, adopts the bardic mantle, and sees as Blake sees. But for Wordsworth such seeing is a personal matter, and this really underscores the contradiction within *Lyrical Ballads*. On the one hand he is writing poems of social protest – 'Goody Blake and Harry Gill', 'The Last of the Flock', 'Simon Lee', 'The Old Cumberland Beggar'; but on the other hand he concludes the first edition with one of his most personal poems, 'Lines Written a Few Miles above Tintern Abbey', a poem that anticipates in its concerns the broad, grand sweep of *The Prelude*, and in the second edition he not only includes lines that eventually form part of that personal epic, he also writes poems – such as the 'Matthew' or 'Lucy' poems – which quite clearly owe their power to his own sense of self, to that 'sort of half-consciousness of unsubstantial existence' he speaks of in the Preface. As a sign of his own ability to at least bridge this gap between public and private, 'Michael' stands at the conclusion of the second volume, almost as though it were a dramatisation, a working-out in narrative terms, of the emotional fluxes and refluxes of 'Tintern Abbey': yet even in 'Michael' he cannot help but draw attention to his awareness of himself as a poet. In its recognition, or perhaps hope, of his 'second self', it is a remarkable latter-day version (and the subtitle of 'Pastoral Poem' points in this direction) of Milton's *Lycidas*, perhaps the most perfect fusion, *pace* Johnson, of highly ornate literary tradition and personal grief. But in Wordsworth's case, generic concepts, whether pastoral or epic, lend only as much support as they take away – both for poet and reader. By a similar token, when in later versions of his 'Immortality Ode' he adds as an epigraph the Virgilian 'paulo majora canamus', the echo presents as many problems for the reader as it purports to solve.

There are varieties of absence and emptiness in *Lyrical Ballads*: many of the poems deliberately deny themselves any real sense of narrative, and thereby undercut their own rationale. This in fact is one of the central characteristics of poems which, whilst offering themselves as ballads, undermine our expectations at every turn. Bewilderingly for the reader, humour often plays a part in the anti-narrative strategy, and aesthetic bearings can be lost along with a sense of where the poet is going. 'Simon Lee' is a classic example of this technique.[11] It is hard to believe, from the opening stanza, that we are entering a 'serious' poem:

> In the sweet shire of Cardigan,
> Not far from pleasant Ivor-hall,
> An old man dwells, a little man,
> I've heard he once was tall.
> Of years he has upon his back,
> No doubt, a burthen weighty;
> He says he is three score and ten,
> But others say he's eighty.

The effect of the pathetic and quirky detail, of the rhyme, is inevitably comic, but in a way which is hard to pin down. As the poem proceeds, our feelings for the old man are nursed by a continually shifting accumulation of detail which all goes to emphasise his old age, his former glory set against his present dire circumstance. The poem ends with the old man's tears of gratitude, as the poet helps him cut through the 'tangled root' of an old tree-stump. The emotion of the final lines seems a far remove from the apparent jauntiness of the opening, and this is precisely the test of the poem, how Wordsworth carries his reader with him from first stanza to last:

> – I've heard of hearts unkind, kind deeds
> With coldness still returning.
> Alas! the gratitude of men
> Has oftner left me mourning.

Apart from the humour, two other points deserve comment: firstly the absence of any narrative as such: we are brought up against our own expectations, and gently mocked. This is 'no tale', and yet we feel the need to give it a narrative structure, the very thing Wordsworth has denied himself and the reader. The poem is about a lack in the aesthetic sense: all that happens is at the deeply emotional level. By a similar token, the poem itself circles around the absence of Simon Lee, in that all the things – work, employment, friends, animals, his own strength – by which he used to be defined, by which he defined himself, have gone. He is now, to all intents and purposes, as useless as the 'stump of rotten wood' which mocks his efforts to cut through it. He cannot, it would seem, even get rid of the emblem of himself; he is taunted by his own failure, and by the cruel image of that failure. The poet (or at least his spokesman) suffers in a rather different way: by helping him, he has in fact simply emphasised the old man's helplessness. And, once the connection is made between Simon Lee and the old tree, then it is not fanciful to see that the poet has cut him down, has destroyed him, reduced him to a helpless stream of tears.

Other poems play with similar effects: 'The Idiot Boy', with its greater length, appears to risk more, for nothing happens here either. Once again, there is a total avoidance of actual narrative; what Betty Foy imagines to have happened to her simple son on his quasi-epic journey turns out to be just that, fanciful imaginings fed by superstition and fear, by the anticipation, this time, of the loss of what she truly cares for. To that extent, the poem is almost a complete reversal of the drift of 'Simon Lee': it circles around the idea of loss, and Wordsworth once again draws attention to his own role as a poet, a poet let down by his muse.

> I to the muses have been bound,
> These fourteen years, by strong indentures;
> O gentle muses! let me tell
> But half of what to him befel,
> For sure he met with strange adventures.
>
> O gentle muses! is this kind?
> Why will ye thus my suit repel?
> Why of your further aid bereave me?
> And can ye thus unfriendly leave me?
> Ye muses! whom I love so well.

It is at this point that Johnny appears, unharmed, to be embraced by his deleriously happy Mother. It is a moment of great poignancy which, as so often with Wordsworth, depends upon a careful reading of the whole poem. For most of the poem the boy – the subject of the ballad – has disappeared, apparently as a direct result of his Mother's sending him on an impossible errand; but whereas Simon Lee remains lost, a figure with no identity, here Johnny is found, in an outburst of glory, celebrating his adventure:

> 'The cocks did crow to-whoo, to-whoo,
> And the sun did shine so cold.'

But the poet has failed: he has been no more use than Betty or Susan Gale. Furthermore, there is something terribly unsettling about the boy's own vision: whatever he has seen is not the normal world, it chills in its reminder of Harry Gill's curse beneath the cold moon, a Tom-like figure in a surprising echo of *Lear*. Although there is no doubting Johnny's moment of glory, in what that glory consists is left a mystery. The mother, the friend, the poet, have all been asking questions, expecting something wonderful; but at the end, they, like the reader, are kept at a distance, out of range of full understanding of Johnny's story. His vision – and it is as though he has become the surrogate poet by the end – is both glorious and disturbing. That complex of pain and pleasure that Wordsworth mentions in the Preface emerges here: it is as though we are led to stare into a world of confusion, and the closest that anything comes to the poet's voice in fact keeps us out, throwing back at us our own bafflement and incomprehension.

A similar point could be made of 'The Thorn', one of the most teasing of these non-narrative ballads, made the more so by Wordsworth's insistence on the nature of the narrator, which lends credence to the argument that many of these poems are early forms of dramatic monologue, anticipating precisely those gaps and ambiguities Browning was to find so tempting in his exploration of the uncertainties of human psychology. Not only does nothing really happen in 'The Thorn', the poem traces the ineffective attempts of the aged narrator, the retired sea-captain, to find out, with a dogged matter-of-factness with which Wordsworth must in part identify, what has, or might have, happened in the past. The present – represented by the ambiguous thorn and the apparently eternal image of Martha Ray, simultaneously part of and set apart from the natural world – can only be explained by the past, but that past is in itself incomplete.

Wordsworth speaks in the Preface of 'truth', but many of these poems seem to challenge that very notion: however steady and determined the narrator's gaze (again echoing the Preface's emphasis on the poet's need to look at things 'steadily'), the truth is elusive. Certainly the community's rush to rash judgement is to be condemned (one of his poems on the naming of places makes the point directly): we are left with images of isolation – Martha Ray ('quietly sitting by the quiet thorn', as he puts it in *The Prelude*), but also the narrator, another kind of poet-figure, a strange echo of the Ancient Mariner (and the wedding-guest), trying to comprehend what is beyond comprehension.

Given the extremes of suffering to which so many of these characters are doomed, it is scarcely surprising that the balance of their minds often tilts over into forms of madness. The shepherd in 'The Last of the Flock' puts it well enough:

> No peace, no comfort could I find,
> No ease, within doors or without.
> And crazily, and wearily,
> I went my work about.
> Oft-times I thought to run away;
> For me it was a woeful day.

Martha Ray in 'The Thorn' is, in her repetitive harping on her own miserable state, on the verge of madness, beyond any rational control; Johnny Foy's very nature is characterised by an idiocy that Wordsworth explains, outside the poem, as some kind of closeness to God: but within the poem itself, such insight as derives from this 'idiocy' is, as I have suggested, deeply unsettling. 'The Female Vagrant' is more than a carefully delineated portrait of a social outcast; she has her 'inner self abused'; she stops her narrative 'because she had no more to say / Of that perpetual weight which on her spirit lay'. In her state of desperation and failure she is close to the 'Mad Mother'.

> Her eyes are wild, her head is bare,
> The sun has burnt her coal-black hair,
> Her eyebrows have a rusty stain,
> And she came far from over the main.

If this seems like something out of a traditional ballad (and anticipating the 'wild eyes' of Keats's 'Belle Dame'), Wordsworth transforms her madness into a dreadful form of self-delusion, which on one level offers her solace; but her child's dependency on her, in particular his frantic sucking at her breast, brings her madness upon him, and she senses, albeit tenuously, that she has lost him:

> – Where art thou gone, my own dear child?
> What wicked looks are those I see?
> Alas! alas! that look so wild,
> It never, never came from me:
> If thou art mad, my pretty lad,
> Then I must be for ever sad.

She has lost her husband, and she is about to lose the child who defines her. 'Without me my sweet babe would die', she has said earlier, but she tells him not to fret as she plans to hurl them both over the cliff's edge. The poem ends with her manic cry:

> 'Now laugh and be gay, to the woods away!
> And there, my babe, we'll live for aye.'

For all its brevity, this poem is an extraordinary psychological portrait of insanity: Wordsworth twice uses the rhyme of 'boy' / 'joy' he had played with in 'The Idiot Boy', and we are reminded, yet again, of the cruelly ambivalent nature of joy.

It seems almost wilfully perverse of Wordsworth, in view of the Preface's emphasis on permanence, to devote so many of the ballads to undermining the concept. The 'Lucy' poems are perhaps the obvious examples here: in a sequence of poems that offers its own grimly imagined narrative of death, he demonstrates what, indeed, 'simplicity' can achieve, and he provides his own version of the compression Blake had mastered in poems like 'London' and 'The Sick Rose'. Not everyone has responded to the risks Wordsworth takes here (these poems received their fair share of parodies from those who found his eschewal of 'poetic diction' as risible here as elsewhere), but it seems to be the case that the briefer these poems become, the more powerful and moving they are. So frequently have these poems been analysed that I hesitate to do more than place the emphasis on the paradoxes of permanence: once the poet has allowed into his head the thought 'If Lucy should be dead!' it becomes a fact, and that cosy domestic scene, deliberately traditional in its initial affirmation, is swept away. What had seemed so sure and permanent, partly because of its very traditional qualities, and its apparently easy merging of people and landscape (poet, lover, cottage, moon), has gone. And the second poem in the sequence shows just how delicate and fragile a figure Lucy was – magnificent, the only star in the firmament, and yet already a creature unknown: the cruel truth is that she was as insignificant alive as she is when dead, and the only person to register this loss is the poet, in words the more powerful because of their bathos, their total inadequacy:

> She lived unknown, and few could know
> When Lucy ceased to be;
> But she is in her grave, and oh!
> The difference to me.

'A Slumber did my Spirit Seal', with its apparently parallel, spare stanzas, in which nothing, and everything, is said, makes clear how deceptive is the very idea of something lasting: that earlier celebration of convergence in 'Strange Fits of Passion' has become a dreadful admonishment of his own solitude and deprivation. With her 'ceasing to be' Lucy has effected the poet's loss of identity, for his depended on her, who now 'neither hears nor sees': in being 'rolled round in earth's diurnal course' she is forever separate from him, excluding him. He has no place in his own poem: whereas it is often we, the readers, who are kept out, here the poet too has written himself out of existence. As he puts it in 'Three Years She Grew', where nature hugs Lucy to her bosom:

> She died, and left to me
> This heath, this calm and quiet scene;
> The memory of what has been,
> And never more will be.

If, as Wordsworth suggests in the Preface, the poet in general is concerned with absence, then the role of memory is clearly crucial. To unravel the implications of memory becomes the major task of *The Prelude*; but there are several other poems in *Lyrical Ballads* which dwell, increasingly, on this conundrum, and which deserve some detailed attention, especially as they pursue the line of thought that begins to emerge in the 'Lucy' poems, the concentration on the self. Whatever the social impetus behind many of the ballads, the nature of Wordsworth's role as a poet, and of the possibilities of poetry, is raised in such a way that questions of identity that originally might be attached to some of the characters in his own poems become questions about his own identity. 'Tintern Abbey' is the poem that charts this argument most fully, but there are others, too, where several of these concerns meet.

'The Brothers', like 'Michael', is subtitled 'A Pastoral Poem', and employs the same kind of musing blank verse which is to take Wordsworth away from the 'simplicity' of the ballad poems towards the assured and measured tread of *The Prelude*. Leonard, indeed, as he hears 'The tones of waterfalls, and inland sounds / Of caves and trees', can seem like a Wordsworthian alter ego, rather like the subject of 'There was a Boy' (a passage from *The Prelude* that was incorporated in *Lyrical Ballads* as an unexplained fragment), who is imagined by the poet to have died, and whose grave he visits (the personal significance of this only becomes clear in the version that appears in *The Prelude*). Leonard

> in those hours
> Of tiresome indolence would often hang
> Over the vessel's side, and gaze and gaze,
> And, while the broad green wave and sparkling foam
> Flashed round him images and hues, that wrought
> In union with the employment of his heart,
> He, thus by feverish passion overcome,
> Even with the organs of his bodily eye,
> Below him, in the bosom of the deep,
> Saw mountains, saw the forms of sheep that grazed
> On verdant hills, with dwellings among trees,
> And Shepherds clad in the same country grey
> Which he himself had worn.[12]

Such literally reflective introversion is at the core of *The Prelude*, and it is important to register Wordsworth's desire to dramatise it here, just as 'Michael' dramatises so much of 'Tintern Abbey': however much he wants to write about himself, he also needs to keep himself at a distance.

Intriguingly, in adopting Leonard as his other self, he makes himself an enquirer after the truth (and therefore a poet figure), but also someone who represents the audience: it is, importantly, the Priest who is the teller of the tale within the tale. Not for the first time in this collection, the central image is that of the grave; Wordsworth's landscape is peopled, literally and metaphorically, by the dead. Leonard is puzzled that in the graveyard there are no headstones, 'type of our earthly state / Or emblem of our hopes'; for the Priest and his parishioners there is no need – '"*we* want / No symbols, sir, to tell us that plain tale"'. The poem becomes a curious kind of *danse macabre*, as the two men circle around the past, around the dead beneath their feet. Leonard wants to know if his brother, James, is still alive, but any approach to a simple, direct question is sidestepped by the Priest, until the truth comes out, that James had, walking in his sleep, fallen to his death in the mountains. Leonard's fears are confirmed, and he realises that the unmarked grave that had aroused his suspicions is that of his brother. But the poem has an added darkness, in that even Leonard's briefly uttered recognition of the grave – '"My brother"' – is not heard by the Priest, and the two men part. Not only does the poem explore, in its deeply affecting way, the sense of loss and, again, the loss of identity, for in losing James Leonard has lost part of himself ('they were such darlings of each other'); the poem also explores the great chasm between the two protagonists (spelt out in symbolic terms early in the poem, 'that dark cleft', the 'chasm', is not as it was, as Leonard rightly conjectures). This bleak poem appropriately ends with Leonard's leaving the home he had returned to with such hope:

> All pressed on him with such a weight, that now,
> Yon vale, where he had been so happy, seemed
> A place in which he could not bear to live.

It is the 'heavy and the weary weight / Of all this unintelligible world' to which Wordsworth attends in what many would claim to be the weightiest poems of *Lyrical Ballads* , 'Tintern Abbey' and 'Michael'. As I have suggested, part of the importance of 'Tintern Abbey' lies in its autobiographical nature, emphasised by its placing at the end of the 1798 edition: after so many ballads which had centred on human suffering, on poverty and old age, Wordsworth turns to himself, and to a particular, precisely dated moment in his life: 13 July 1798. Whatever the conventions of the poetic persona, we do not question (and his note encourages us not to) the identity of the speaker, any more than we are to when it comes to *The Prelude*. Once we have read Coleridge's conversation poems it is quite clear that 'Tintern Abbey' is one of the major 'self-conscious poems' to which Michael O'Neill has recently given such close and careful attention.

New historicists have pointed to some of the obvious absences of the poem: the 'vagrant dwellers in the houseless woods' get a mention, but are to some extent blotted out by the more picturesque 'hermit's cave, where by his fire / The hermit sits alone'. Even William Gilpin in his comments on the picturesque beauties of the Wye Valley had given more than a nod to the beggars on the bank, to the noise and clamour of the forges that would have disturbed the quietude by which Wordsworth wants to set such store.[13] But to charge him with dishonesty or lack of realism seems to be beside the point in a poem which, from the ambiguities of the title onwards, challenges all our expectations, both aesthetic and historical. It is as though Wordsworth deliberately hints at the possibilities, only to avoid them: for example, Tintern Abbey itself does not appear in the poem, but once it has been mentioned the reader cannot rid herself of the connotations; similarly the date undoubtedly alludes to the eve of the fall of the Bastille, and we know that five years earlier Wordsworth had indeed been weighed down by the prospect of war, as he gazed balefully across the Bristol Channel.[14] But, in turning away from the obvious, he emphasises his own desire for 'tranquil restoration', which has nothing to do with a particular landscape remembered, but with the implications of that natural world. More than many of the *Lyrical Ballads*, this poem tries to make the connection between the landscape and the impression it makes on the individual mind, but that this is no easy matter is clear from the opening lines, which are quite extraordinary in their ramifications and repetitions, far indeed from the 'matter-of-factness' of which Coleridge complained:

> Five years have passed; five summers, with the length
> Of five long winters! and again I hear
> These waters, rolling from their mountain-springs
> With a sweet inland murmur. Once again
> Do I behold these steep and lofty cliffs,
> Which on a wild secluded scene impress
> Thoughts of more deep seclusion; and connect
> The landscape with the quiet of the sky.

He 'hears' before he 'sees'; both verbs have metaphoric force. With hindsight we think of the River Derwent in *The Prelude*, of the children sporting on the shore in the 'Immortality Ode', of the inland waters of 'The Brothers': these rolling waters anticipate '[the] motion and [the] spirit, that ... rolls through all things' later in the poem. Within a few lines we are taken back into the past, and then brought into the present; but in the process we are made aware of the complexity (the syntax underlines this) of words like 'impress' and 'connect'. There is mystery here, as much as relief. In the Preface Wordsworth talks of the role of repetition in poetry, and its function in recreating the repetition of experience: so here, the very repetition of 'again' draws attention to itself, and in doing so reminds us that repetition involves change. Just as 'these orchard-tufts ... lose themselves / Among the woods and copses', so the poet loses and finds and then loses himself again as the poem unfolds.

Wordsworth wants to affirm that for all the loss of the past, of his youthful self, his 'aching joys' and 'dizzy raptures', he has, in fact,

> Abundant recompense. For I have learned
> To look on nature, not as in the hour
> Of thoughtless youth, but hearing oftentimes
> The still, sad music of humanity,
> Nor harsh nor grating, though of ample power
> To chasten and subdue.

This becomes the drift of the rest of his mature poetry, how to urge that connection between 'nature' and the 'music of humanity': the whole of *The Prelude* is devoted to that task, the complexity and difficulty of which soon become apparent. The sheer effort is more than hinted at here, as he talks longingly of the 'burden of the mystery' being 'lightened', a passage which drew from Keats one of the truest and finest responses we have to Wordsworth's dread verse:

> I compare human life to a large Mansion of Many Apartments, two of which I can only describe, the doors of the rest being as yet shut upon me. The first we step into we call the infant or thoughtless Chamber, in which we remain as long as we do not think ... we no sooner get into the second Chamber, which I shall call the Chamber of Maiden-Thought, than we become intoxicated with the light and the atmosphere, we see nothing but pleasant wonders, and think of delaying there for ever in delight: However among the effects this breathing is father of is that tremendous one of sharpening one's vision into the heart and nature of Man – of convincing one's nerves that the world is full of Misery and Heartbreak, Pain, Sickness and oppression – whereby this Chamber of Maiden Thought becomes gradually darken'd and at the same time on all sides of it many doors are set open – but all dark – all leading to dark passages – We see not the ballance of good and evil. We are in a

> Mist. *We* are now in that state – We feel the 'burden of the Mystery', To this Point was Wordsworth come, as far as I can conceive when he wrote 'Tintern Abbey' and it seems to me that his Genius is explorative of those dark Passages.[15]

Neither Wordsworth nor Keats is willing to downplay the tenuousness of the process. The darkness of which Keats speaks so movingly echoes Wordsworth's halting acknowledgement that he might be wrong:

> If this
> Be but a vain belief, yet oh! how oft,
> In darkness, and amid the many shapes
> Of joyless daylight; when the fretful stir
> Unprofitable, and the fever of the world,
> Have hung upon the beatings of the heart,
> How oft, in spirit, have I turned to thee,
> O sylvan Wye! Thou wanderer through the woods,
> How often has my spirit turned to thee!

But even this declaration is short-lived, and we are back with the doubts he would like to have banished, but cannot:

> And now, with gleams of half-extinguished thought,
> With many recognitions dim and faint,
> And somewhat of a sad perplexity,
> The picture of the mind revives again ...

'Again', again, to remind us of the necessity of repetition, even as, in doing so, it reminds us of repetition's ultimate fickleness. Things in Wordsworth, as the 'Immortality Ode' puts it, 'come and go': the 'fitting' of the mind to nature does not imply 'fixing'.

For two thirds of this poem, the reader's natural assumption is that Wordsworth is talking to himself: we are intruders, as it were, 'overhearing' (to use Mill's term in describing poetry as opposed to rhetoric),[16] rather as the poet himself listens to the river, feeling 'in the blood ... and along the heart' the 'sensations sweet'. In the process, as I have suggested, we hear and watch him as he moves back and forth between present and past, trying to impose a coherence on things. In the Preface, the poet is, amongst other things, a 'man speaking to men', but this does not seem to be the case here. The whole idea of audience has changed, and with it Wordsworth's declared aesthetic:

just as with Leonard and the Priest in 'The Brothers', or the poet and the old man in 'Old Man Travelling', there is a gap between speaker and audience, a rhetorical echo of the gap between present and past. These distances are dramatically refocused in the final verse paragraph of 'Tintern Abbey', where it transpires that the immediate audience is, in fact, his sister Dorothy:

> in thy voice I catch
> The language of my former heart, and read
> My former pleasures in the shooting lights
> Of thy wild eyes. Oh! yet a little while
> May I behold in thee what I was once,
> My dear, dear sister!

She represents his loss: 'abundant recompense' was not, after all, so abundant. Her simple, direct relationship with the natural world is indeed something that he wishes he still had, and the poem ends with his emotional investment in her for the future. He reverts to the very concept of absence in the final lines, and we realise that the future, like the past, and like the present, has to do, as much as anything, with absence. The major absence anticipated here is the poet's own: at the end he, like his own past, will have gone. He becomes his own Lucy figure, in that he too will require memorialising.

This is a most strange and disturbing turn, and clearly much more could be said about it; for present purposes, what is most striking is the very undercutting of the poem's foundations, a process dramatised in the answering poem, 'Michael'. As with so many of the narrative poems, Wordsworth offers a long poem which avoids narrative until the very end: the bulk is given over to the aged Michael, his wife, and their son Luke, and their hard, strenuous life on a small-holding: anyone who talks of Wordsworth's sentimentalising the 'shepherd's sweet lot' should be pointed to 'Michael', a gruelling study of the way in which poverty can be kept at arm's length only for so long. Luke is sent to the anonymous city, and as he drops into wicked ways, drops out of the poem – it all takes a mere handful of lines, after which Michael is left alone, to do what he can to finish the sheepfold they had started to build, as a 'covenant' between them.

> There is a comfort in the strength of love;
> 'Twill make a thing endurable, which else
> Would break the heart: old Michael found it so.

The resort to 'endurable' underlines the slightness of the 'comfort': hard things can, just about, be borne, for some time. Michael carries on the work for seven years, but completion is impossible.

> 'Tis not forgotten yet
> The pity which was then in every heart
> For the old man – and 'tis believed by all
> That many and many a day he thither went,
> And never lifted up a single stone.

When Arnold chose this final line of the penultimate paragraph as, ironically, one of his 'touchstones', he failed to point out that its effect depends – Wordsworth would have said 'hangs' – on all that has gone before. Wordsworth's is a cumulative art, and the paradox here is that the accumulation leads to nothing: 'great changes have been wrought / In all the neighbourhood'. The cottage has gone, all the characters have gone: all that is left is the oak tree by the door, and the unfinished sheepfold.

This is where the poem had in fact started, with the 'straggling heap of unhewn stones'. Wordsworth begins with the 'utter solitude', the very solitude of the poem's end. Not for the first time in his work the poem comes full circle, and the reader is left to register that all that the poem goes on to contain has gone, that the poem recognises from the very beginning the loss and emptiness at its core. This framing device allows Wordsworth to engage, as I hinted earlier, in the literariness of the pastoral elegiac tradition to which this poem, perhaps surprisingly, belongs. As Milton looks ahead, in *Lycidas*, to his own possible death, so Wordsworth thinks, as he had in 'Tintern Abbey', of a time when he will have gone: the poem is, as he says,

> for the sake
> Of youthful poets who among these hills
> Will be my second self when I am gone.

Wordsworth is fascinated by this idea of his 'second self'; although, here, it might seem no more than a gesture towards posterity, in that he will live on in another generation of poets, he is in fact, by projecting himself forwards, reminding himself and the reader the more fully of how in fact he will not survive. True, the poem might be seen as his own epitaph, one of those memorials scattered across his bleak poetic landscape: others will come and read his poem, his epitaph, and in so doing they will be both audience and poet; that is the significance of his 'second self' here. But by the end of the poem, there is nothing left, except insofar as he has memorialised it: and the 'emblem' of the cottage, of the 'evening star', has gone, passed into other hands. The emblem of the sheepfold is deeply ambiguous: it has survived, but it has survived unfinished, 'the memory', as he puts it at the end of one of the 'Lucy' poems,

> The memory of what has been
> And never more will be.

Poe's raven was never to chant 'never more' with such pathos. Neither a fool nor a wise man, to refer back to Hazlitt's terms, would want to say whether Wordsworth presents us, in 'Michael', with an emblem of success or of failure. Like Wordsworth's soul in 'Tintern Abbey', 'These fields were burthened when they came to me.' Keats, like Wordsworth, knew how rarely that burden could be lifted. Permanence has proved elusive, whatever the Preface might have said:

> the remains
> Of the unfinished sheepfold may be seen
> Beside the boisterous brook of Green-head Gill.

So much for the restorative powers of nature – and, therefore, of poetry.

2
Coleridge: 'The self-consuming breast'

Coleridge prefaces his *Biographia Literaria* (1817) with a quotation from Goethe: 'He wishes to spare the young those circuitous paths, on which he himself had lost his way.' But it is virtually impossible to think of him without thinking of those 'circuitous paths', and he is a prime example of the Romantic poet who has 'lost his way'. This is a source of his fascination for the modern reader, but also of the frustration he can induce: the subtitle of his crucial autobiographical work (so very different from Wordsworth's aims in the Preface to *Lyrical Ballads*) is misleading in its apparent clarity – 'Biographical Sketches of My Literary Life and Opinions'. As he acknowledges in his opening paragraph, both proud and self-deprecatory, 'the least of what I have written concerns myself personally'; he is interested primarily in stating his 'principles in politics, religion, and philosophy, and the application of the rules ... deduced from philosophical principles, to poetry and criticism'. He goes on to say that he is concerned in particular with the 'true nature of poetic diction', and then to 'define with the utmost impartiality the real *poetic* character' of Wordsworth; intriguingly, Coleridge is, in fact, planning to define himself against, as it were, his old friend. In spite of their quarrels and disagreements the two poets speak across the gap that opens between them, just as they had in so many of their major poems; as Patrick Parrinder puts it, *Biographia Literaria*, despite Coleridge's disclaimers, is 'a remarkable product of romantic egotism'.[1]

When he refers to his own early work, Coleridge does so in terms of the florid style: 'these parasite plants of youthful poetry had insinuated themselves into my longer poems with such intricacy of union, that I was obliged to omit disentangling the weed, for fear of snapping the flower.' This distinguishes his view of poetry, as he goes on to recognise, from that of Pope, whose 'matter and diction seemed to me characterised not so much by poetic thoughts, as by thoughts translated into the language of poetry'. At the same time, even when young, he could admire the 'manly simplicity of the Grecian, and of our own elder poets', and he was encouraged in this by one of his schoolmasters, who remorselessly scoffed at his poeticisms. The importance to Coleridge of the sonneteer William Lisle Bowles might be difficult for the modern reader to understand: 'the genial influence of a style of poetry, so tender, and yet so manly, so natural and real, and yet so dignified, and harmonious'. But his problems with style should not be underestimated: far from being a mere matter of escaping an unsuitable, high-flown style, it is for him, as Hazlitt realised when he compared him with Godwin, a reflection of his questioning nature, and in particular his constant agonising about his sense of himself. Whereas, according to Hazlitt, Godwin just got on with the task in hand, 'with spirit and fortitude', having 'the happiness to think an author the greatest character in the world, and himself the greatest author in it', Coleridge, 'in writing an harmonious stanza, would stop to consider whether there was not more grace and beauty in a *Pas de trois*, and would not proceed till he had resolved this question by a chain of metaphysical reasoning without end'.[2] Put in those terms, Coleridge's heightened selfconsciousness is his own worst enemy.

A slight early poem, 'On observing a Blossom on the First of February 1796', contains this revealing passage:

> Dim similitudes
> Weaving in moral strains, I've stolen one hour
> From anxious Self, Life's cruel taskmaster!
> And the warm wooings of the sunny day
> Tremble along my frame and harmonise
> The attempered organ, that even saddest thoughts
> Mix with some sweet sensations, like harsh tunes
> Played deftly on a soft-toned instrument.

He has not quite worked out of his system the image of the aeolian harp, for which he had, less than a year earlier, earned Sarah's cool rebuke, and the result is yet another awkward poem. The weight put on 'self' here is notable, not just for the openly stated desire to escape from himself, nor for the anticipation of the much more complex shift attempted by Keat in his 'Ode to a Nightingale', nor even for the earlier reference to Chatterton ('Bristowa's bard') which makes the poem, because of the contrast, more rather than less self-conscious (and therefore curiously self-defeating) – but because of the connection made between the wish to leave self behind, and the quaintly old-fashioned, 'poetic' means used. Hazlitt finishes his account of Godwin and Coleridge with an ironic flourish: 'Each has met with his reward: for justice has, after all, been done to the pretensions of each; and we must, in all cases, use means to ends!' There speaks the bitter anti-Utilitarian, whose earlier chapter had been on Bentham, and who had made the point that whereas Godwin arrives at his destination, Coleridge's bark, 'the sport of every question, dancing to every wave,... flutters its gaudy pennons in the air, glitters in the sun, but we wait in vain to hear of his arrival in the destined harbour.' One of the remarkable facts about Coleridge is just how much of his writing is bad.

He is often quite open about this, having to admit, in so many words, that he has not learnt his schoolmaster's lesson. When he sent a copy of 'The Rose' to his brother George in 1793, calling it an 'effusion', he dismissed it rightly as 'of the namby-pamby genus'.[3] That was one of the terms of abuse hurled by unsympathetic reviewers at some of Southey's work, and it has to be said that many of Coleridge's poems come into this category. A poem with the title, 'Resignation: A Travelling Eclogue' (1794), does not promise much, but there is no guarantee that the poet is mocking his own high-flown diction:

> Or, where the worn sides of the chalky road
> Yield their scant excavation (sultry grots!),
> Emblem of languid patience, we behold
> The fleecy files faint-ruminating lie.

When 'Reflections on Having Left a Place of Retirement' appeared in the *Monthly Magazine* in 1795, he added, 'A Poem which affects not to be Poetry'. Whilst raising many questions, this alerts us to Coleridge's awareness of an audience, and to his strong sense that there is such a thing as poetry. What we are to make of a poem that denies its own status is the kind of conundrum we face with so many of the *Lyrical Ballads*; at this point in his career, part of Coleridge's work is aimed at moving away from that which did so obviously 'affect to be Poetry', moving towards the blank verse of his conversation poems. A note added to one manuscript version of 'Fears in Solitude' (1798) informs us, 'N.B. The above is perhaps not Poetry, – but rather a sort of middle thing between Poetry and Oratory – sermioni propriora. Some parts are, I am conscious, too tame even for animated prose.' [4] This 'middle thing' is in fact a perfect description of 'Frost at Midnight', and then of course of Wordsworth's 'Tintern Abbey'. Those conversation poems, it could be said, rescue Coleridge from the worst of himself; poems with titles like 'The Destiny of Nations', or 'Ode to the Departing Year', cannot live up to their grandeur. It is true, as Max Schultz pointed out long ago, that there is a considerable variety of poetic voices in Coleridge's *œuvre*, but I am not persuaded that the variety, in itself, is necessarily a virtue.[5] That a mere handful of poems is all that Coleridge tends to be remembered by has its own significance: he could not sustain the sense of integrity and wholeness that was his cherished aim, except in that little clutch of poems to which all readers have returned.

Whatever Coleridge's desire to speak of style as though it were a separable commodity, he soon finds himself talking in those vaguer terms that characterise so much Romantic theorising. It is not, then, quite such a surprise when he proceeds to discuss, in *Biographia Literaria*, the 'supposed irritability of men of genius': this is a charge he naturally wishes to refute, whilst at the same time having to acknowledge the fineness of the dividing line. Those who 'possess more than mere talent ... yet still want something of the creative, and self-sufficing power of absolute genius' , become, in 'times of tumult ... the men destined to come forth as the shaping spirit of ruin, to destroy the wisdom of ages in order to substitute the fancies of a day, and to change kings and kingdoms, as the wind shifts and shapes the clouds'. The echoes of 'Dejection' and 'The Ancient Mariner' ring loud and clear.

What is of particular interest here is that, in his attempt to explain why genius has been wrongly characterised, Coleridge talks very directly about the professionalisation of literature. As several critics have pointed out, there is a central and apparently irreconcilable clash here, between the idea of genius (and whatever that might mean) and the recognition that there is a growing (and therefore for many demeaning) sense of literature as a trade.[6] Coleridge refers to this several times, but here, in the second chapter, is his first tirade:

> But, alas! the multitude of books, and the general diffusion of literature, have produced other, and more lamentable effects in the world of letters, and such as are abundant to explain, though by no means to justify, the contempt with which the best-grounded complaints of injured genius are rejected as frivolous, or entertained

> as matter of moment … now, partly by the labours of successive poets, and in part by the more artificial state of society and social intercourse, language, mechanized as it were into a barrel-organ, supplies at once both instrument and tune … of all trades, literature at present demands the least talent, or information; and, of all modes of literature, the manufacturing of poems.

In such a climate, Coleridges urges the necessity of the idea of poetry as hard work. The more the creative writer is open to ridicule (and criticism, as he goes on to argue, has become the tool of the many to ridicule the few who are geniuses), the more the creative act, the act of genius, has to be treasured. His own experience tells a different story:

> I have laid too many eggs in the hot sands of this wilderness the world, with ostrich carelessness and ostrich oblivion. The greater part indeed have been trod under foot, and are forgotten; but yet no small number have crept forth into life, some to furnish feathers for the caps of others, and still more to plume the shafts in the quivers of my enemies, of them that unprovoked have lain in wait against my soul.

Whatever he might have wanted to say about the absurdity of the idea of the irritable genius, quite clearly it is a thankless task. Coleridge appeals to the notion of writing as a religious act – which for so many of his contemporaries, including Wordsworth, it becomes. But the market is in stark contradiction to all this:

> In times of old, books were as religious oracles; as literature advanced, they next became venerable preceptors; they then descended to the rank of instructive friends; and as their numbers increased, they sunk still lower to that of entertaining companions; and at present they seem degraded into culprits to hold up their hands at the bar of every self-elected, yet not the less peremptory, judge, who chooses to write from humour or interest, from enmity or arrogance, and to abide the decision (in the words of Jeremy Taylor) 'of him that reads in malice, or him that reads after dinner.'

We have moved from the 'lofty address of Bacon' to patronage, to the free-for-all of the present. The changing nature of the readership has inevitably changed the nature of the relationship between author and audience, and hence of the status of the author: hence, too, the self-conscious nature of poetry.

When Coleridge addresses himself to Wordsworth's first publication, the *Descriptive Sketches* of 1793, he responds to all the complexities of a kind of writing that on one level might have seemed almost old-fashioned.

> In the form, style, and manner of the whole poem, and in the structure of the particular lines and periods, there is an harshness and acerbity connected and combined with words and images all a-glow, which might recall those products of the vegetable world, where gorgeous blossoms rise out of the hard and thorny rind and shell, within which the rich fruit was elaborating.

His use of the idea of some lines as 'an emblem of the poem itself' anticipates his belief in poetry itself as emblematic, and helps to make sense of Wordworth's practice. This leads him on to a further discussion of the nature of poetic genius, whereby he is able to do what Wordsworth had attempted in his Preface, to unite general observations with the particularities of his own verse. The crucial concept of the Imagination is brought into play, and Coleridge begins to work towards a 'desynonymisation' of Imagination and its apparent synonym, Fancy.[7] This is one of the most teasing of Coleridgean cruces, to which he returns in the famous passage in chapter 13; rather like the person from Porlock, he resorts to an interruption which allows him to leave the distinction without its being fully explained.

One of Coleridge's problems is that his definition of poetry depends on his own experience, which includes the turmoil of the French Revolution: like Southey, he had initially embraced it, seeing in it the political and philosophical culmination of all that had gone before. But he was quicker than Southey to kick over his revolutionary traces, and he speaks in the *Biographia* of how 'my mind sunk into a state of thorough disgust and despondency, both with regard to the disputes and the parties disputant.' In 'France, an Ode' he had, in 1798, inveighed against the desperate turn of events; the final stanza of the poem is quoted in the *Biographia.*

> The sensual and the dark rebel in vain,
> Slaves by their own compulsion! In mad game
> They break their manacles, to wear the *name*
> Of freedom, graven on an heavier chain ...

The sense of despair is put more forcefully two stanzas earlier:

> 'And what', I said, 'though Blasphemy's loud scream
> With that sweet music of deliverance strove!
> Though all the fierce and drunken passions wove
> A dance more wild than e'er was maniac's dream!

The vocabulary here is that of many familiar poems: the wild dance appears as an image of poetry in 'Kubla Khan', in 'The Aeolian Harp', in 'The Ancient Mariner'. But such madness, as Wordsworth realised in a very different context, easily leads to the desire to escape all such extremes. Coleridge summarises his own retreat from political engagement, to marriage and domesticity (not to mention – which he does not – the whole saga of Pantisocracy and his quarrels with Southey, his lectures in Bristol, his fervent magazine *The Watchman*), in terms that are recognisable: religious and moral questions are always in his mind, and for him poetry is a means of exploring them. What is fascinating is how, at this juncture, all these disparate elements – politics, despair, retreat, madness, poetry, religion – come together. Nothing can better the wonderful description Hazlitt gives of his first meeting with Coleridge, when he heard him preaching at Shrewsbury in 1798:

> When I got there, the organ was playing the 100th psalm, and, when it was done, Mr Coleridge rose and read out his text, 'and he went up into the mountain to pray, HIMSELF, ALONE.' As he gave out his text, his voice 'rose like a steam of rich distilled perfumes,' and when he came to the two last words, which he pronounced loud, deep, and distinct, it seemed to me, who was then young, as if the sounds had echoed from the bottom of the human heart, and as if that prayer might have floated in solemn silence through the universe. The idea of St John came into mind, 'of one crying in the wilderness, who had his loins girt about, and whose food was locusts and wild honey.' ... I could not have been more delighted if I had heard the music of the spheres. Poetry and Philosophy had met together. Truth and Genius had embraced, under the eye and with the sanction of Religion.[8]

That ringing affirmation of solitude and isolation is strikingly consonant with how Coleridge saw himself.

In describing his retreat to Somerset, Coleridge is honest enough:

> Here I found myself all afloat. Doubts rushed in; broke upon me 'from the fountains of the great deep,' and fell 'from the windows of heaven.' The fontal truths of natural religion and the books of Revelation alike contributed to the flood; and it was long ere my ark touched on an Ararat, and rested.

Although he accepted as necessary the 'idea of the Supreme Being', he 'was not wholly satisfied'. This is perhaps his greatest virtue, his refusal to be satisfied. 'I began then to ask myself, what proof I had of the outward existence of anything.' What matters for Coleridge is that he sees the connection between this philosophical questioning and his role as a poet, and the connection between both and the search for freedom as acted out in political terms (but also, and dreadfully, as 'France' had shown, in terms of death and destruction, in terms of that very madness that is so closely allied to the idea of the poet). This explains his despair when things go so hopelessly wrong: if poetry, if imagination, cannot make sense of the aftermath of the French Revolution, then what can? Wordsworth, as Coleridge knew only too well, wrestled with the same problem in *The Prelude*. As Coleridge goes on to say, in that grand sweeping way with history that was to characterise Shelley's *Defence of Poetry,* not many years later, 'In Pindar, Chaucer, Dante, Milton, etc. etc. we have instances of the close connection of poetic genius with the love of liberty and of genuine reformation.' He rather touchingly adds to this list ('etc. etc.') the cobbler of Nuremburg, Hans Sachs (without, Robert Bloomfield might have ruefully noted, making any reference to his contemporary cobbler-poet of Suffolk). However much a reactionary he became, Coleridge wants his credentials to be widely known.

He spells out the concerns of poetry in a remarkable passage in Chapter 12, before his befuddling chapters on the nature of the Imagination. Just as Wordsworth, in his Preface, had made an almost passing allusion to Imlac and the streaks of the tulip in Johnson's *Rasselas*, so here, Coleridge seems to be alluding to the limitations of the 'Happy Valley': the 'higher ascents are too often hidden by mists and clouds'. The poet's task is to explore beyond the horizon: this becomes true for most of the major Romantic writers, in that what might have started out as a picturesque trope becomes an essential part of their self-definition – Wordsworth, Byron, Shelley, all use literal mountains as metaphors, to test what Wordsworth, quoted here by Coleridge, says of 'the vision and the faculty divine'.

> But in all ages there have been a few, who measuring and sounding the rivers of the vale at the feet of their furthest inaccessible falls have learnt, that the sources must be far higher and far inward; a few, who even in the level streams have detected elements, which neither the vale itself or [sic] the surrounding mountains contained or could supply. How and whence to these thoughts, these strong probabilities, the ascertaining vision, the intuitive knowledge, may finally supervene, can be learnt only by the fact. I might oppose to the question words with which Plotinus supposes Nature to answer a similar difficulty. 'Should any one interrogate her, how she works, if graciously she vouchsafe to listen and speak, she will reply, it behoves thee not to disquiet me with interrogatories, but to understand in silence, even as I am silent, and work without words.'

That extraordinary acknowledgement of the insufficiency of words, of the need for silence, illuminates much of the poetry of this period, even as it undermines the very reason for poetry's existence. Poetry both is, and is not, its own justification. This solipsism extends to Coleridge's abbreviated discussion, in Chapter 12, of the nature of self-knowledge:

> If then I know myself only through myself, it is contradictory to require any other predicate of self, but that of self-consciousness. Only in the self-consciousness of a spirit is there the required identity of object and of representation; for herein consists the essence of a spirit, that it is self-representative. If therefore this be the one only immediate truth, in the certainty of which the reality of our own collective knowledge is grounded, it must follow that the spirit in all the objects which it views, views only itself. (Thesis VII)

Coleridge goes on to reiterate his point about the deadness and finiteness of any object; hence the function of the 'esemplastic' imagination, or, as he puts it here, 'the spirit (originally the identity of object and subject) must in some sense dissolve this identity, in order to be conscious of it: *fit alter et idem* [it becomes another and yet the same].' This in turn involves an act of will, and it is that will for which Coleridge is so often desperately searching. In this way he confronts what would otherwise be a central problem: just as poetry would, in effect, be self-defeating, so the self would make up the whole world, and everything viewed would be nothing other than itself. He gets around this (and there is a sense of rather tenuous logic about this) by arguing that the original identity of subject and object has to be dissolved, and only then can there be any awareness of that very identity; it is rather like having the best of both worlds. The religious terminology he uses can begin to explain what is happening: 'self cause and effect: father of himself, Son of himself',

Coleridge's account of the Imagination is astonishing both for its brevity and for the claims he makes.

> The imagination then I consider either as primary, or secondary. The primary imagination I hold to be the living power and prime agent of all human perception, and as a repetition in the finite mind of the eternal act of creation in the infinite I AM. The secondary I consider as an echo of the former, coexisting with the conscious will, yet still as identical with the primary in the kind of its agency, and differing only in degree, and in the mode of its operation. It dissolves, diffuses, dissipates, in order to recreate; or where this process is rendered impossible, yet still at all events it struggles to idealize and to unify. It is essentially vital, even as all objects (*as* objects) are essentially fixed and dead.

But, once again, these claims are more comprehensible when set in the context of the religious/philosophical arguments I have just mentioned, in particular the paradoxical nature of God as Father and Son of Himself (the *Frankenstein* version of this is obviously central to the period); here, reviving his earlier talk of the relation between poetry and repetition, and arguing that the imagination is a 'repetition in the finite mind of the eternal act of create in the infinite I AM', he is equating the poet with God. We can see how this happens, once he has asserted that it is the primary Imagination that is the active agent in 'all human perception', that faculty that has gone beyond the horizon's limits: poetry has, as it were, ousted philosophy and religion, in so far as they can be separated. For Coleridge's purposes, it is as though they require separation before they can be seen for what they are, and then reunited.

It is worth noting here the sonnet he wrote in 1796, 'On Receiving a Letter Informing Me of the Birth of a Son'. Coleridge is clearly not only deeply moved, but perplexed by this particular form of creation; nothing, however, quite prepares us for the turn of the sestet:

> And now once more o Lord! to thee I bend,
> Lover of souls! and groan for future grace,

That ere my babe youth's perilous maze have trod,
Thy overshadowing Spirit may descend,
And he be born again, a child of God.

This is so strange that it becomes weird. A second poem, written on the same day on the way home, imagines that he will be greeted by the news of the child's death:

O my sweet baby! when I reach my door,
If heavy looks should tell me thou art dead
(As sometimes, through excess of hope, I fear)
I think that I should struggle to believe
Thou wert a spirit, to this nether sphere
Sentenc'd for some more venial crime to grieve;
Did'st scream, then spring to meet Heaven's quick reprieve,
While we wept idly o'er thy little bier!

This correlation between creativity and death is a recurrent theme of much Romantic writing: once again *Frankenstein* provides an obvious model.

However much the shift to God can be explained, the very brevity and suddenness of its statement comes as a shock. If the poet is God, then all poets are God: Coleridge is God. The blasphemy of such a thought is recognised by the move to a discussion of the origins of *Lyrical Ballads,* in which he seems happier to range between the natural (Wordsworth) and the supernatural (himself). On the other hand, it is still within this religious context that he attempts a definition of poetry and the poet.

The poet, described in ideal perfection, brings the whole soul of man into activity, with the subordination of its faculties to each other, according to their relative worth and dignity. He diffuses a tone, and spirit of unity, that blends, and (as it were) fuses, each into each, by that synthetic and magical power, to which we have exclusively appropriated the name of imagination. This power ... reveals itself in the balance or reconciliation of opposite or discordant qualities: of sameness, with difference; of the general, with the concrete; the idea, with the image; the individual, with the representative; the sense of novelty and freshness, with old and familiar objects; a more than usual state of emotion, with more than usual order; judgment ever awake and steady self-possession, with enthusiasm and feeling

> profound or vehement; and while it blends and harmonizes the natural and the artificial, still subordinates art to nature; the manner to the matter; and our admiration of the poet to our sympathy with the poetry.

The claims he makes are indeed awesome, and had never before been made in these terms. If much of this might seem mere rhetoric, then there is a sense in which rhetoric is all that is left to those who address such topics. All his close critical readings of Wordsworth stem from his own general premises, and from the fact that from the very beginning people's admiration of *Lyrical Ballads* 'was distinguished by its intensity, I almost might say, by its *religious* fervour'. For Coleridge this is a natural consequence of a theory that sees poetry and religion as such close allies: it helps to explain the genuflexions of his poem addressed to Wordsworth after that lengthy reading of what was to become *The Prelude*. To read, as to write, poetry has become a religious act; it was perfectly natural, therefore, for Wordsworth to talk of his life's work in terms of a cathedral, still in the process of being built. When Wordsworth speaks about the 'awful truth' that 19 out of 20 people do not enjoy poetry, he goes on to explain: 'the truth is an awful one because to be incapable of a feeling for Poetry in my sense of the word is to be without love of human nature and reverence for God.'[9]

Another consquence for Coleridge is that sense of panic and emptiness, which is one of the main themes of this study: the simple fact is that in Christian terms there can be only one God, and all that poets and philosophers can do is to play at being God. As I have hinted, Mary Shelley tackles this theme in *Frankenstein* (published within a year of *Biographia*), which sheds devastating light on Romantic myths of creation. Coleridge is only too uncomfortably aware of the vanity of the claims he so repeatedly makes: he counters the high-flown rhetoric of the *Biographia* with a letter to Thelwall of 1796, in which he dismisses Plato's view of life as

> *Harmony* – he might as well have said, a fiddle stick's end – but I love Plato – his dear *gorgeous* Nonsense! And *I, that last not least, I* do not know what to think about it – on the whole, I have rather made up my mind that I am a mere *apparition* – a naked Spirit! – And that Life is I myself I![10]

This is the solipsism from which he does his best to escape in the

Biographia. As he writes to Godwin in a famous letter of 1801, a mere year before the 'Dejection Ode', he has ceased to be a poet, and therefore, like the Lucy whose 'epitaph' Wordsworth had sent him, ceased to be at all. Ironically, in that he had written the *Biographia* with Wordsworth as a sounding-board, as it were, for his own development, he finishes the letter to Godwin by offering his own epitaph: 'Wordsworth descended upon him, like the Γνϖθν σεαυτόν [know thyself] from Heaven; by shewing to him what true Poetry was, he made him know, that he himself was no Poet.'[11] There are several cruel paradoxes here, not the least that Wordsworth was going through similar torments at the same time; but also that God knows that 'we are not capable of knowing ourselves – it is not impossible, that this perfect (as far as in a creature can be) Self-Knowledge may be among the spiritual punishments of the abandoned, as among the joys of the redeemed Spirits.'

Coleridge had written a poem as early as 1789, making fun of the nose of the Lord Mayor of London: even then, at that tender age, he had used the comic form to make a point about inadvertent, but inevitable, self-destruction:

> The Furies to madness my brain devote –
> 	In robes of ice my body wrap!
> On billowy flames of fire I float,
> 	Hear ye my entrails how they snap?
> Some power unseen forbids my lungs to breathe!
> 	What fire-clad meteors round me whizzing fly!
> I vitrify thy torrid zone beneath,
> 	Proboscis fierce! I am calcified! I die!
> Thus, like great Pliny, in Vesuvius' fire,
> I perish in the blaze while I the blaze admire.

Perhaps, more than any of the other Romantic writers, Coleridge lives in the mist that covers the mountain tops ('this total Mist', he calls it at the end of 1803). His late poem 'Self-Knowledge' is an acknowledgement that such a thing is impossible:

> Γνϖθν σεαυτόν! – and is this the prime
> And heaven-sprung adage of the olden time?
> Say, canst thou make thyself? – Learn first that trade; –
> Haply thou mayst know what thyself had made.
> What hast thou, Man, that thou dar'st call thine own? –

What is there in thee, Man, that can be known? –
Dark fluxion, all unfixable by thought,
A phantom dim of past and future wrought,
Vain sister of the worm, – life, death, soul, clod –
Ignore thyself, and strive to know thy God!

Two notebook entries for November 1809 sum up his sheer desperation:

> Where am I? What and for what am I? What are the duties, which arise out of the relations of my Being to itself as heir of futurity, and to the World which is its present sphere of action and impression?...
>
> Important remark just suggests itself ... That is by a negation and voluntary Act of *no*-thinking that we think of earth, air, water &c as dead – It is necessary for our limited powers of Consciousness that we should be brought to this negative state, & that should pass into Custom – but likewise necessary that at times we should awake & step forward – & this is effected by Poetry & Religion / – . The Extenders of Consciousness – Sorrow, Sickness, Poetry, Religion.[12]

*

To open his first volume of 1796 with a 'Monody on the Death of Chatterton' was, partially, to make a point repeated by several other Romantic writers. Chatterton was the archetypal unfulfilled, unrecognised genius, with the added political advantage of coming from the radical city of Bristol. For Wordsworth, Keats and Clare he was something of an ambiguous figure, in that his importance was intimately bound up with his early suicide. Although he had written a vast amount of verse, most of it was bogus; in the sense that Chatterton's claims on posterity were to rest on the pretence that these 'discovered' poems, the so-called 'Rowley' poems, were the work of a forgotten medieval writer, he was also largely forgotten (hence the suicide). Those poets who later imagined in various ways their own deaths were acting out in literary fashion the death that Chatterton had so brutally visited upon himself. As Wordsworth discovers in 'Resolution and Independence', the recollection of Chatterton can bring 'despondency and madness'. Coleridge, in 1796, is aligning himself with a poet whose fame depends on his failure. There is something both peculiar and prophetic about this.

The volume as a whole represents a certain unease: in technical terms, Coleridge acknowledges that whilst he could have called many of these poems 'sonnets', he settled for 'effusions', because 'they do not possess that *oneness* of thought which I deem indispensible in a Sonnet', and because the inevitable comparison with Bowles would be to his disadvantage. It is certainly true that, with a few exceptions, Coleridge was right about the lack of 'oneness': but then, his aim at the 'Vast' and the 'Whole', whilst a distinctive feature of his thought and writing, was often an aspiration as much a fulfilment. In fact, as he discovers in some of the poems that look ahead to the conversation poems, he creates a form that is much more suitable than the sonnet to his processes of poetic thought. When Wordsworth refers, in 1808, to some stanzas he had composed after visiting a grave, he draws himself up: '*composed* I have said. I ought rather to have said effused, for it is the mere outpouring of my own feeling ...'[13] It is of course Wordsworth who concentrates on the sonnet as an ideal means of imposing form on what might otherwise seem 'loose' emotion. Not all of Coleridge's effusions are successful, but nor should we expect them to be – this is prentice work, 'Songs of the Pixies' mingling with poems to famous statesmen and writers of his age, and the volume culminating with the extraordinary 'Religious Musings' (to which I shall return). Quite what kind of poem he is writing is not just a matter of technique: it is also to do with his own place in his poetry, his consciousness of which emerges in the unusual Preface to the volume.

> Compositions resembling those of the present volume are not unfrequently condemned for their querulous egotism. But egotism is to be condemned then only when it offends against time and place, as in an History or an Epic Poem. To censure it in a Monody or Sonnet is almost as absurd as to dislike a circle for being round.

The very idea of an 'effusion' allows for concentration on the self, and, for Coleridge, this is perfectly allowable. He scoffs at his contemporaries who do their utmost to avoid

> the word *I* ... all this is the watchfulness of guilt. Conscious that this said *I* is perpetually intruding on his mind and that it monopolises his heart, he is prudishly solicitous that it may not escape from his lips.

Coleridge then inserts, teasingly, a sentence which neatly advocates a different kind of aesthetics: 'This disinterestedness of phrase is in general commensurate with selfishness of feeling: men old and hack-neyed in the ways of the world are simple avoiders of Egotism.' Not only is this a declaration of youth's freedom, it spells out what Coleridge is actually doing: poetry requires an openness of feeling, a concentration on the self that is paradoxically unselfish, as opposed to those old curmudgeons who keep their secrets to themselves.

The 'Monody' appears to embrace the pleasures of peace, before undercutting them. The poem, in its 1796 version, begins in the tones of the late 18th century, as we would expect, with a dash of Southey thrown in: it is grand, lofty, generalised, and at the same time located in some seemingly Oriental setting.

> When faint and sad o'er Sorrow's desart wild
> Slow journeys onward poor Misfortune's child;
> When fades each lovely form by Fancy Drest,
> And inly pines the self-consuming breast;
> No scourge of scorpions in thy right arm dread,
> No helmed terrors nodding o'er thy head.
> Assume, *O death!* the cherub wings of *Peace*,
> And bid the heart-sick Wanderer's anguish cease!

The more we contemplate this, the more the puzzlement: do we associate the Wanderer with Misfortune's child, and then with the poet? It is hard not to register the 'self-consuming breast', and to make some connection with those words in the Preface about feeling, sorrow and the self. (Readers of Clare will pick up the pre-echo of his asylum poem, 'I Am', with its description of himself as the 'self-consumer of my woes'.) Death is solace, 'When fades each lovely form by Fancy Drest': it is not just that the choices offer little comfort, but that death is in fact preferable to what it might replace, that lines 3–4 describe the act of failed poetry. Clarification comes in the second stanza, where it transpires that Chatterton has been saved by his own death: those daunting personifications are left behind, as the poet emerges, 'Perchance, thou raisest high th'enraptur'd hymn / Around the blaze of Seraphim.' But as the third stanza shows, the realities of Chatterton's suicide are a high price to have paid. In its movement, its pushing of his argument along the lines of feeling, Coleridge's poem, anticipating Keats's troubled relationship with his nightingale, seems at times to consist of a whole series of cancellations. In the 1834 version, this becomes much clearer, giving us a rare instance of

Coleridge learning from, and echoing, Keats, rather than the other way around:

> Thee Chatterton! these unblest stones protect
> From want, and the bleak freezings of neglect.
> Too long before the vexing Storm-blast driven
> Here hast thou found repose! beneath this sod!
> Thou! O vain word! thou dwell'st not with the clod!
> Amid the shining Host of the Forgiven
> Thou at the throne of Mercy and thy God
> The triumph of redeeming Love dost hymn
> (Believe it, O my Soul!) to harps of Seraphim.

This is a much worked-over poem, and not all the alterations are improvements; what is striking here (and the central rhyme reinforces it) is the sense of contradiction, of something rather desperate about that appeal, in the last line, to his soul.

The whole poem is, in fact, one of assertion and counter-assertion; increasingly, it is a poem about poetry. As Byron, twenty years later in *Childe Harold's Pilgrimage*, was to question the noble lineage of his country's poetry, so here Coleridge emphasises Chatterton's place in a long tradition of neglect:

> Is this the land of song-ennobled line?
> Is this the land, where Genius ne'er in vain
> Pour'd forth his lofty strain?
> Ah me! yet *Spenser*, gentlest bard divine,
> Beneath chill *Disappointment's* shade,
> His weary limbs in lonely anguish lay'd.
> And o'er her darling dead
> *Pity* hopeless hung her head,
> While "mid the pelting of that merciless storm,"
> Sunk to the cold earth Otway's famish'd form!

Just as Coleridge places Chatterton in this sad line, so he places his own poem in that line of hope and despair. There are several passages where a modern reader might feel she is reading a palimpsest of other Romantic poems. For example, in celebrating Chatterton's verse, he anticipates his own 'Kubla Khan':

And, as floating high in air
Glitter the sunny visions far,
His eyes dance rapture, and his bosom glows!

In 1834 Coleridge, no doubt hearing his own echo, alters these lines to something much more Wordsworthian, as the poem itself moves into an emphasis on Chatterton's own sense of community, his sympathy for the poor and the suffering. Rather curiously, in this change nearly 40 years later, it is as though we also see something of Wordsworth's shift:

And now his cheeks with deeper ardour flame,
His eyes have glorious meanings, that declare
More than the light of outward day shines there,
A holier triumph and a sterner aim!
Wings grow within him; and he soars above
Or Bard's or Minstrel's lay of war or love.

Within a few lines, there is another pre-echo, as it were (depending on which version we are reading) of Wordsworth and Keats, as well as Coleridge's own struggle with 'Dejection':

Ah! where are fled the charms of vernal Grace,
And Joy's wild gleams, that lighten'd o'er thy face?
Youth of tumultuous soul, and haggard eye!
Thy wasted form, thy hurried steps I view,
On thy cold forehead starts the anguish'd dew
And dreadful was that bosom-rending sigh!

Coleridge was to have his own contact with such a cold forehead when Robert Lovell died in 1796, as was Keats, when his brother died in 1818: it is easy to see why both poets had their own personal reasons for looking in helplessness to the image of the dying poet. At this stage in his career, Coleridge is not thinking of that terrible gap between present and past, which both he and Wordsworth were to contemplate in their respective Odes of 1802–04, but he is only too aware, in a Keatsian way, of the transience of the 'charms of vernal Grace', of the fact that the young poet is no more. There is a particularly interesting divergence between the 1796 version and later ones when Coleridge imagines the young poet beside the Avon:

> And here, in Imagination's eager hour,
> When most the big soul feels her madning power;
> These wilds, these caverns roaming o'er
> Round which the screaming seagulls soar,
> With wild unequal steps he pass'd along
> Oft pouring on the winds a broken song ...

In 1834, 'madning' becomes 'mastering', which helps to make more sense of a 10-line insertion a little before this, in which he hopes that he would have faced such desolation with more fortitude than did Chatterton. In other words, in 1796 Coleridge was much more alert to the impossibility of things, and also to the relation between poetry and madness: he spent all his life aiming at the mastery, the control, of which he speaks in 1834, but his best work shows how forlorn a task it was. It is surely significant that he still acknowledges that the poet's song is 'broken', that his steps are 'wild' and 'unequal'. Hazlitt spoke, in 1825, of Coleridge's peculiar gait, of how he lurched from one side of the path to the other, and of how this was something he, Hazlitt, remembered in later life as he saw Coleridge lurch from crisis to crisis, from one belief to another.[14] At this point in the poem, Coleridge seems to have made the connection, and beaten Hazlitt to the image. And it is the likening of himself to the dead poet that urges him away:

> O'er the ocean swell
> Sublime of Hope I seek the cottag'd dell
> Where virtue calm with careless step may stray;
> And, dancing to the moonlight roundelay,
> The wizard Passions weave an holy spell!

The poet has become the inspired bardic figure of 'Kubla Khan', the figure that in 'The Aeolian Harp' he laughs at, when reproved by the young Sarah (this poem is in the same 1796 volume). But the 'cottag'd dell' implies, as does the 'cot' in 'The Aeolian Harp', a retreat from the world. Already Coleridge's political bent seems to have become somewhat warped: he had spent much time and energy agonising over the role of the poet and the lecturer, and yet he seems ready, even now, to talk of the grand scheme of Pantisocracy as though it were not a serious gesture against the notion of property so much as an escape. He fantasises about Chatterton being with them all in their colony in America:

> And love with us the tinkling team to drive
> O'er peaceful Freedom's undivided dale ...
>
> Alas, vain Phantasies! the fleeting brood
> Of woe self-solac'd in her dreamy mood!
> Yet will I love to follow the sweet dream
> Where Susquehanah pours her untam'd stream.
>
> And there, sooth'd sadly by the dirgeful wind,
> Muse on the sore ills I had left behind.

There is no question here of Coleridge's altering his verse: what was good enough for him in 1796 was good enough in 1834. The problem, in fact, is that it is not quite good enough for us, in that there is too much jostling for attention here. Pantisocracy is tossed in, but also tossed aside; the hard-working, idealistic commune has become as unreal as Lycidas' sheep; yes, the Susquehannah is 'untam'd' (as against Blake's 'chartered Thames'), but there is a practical sense in which it might well require some taming; in any case, it is merely a 'sweet dream', somewhere to escape to, where he can look back on the 'sore ills' of England. Few readers would have much idea of what all this was about, and the embarrassed comment in the Preface provided little enlightenment: 'Some of the verses allude to an intended emigration to America on the scheme of an abandonment of individual property.' There was much more to it than that. As it is present in the poem, the scheme becomes as much a vain fantasy as the idea of having Chatterton there to sing for them in the evenings, 'the young-eyed Poesy / All deftly mask'd, as hoar Antiquity'. The poem ends, then, on this note of unreality, anticipating Sarah's dismissal of such things in 'The Aeolian Harp'. But it also returns us to the opening, with 'woe self-solac'd in her dreamy mood' a sharp reminder of the 'self-consuming breast' of the first stanza. By raising another 'cenotaph' to Chatterton, the youthful poet dead ere his prime, Coleridge is curiously re-enacting the whole process of the poem, whereby we are reminded the more forcibly of the failure, not only of Chatterton, but of poetry itself.

'Religious Musings', the last poem in the 1796 volume, is far from being the 'desultory' poem its subtitle claims: as the epigraph from Akenside more appropriately hints, the poem represents, from its opening Miltonic cadences onwards, a change of tack.

> What tho' first
> In years unseason'd, I attun'd the lay

To idle Passion and unreal Woe?
Yet serious Truth her empire o'er my song
Hath now asserted: Falshood's evil brood,
Vice and deceitful Pleasure, she at once
Excluded, and my Fancy's careless toil
Drew to the better cause!

Although Coleridge removed the epigraph after 1796, he could not deny the general effect of this poem, which is to counter the movement of most of the volume. It is rather like his placing a headstone at the end of the book, announcing that all the other poems lie in the shadow cast backwards by this apocalyptic piece: an 'Argument', ranging from the 'Passion of Christ' through 'The Present State of Society' and 'The French Revolution' to the 'Millennium' and 'Universal Redemption', gives a daunting indication of what is to be expected. The poem itself (there are several different versions) begins with a celebration of the Nativity at Bethlehem:

there ... to sit
Sublime of extacy, and mark entranc'd
The glory-streaming Vision throng the night.
Ah, not more radiant, not loud harmonies
Hymning more unmanly sweet
With choral songs around th'Eternal Mind
The constellated company of *Worlds*
Danc'd jubilant: what time the startling East
Saw from her dark wound leap the flaming Child!
Glory to God in the Highest! Peace on Earth!

In reducing this passage in 1834, Coleridge loses some of its power and intensity, in particular the religious sense of ecstasy and of sublimity: these terms lurk beneath the surface of many Romantic poems, but Coleridge is the first to bring out their specifically Christian (as opposed to Blake's religious) force. The music of the spheres, the dance of the natural world – all touched upon in other poems, often in similar fashion, and often with reference to the poet and the poetic impulse – have been translated into the Christian harmony of Milton's 'Nativity Ode'. The central paradox of Christ's birth is, for Coleridge, that the vision of perfect self-hood is invisible: ecstasy is important for the Romantics because it allows them to talk in quasi-religious terms of those moments when the soul gets outside itself. Here the 'Despised

Galilaean! Man of Woes' (Chatterton, too, a man of woes, like the poet, had been despised) takes over the 'flaming Child':

> For chiefly on the oppressed God Man's face
> The Great Invisible (by symbols seen)
> Shines with peculiar and concentrated light,
> When all of self regardless the scourg'd Saint
> Mourns for the Oppressor, O thou meekest Man!
> Meek Man and lowliest of the Sons of Men!
> Who thee beheld thy imag'd Father saw.

The child is already the man, the Man who will die on the cross (as the next passage explains): the great Vision is the Great Invisible (to be seen, as Coleridge was to speak of poetry, in terms of symbols), self and non-self, life and, therefore, death.

> Lovely was the Death
> Of Him, whose Life was Love! Holy with power
> He on the thought-benighted Sceptic beam'd
> Manifest Godhead, melting into day
> What Mists dim-floating of Idolatry
> Split and mishap'd the Omnipresent Sire:
> And first by *terror*, Mercy's stumbling prelude,
> Uncharm'd the Spirit spell-bound with earthy lusts
> Till of its nobler Nature it gan feel
> Dim recollections; and thence soar'd to Hope,
> Strong to believe whate'er of mystic good
> Th'Eternal dooms for his Immortal sons,
> From Hope and stronger Faith to perfect Love
> Attracted and absorb'd: and center'd there
> God only to behold, and know, and feel,
> Till by exclusive consciousness of God
> All self-annihilated it shall make
> God its Identity: God all in all!
> We and our Father one!

Once agan, the anticipations of later writers are remarkable: the 'mists' are to be found in later Coleridge, but also in Wordsworth, in Keats, in Clare, and their function similar in that they conceal the true shape. The difference lies in Coleridge's emphasis on the active role the Godhead plays in dispelling such mists; and in seeing the truth, we end up self-annihilated, consumed by and with God, as opposed to the self-consumption of and by our woes in the 'Monody on the Death of Chatterton'.

> Thus from the Elect, regenerate through faith,
> Pass the dark Passions and what thirsty Cares
> Drink up the Spirit, and the dim regards
> Self-centre. Lo they vanish! or acquire
> New names, new features – by supernal grace
> Enrobed with Light, and naturalized in Heaven.
> As when a shepherd on a vernal morn
> Through some thick fog creeps timorous with slow foot,
> Darkling he fixes on the immediate road
> His downward eye: all else of fairest kind
> Hid or deformed. But lo! the bursting Sun!
> Touched by the enchantment of that sudden beam
> Straight the black vapour melteth, and in globes
> Of dewy glitter gems each plant and tree;
> On every leaf, on every blade it hangs!
> Dance glad the new-born intermingling rays,
> And wide around the landscape streams with glory!

The 'omnipresent Mind' flies from himself, as opposed to Keats's nightingale's flight from the poet; we 'know ourselves / Parts and proportions of one wondrous whole ... tis God / Diffused thro all, that doth make all one whole.' Coleridge presents his own version of the complete Blakean myth, in which the self is so divided that it loses its sense of wholeness. For Blake at this point, war descends, and his myth of falling gods looks back to Christian and classical myth, enabling him to play with similarities between Christ and Prometheus; for Coleridge to invoke the myth is to invoke the realities of war. A footnote to the line 'But first offences needs must come' (line 159), points to the current debate on whether or not war should be joined with France, and the poem lurches into the cruelty and horror of war. Just as he had done in his 'Monody', he here casts a baleful eye over a landscape where 'childless widows o'er the groaning land / Wail numberless: and orphans weep for bread'. It is an alarming and shocking moment, as Coleridge addresses the effects of a war pursued in the name of Christ. He cannot accept what has happened, and launches into a history of mankind to demonstrate that the blame lies with desire, fuelled by the Imagination. We are presented with the Enlightenment reasons for Pantisocracy:

with busy aim,
Each for himself, earth's eager children toiled,
So property began, twy-streaming fount,
Whence Vice and Virtue flow, honey and gall.
Hence the soft couch, and many-coloured robe,
The timbrel, and arch'd dome and costly feast,
With all the inventive arts, that nursed the soul
To forms of beauty, and by sensual wants
Unsensualised the mind ...

As the poem dwells on the awfulness of earth's overthrow, in strains similar to the apocalyptic poems of Byron and Clare (discussed later), Coleridge indulges in a disturbing directness:

Believe thou, O my soul,
Life is a vision shadowy of Truth;
And vice, and anguish, and the wormy grave,
Shapes of a dream! The veiling clouds retire,
And lo! the Throne of the redeeming God
Forth flashing unimaginable day
Wraps in one blaze earth, heaven, and deepest hell.

At the poem's end, he looks ahead to being part of the 'mystic choir':

Till then
I discipline my young and novice thought
In ministeries of heart-stirring song.

There is, in this remarkable poem, a sense of pressures that cannot be resisted. Coleridge aims, as the epigraph implies, at Truth, and yet the poem ends by discounting Life as 'a vision shadowy of Truth'. His own notes refer to the Revelation of St John, but the poem itself seems to reach rather emptily for the delights of 'Pure Faith' and 'meek Piety'. The Argument might refer to 'Universal Redemption', but a close reading of the poem renders this less than convincing: the poem cannot fulfil its own claims. Ostensibly about the love of God, it confronts mankind's failure, and cannot explain the apparently absurd paradox of the premise that peace can be won by force: what aspires to be about peace becomes an extraordinary tumult, a chaos of images. In this it is like 'Kubla Khan', where the voices 'prophesying war' are never far away. Just as we could argue that the desired 'plastic power' deserts him in 'Kubla Khan', so here the 'plastic might' that can '[mould] confusion to such perfect forms' is something that can be looked forward to, in a vague future. The reality is another matter.

To the 1817 version of 'The Ancient Mariner', Coleridge added, not just the prose gloss, but a quotation from the philosopher Thomas Burnet. There too there is talk of an 'image of a grander and better world', as there is of the necessity of being 'on the watch for truth'. But the firm emphasis on the multiplicity of 'invisible creatures, of a world elsewhere – 'What do they do? Where do they live? Human wit has always circled around a knowledge of these things without ever attaining it.' – this emphasis seems to underscore the poem itself. Perhaps one of the reasons for its endless fascination for readers of all persuasions (apart from so many of his unpersuaded contemporaries) is the poem's multifariousness, its refusal to yield its secrets to any one reading. Whatever the Gothic attractions of the narrative, the hypnotic quality of the verse, the religious connotations, there can be no doubt about the poem's metaphysical core: just as he blesses the watersnakes 'unawares', so he kills the albatross in a completely arbitrary fashion. Wordsworth is also drawn to the arbitrary nature of events, of how things happen by surprise, unassisted, 'unaware': he is a poet, indeed, of 'strange fits of passion'. It was Wordsworth, as we know, who suggested, when the poem was still a joint enterprise, the killing of the albatross as the essential act of the poem. Coleridge explores the dreadful ramifications of this act and, in so doing, gives one of the most powerful accounts in literature of the awfulness of the ensuing nightmare. The moral, which Mrs Barbauld found wanting, Coleridge wished away. The wisdom of the wedding guest is bought at the expense of sorrow; Keats, who in some of his letters and in *Hyperion* urged upon himself the connection between sorrow and knowledge, echoes, at the end of his 'Ode on a Nightingale', Coleridge's 'forlorn'. The poem, far from celebrating the virtues of community, the pleasures of the marriage-feast, keeps at its fore the terrible sense of isolation; the mariner is cursed, both by the 'dead man's eye', but, worse, by his experience. His 'strange power of speech' is akin to that of the poet's (Coleridge makes the connection in his late epitaph on himself): as the gloss puts it bluntly: 'the penance of life falls on him.'

There are times when, for Coleridge, the burden of life can be lifted. In some of his conversation poems, for example, he manages, more directly than Wordsworth, to bridge the gap at the heart of the poem: the prison of 'This Limetree Bower' becomes, through the power of the

Imagination, a source of 'delight'; when he blesses the 'last rook' as it flies across the setting sun, he does so in the knowledge, not available to the Mariner, that 'Nature ne'er deserts the wise and poor'; he is united with his 'gentle-hearted Charles, to whom / No sound is dissonant which tells of Life'. 'Frost at Midnight' is a most wonderful testimony to his belief in repetition, in the circularity that takes us, when we reach the end of the poem, back to the beginning. But if Coleridge seems more confident than Wordsworth of the reciprocity between inner and outer, in 'the lovely shapes and sounds intelligible / Of that eternal language, which thy God / Utters, who from eternity doth teach / Himself in all, and all things in himself', the poem is one, ultimately, of silence and of dreams. The frost's 'secret ministry' has its political and religious implications, but that quiet secrecy is self-confessedly unsettling and inward-looking, as the film on the grate acts as 'Echo and mirror seeking of itself'.[15] There is a chill stillness about the poem, comparable to Keats's 'cold Pastoral' of the Grecian Urn; but there is the marvellous warmth of the final paragraph:

> Therefore all seasons shall be sweet to thee,
> Whether the summer clothe the general earth
> With greenness, or the redbreast sit and sing
> Betwixt the tufts of snow on the bare branch
> Of mossy apple-tree, while the nigh thatch
> Smokes in the sun-thaw; whether the eave-drops fall
> Heard only in the trances of the blast,
> Or if the secret ministry of frost
> Shall hang them up in silent icicles,
> Quietly shining to the quiet Moon.

This apparent 'reconciliation of opposites' is what Coleridge seems to want to capture in 'Kubla Khan'. But just as the caves are 'measureless to man', so the poet cannot rise to the measure of 'That sunny dome! those caves of ice!' He would dearly love to be the idealised, slightly crazed poet of Platonic tradition. But whereas Wordsworth is able to say in 'Tintern Abbey' that 'the picture of the mind revives again', Coleridge can get no further than the subjunctive: 'Could I revive within me / Her symphony and song / I would build that dome in air.' For all its detail, for all its seething waters, it remains at one remove: what he calls in 'Dejection' the 'shaping spirit of imagination' is, not for the first or last time, absent. The poem remains a mystery, in which he glimpses what he might achieve; but the vision is always just beyond his reach. Once again, Coleridge is writing about the act of writing, and the result is essentially introspective and fragile, announcing, for all its wish to inspire 'holy dread', its own anguished privacy. But that is precisely the problem: no imagined 'romantic chasm', no 'mighty fountain' can be sufficent, without the connection he had been able to make in 'Frost at Midnight' between past and present, inner and outer. It is for this reason that, in 'Dejection', although there is a determined celebration of Joy in the final lines, the most poignantly honest stanza is the third, in which he states with devastating candour the underlying fragility of his poetics:

> My genial spirits fail;
> And what can these avail
> To lift the smothering weight from off my breast?
> It were a vain endeavour,
> Though I should gaze for ever
> On that green light that lingers in the west:
> I may not hope from outward forms to win
> The passion and the life, whose fountains are within.

3

The Prelude: 'The wavering balance of my mind'

One of the many intriguing aspects of recent work on Romantic writers is the battle waged over Wordsworth, in terms of the claims we might want to make for him, but also in terms of the claims he might have wanted to make for himself. As Stephen Gill has demonstrated in his *Life* (1989), when the *Lyrical Ballads* first appeared in 1798, Wordsworth's name was not the one to conjure with, alongside that of Coleridge and Southey; the anonymity of the first edition was sufficiently appropriate.[1] By the time Hazlitt came to attempt to comprehend the last quarter of a century, in *The Spirit of the Age* (1825), Wordsworth, for him, represented the 'pure emanation' of that spirit; but that is not necessarily an unqualified compliment from a man reluctant to view any of his contemporaries without qualification.[2] It is true that by the time of his death in 1850 Wordsworth had been Poet Laureate for seven years, and that he had left, for publication, the poem charting the growth of his own mind – the poem we all know him by, but which was, for most of his generation, nothing more than a promise whispered in the hushed cloisters of the Prospectus to the *Excursion* of 1814. The Wordsworth admired by the Victorians was very different from the figure we have tried to get to know.[3] There is some irony in the fact that the writer of the 'egotistical sublime', the writer with epic ambitions, the Milton of his day, became, in the 'influential' scheme of things, less important than Keats, the 'chameleon'-poet of non-identity who had burdened Wordsworth with the soubriquet in the first place.

If *The Prelude* is the poem by which we all, now, know Wordsworth, it is the poem by which, in its various forms, he did his best to know himself. The fact that it is virtually impossible to talk about it as a single construct, that it is, fascinatingly, a poem of process, is as significant for us readers as it was for Wordsworth as writer. For, as Keats realised in his brilliantly casual way, poetic identity is such a problematic concept that he was prepared to discountenance it altogether. Wordsworth confronts the same problem, but instead of letting it slip through his fingers he foregrounds it by making it the subject of his life's work. Well might he say, albeit with a degree of self-mockery, that it was a 'thing unprecedented in literary history for a man to write so much about himself'.[4] The lack of precedent made it that much the harder, the very difficulty reflected in the subterranean nature of the whole enterprise: Coleridge could at least imagine, publicly, the sacred river bursting through the crannies of the constricting world, whereas the most Wordsworth could do was to imagine his own life, his own 'inland waters' matching the Wye or the Derwent, in private to Coleridge. Dorothy, of course, the tender, quiet, loving Dorothy, provided another audience, so silent (and yet so central) that we are scarcely aware of her existence, until, as in 'Tintern Abbey', she appears as if from nowhere, a being in her own right, and at the same time a projection, bewilderingly both backwards and forwards, of the poet himself, as though, without her, he would not exist at all. The psychoanalytical implications of this have been explored, and are not my concern here, except in the sobering sense that however invented or imagined the personal life of the poem, it is also a real life, with real people, who 'lived and moved and had their being' at a particular historical point. Part of this reality is precisely the whispering of sweet everythings to Coleridge and Dorothy (when he is not communing, in silence, with himself). But – and again this point has been well made by others – against this quiet, privileged audience at home in Grasmere, is the audience represented by posterity and acknowledged by Wordsworth, not simply in terms of address, but in terms of the structure of the whole poem, as it grows, along with his mind, from those hesitant early beginnings at the end of 1798 to the published version of 1850 that demands the word 'epic' to describe its status as, at last, a public poem.[5]

The problem, then, is to do with gradations of the private and the public, with that central opposition of so much poetry of the period. One of the reasons for *The Prelude*'s importance in the debate about poetry is that, in trying to know himself, Wordsworth is specifically aiming at knowledge of himself as a poet: against the abstractions of the Preface to *Lyrical Ballads* lie the concretions of *The Prelude*. It is one thing to talk of the poet as a 'man speaking to men'; it is quite another to write a poem in which he is the man doing the talking – to himself, to Coleridge and Dorothy, and to the posterity he will never meet. As the audience keeps changing within the poem, so the poem becomes that oddity, an epic that is private. Stuart Curran has written eloquently about the various resorts to formal props and proprieties in Romantic poetry, but I have sometimes thought he underplays the contradictions, whereby poets' appeals to form can be self-denying if not self-defeating.[6] Whatever Wordsworth might say about antechapels and cathedrals, what *The Prelude* is really a prelude to is itself.

Wordsworth says in his Preface to the *Lyrical Ballads* that poetry depends, amongst other things, on repetition. This is clearly the case, locally, with different parts of *The Prelude*, so that the image of the 'echo' becomes an integral part of the overall structure. But it is also true for the whole poem. If, according to the 'plan', we should move logically on to *The Excursion*, according to the emotional and imaginative logic we should return to the beginning. As we have seen, this pattern of return is to be found in many of his other poems, and also in Coleridge; how appropriate, then, that towards the culmination of *The Prelude*, Wordsworth should address Coleridge in terms that take the poem – and the reader – back to the past, to the private recesses of the mind in which it haltingly began:

> When thou dost to that summer turn thy thoughts
> And hast before thee all which then we were,
> To thee, in memory of that happiness,
> It will be known – by thee at least, my friend,
> Felt – that the history of a poet's mind
> Is labour not unworthy of regard:
> To thee the work shall justify itself. (XIII.404–10; *1805* is the version quoted unless stated otherwise)

Wordsworth no doubt heard the Miltonic echo here, the earlier poet's determination in Book I of *Paradise Lost* to 'justify the ways of God to men', and there is undoubtedly an important sense in which Milton wants to justify himself to God, and sees his poem as the means towards that end. But among the many differences between the two poets is the relentless forward movement of *Paradise Lost*: the spiritual and chronological narratives carry us forward to the expulsion from Paradise. Wordsworth's work shall 'justify itself' to Coleridge only as he, in turn, goes back to that originary moment in memory. As he puts it in Book III, 'each man is a memory to himself', and of course however much recovery of that memory, – or those memories, those 'rememberable things' – might allow him to move on, to move forward, the simple fact is that memory takes him back to where it all began. The paradox is mirrored at a formal level: just as, at the end, Wordsworth allows talk of 'justification' to take us back to the beginning of that other epic of human tragedy, in the 'glad preamble' that he wrote in January 1804, to make sense of those recurrent lines of self-admonishment, he takes us back to the end of *Paradise Lost* – 'the earth is all before me!' – and we realise that behind his 'heart / Joyous, nor scared at its own liberty', lurks the acknowledgement which the literary echo is bound to evoke: paradise has already been lost. From the opening lines of his poem, we are embarking on a journey of return.

Both Milton and Wordsworth use the word 'justify'. Wordsworth is alert to the punning nature of Milton's language, in particular to the quasi-mathematical, accounting, measuring aspects of the Miltonic moral world, whereby, with God as the ultimate accountant, things have to 'balance out'. This kind of moral economy is, in Milton's case, specifically associated with a deity who exacts justification, but also expects it; by the same token Wordsworth resorts to the idea of justification, not just because of the literary allusion, but because of the importance of 'balance' in his poem as a whole. The 'fluxes and refluxes of the mind' bring to him a disturbance that almost destroys him as a poet: what runs through the poem is a desperate need to cling on to the palpable, to assert himself against all the odds. The image of Wordsworth provided by De Quincey is telling, of the poet literally clinging to the earth, or to a nearby wall, to hold on for dear life, as though he would otherwise be hurled off this mortal coil, sent flying by and from the diurnal course on which he depends.[7]

Towards the end of the first Book, Wordsworth turns to Coleridge with one of his disingenuous apologies, before hoping for something more specific:

> Nor will it seem to thee, my friend, so prompt
> In sympathy, that I have lengthened out
> With fond and feeble tongue a tedious tale.
> Meanwhile, my hope has been that I might fetch
> Invigorating thoughts from former years,
> Might fix the wavering balance of my mind,
> And haply meet reproaches too whose power
> May spur me on, in manhood now mature,
> To honourable toil. (I.645–53)

He had earlier announced that 'I may fix my habitation where I will' (I.10). In 1850 this was altered, insipidly, to 'Free as a bird to settle where I will', almost as though he had lost that sense of determination, the fixed habitation becoming something much more conventional. Certainly the poem loses by this act of revision, in that the 1805 version both takes us back to the beginning of the Book, and underlines what we come to recognise as the typical Wordsworthian self-doubts that follow on immediately:

> Yet should these hopes
> Be vain, and thus should neither I be taught
> To understand myself, nor thou to know
> With better knowledge how the heart was framed
> Of him thou lovest ... (I.653–7)

It is hard not to be reminded of those hesitations and pauses of 'Tintern Abbey', and in being reminded to be forced to acknowledge the precariousness of the balancing act. What is more, the attempts at keeping his balance have been, as he puts it in I.646, 'lengthened out', the lengthening a matter both of filling out, as it were, his apparently 'tedious tale', but also of metrically stretching his verse to the end of the line, stretching out the sense into the next line, so that the act of balancing is enacted in the movement of the verse, as it turns (as the Latin 'versus' reminds us that it can).[8] When, in the movement towards doubt quoted above, he steadies himself with a reassuring rhetorical question, he can play more freely with the twists and turns of the verse, as he reverts to

> Those recollected hours that have the charm
> Of visionary things, and lovely forms
> And sweet sensations, that throw back our life
> And almost make our infancy itself
> A visible scene on which the sun is shining. (I.659–63)

'Revert' does then seem the right word: 'throw back' might, given the general reliance on images of recollection and seeing, make us think of the watery mirrors that sparkle through the poem, but the image of juggling is just as persuasive, returning to us (and returning us to) the past he has resorted to, has turned back to, in order to 'fix the wavering balance of [his] mind'.

There are many examples of the way in which the verse mirrors the balancing, and it is significant that so many occur in the early part of the poem, as though he were particularly conscious of the problem as he sets out. Here, for instance, he describes his loitering in the sun, enjoying a 'perfect stillness', and contemplating what he might one day perform as a poet – 'some work / Of glory there forthwith to be begun'.

> Thus long I lay
> Cheered by the genial pillow of the earth
> Beneath my head, soothed by a sense of touch
> From the warm ground, that balanced me (else lost
> Entirely), seeing nought, nought hearing, save
> When here and there, about the grove of oaks
> Where was my bed, an acorn from the trees
> Fell audibly and with a startling sound. (I.87–94)

Wordsworth is emphatic about how lost he would be without this balance provided by the 'warm ground', and this moment is therefore all the more important as one to register. Once again, the movement of the verse spells out the potential terror ('balanced me (else lost / Entirely)'), as does the syntax which in apparently describing the balance can seem to spell out the loss if the balance were not there: 'seeing nought, nought hearing'. This is a hint of many moments in the poem where he is in a world of darkness and despair; for all the talk of sunlit days, there is more than enough to remind us of clouds that take a sober colouring from having watched o'er man's mortality: the ambiguities of the 'Immortality Ode' permeate *The Prelude*, lending it the darkness of dream and nightmare. Here again the 1850 version does more than mar the 'effect', it destroys the whole point of these lines as they are in *1805*.

> Thus long I mused,
> Nor ere lost sight of what I mused upon,
> Save when, amid the stately grove of oaks
> Now here, now there, an acorn, from its cup
> Dislodged, through sere leaves rustled, or at once
> To the bare earth dropped with a startling sound. (*1850*, 1.80–5)

The gap between the two versions is more than a matter of a few words here and there: he has bizarrely transposed a crucial cadence into a different key, losing the very expression of dread of loss in favour of a vague poeticism.

As with Antaeus, so with Wordsworth: balance, whatever else, is a physical thing first and foremost.[9] Many of the childhood episodes of the first two books derive their power from this very physicality, whether or not Wordsworth transforms them into 'spots of time'. When he writes about his role as 'a plunderer ... in the high places' (I. 336), he presents us with an extraordinary image, made the more so by the rhetorical emphasis on the act of balancing:

> Oh, when I have hung
> Above the raven's nest, by knots of grass
> And half-inch fissures in the slippery rock
> But ill-sustained, and almost (as it seemed)
> Suspended by the blast which blew amain
> Shouldering the naked crag, oh, at that time
> While on the perilous ridge I hung alone,
> With what strange utterance did the loud dry wind
> Blow through my ears! The sky seemed not a sky
> Of earth – and with what motion moved the clouds! (I.341–50)

The act of hanging is imaged and reinforced by its repetition at the line breaks, its precariousness reiterated by the suggestion ('almost (as it seemed)') of suspension; he is (almost) an Atlas-figure, with the weight of the world on his shoulders – and, typically in *1805,* the syntax shifts from him to the elements.[10] We forget that this is an episode about birds'-nesting, as it becomes a re-enactment of his desperate attempts to keep his balance, buffeted by a wind that is also a blast. There follows the boat-stealing episode, in which as he strikes the oars 'in cadence', his 'little boat moved on / Even like a man who walks with stately step / Though bent on speed' (I.386–8). This repeats the lines of *1799*, but in the *1850* reworking he removes this passage, as though the passing reference to stately progression had lost its significance for him. Things are not, however, that simple. This passage is so complex that any alteration affects its overall tone and structure; although in the passage that follows, in which the 'huge cliff' strides after him, Wordsworth keeps some of the images of balance – 'measured motion' (I.411), for example, ironically transferring the stately progress to the threatening landscape, or the boat likened to a swan as it sails through the water – he loses an earlier echo of the balance of his own mind: 'I fixed a steady view / Upon the top of that same craggy ridge, / The bound of the horizon' becomes 'I fixed my view / Upon the summit of a craggy ridge'. He had made the same point in *1799*, but by *1850* does not want to make too much of it; he in fact deletes about ten lines, all of which concentrate on the strangeness and the solitude of the episode, his sense of being 'alone', which made the balance, and its difficulty, that much more crucial.

Some of these 'spots of time' are more emblematic, in that the image itself is sufficient to make the point, without elaboration. When he leaves the 'tumultuous throng' (I.476), the power of the verse resides in the act of digging in his heels, and letting the earth spin past:

> – yet still the solitary cliffs
> Wheeled by me, even as if the earth had rolled
> With visible motion her diurnal round! (I.484–6)

To be reminded of Lucy at this point, 'rolled round in earth's diurnal course', is to be made alert to the metaphysical nature of this point of balance, expressed here with such dramatic clarity. But we are also made aware of the strange otherness of this experience, that other world which has such a hold upon him.

> Behind me did they stretch in solemn train,
> Feebler and feebler, as I stood and watched
> Till all was tranquil as a dreamless sleep. (I.487–9)

It is, as so often with Wordsworth, hard to pinpoint the emotional turmoil here. The tenuousness of the experience is emphasised by the subsequent image of the kite, which is reminiscent of the birds'-nesting lines, but this time without any ability to keep the balance:

> – at this hour
> The heart is almost mine with which I felt
> From some hill-top on sunny afternoons
> The kite high up among the fleecy clouds
> Pull at its rein like an impatient courser,
> Or, from the meadows sent on gusty days,
> Beheld her breast the wind, then suddenly
> Dashed headlong and rejected by the storm. (I.517–24)

As he had shouldered the crag, so the kite 'breasts the wind', but is suddenly made passive, literally and grammatically, by the storm. In *1799* Wordsworth had not fully worked through this image, so that it is to some extent passed over too briefly; but by *1805* he has caught its significance the more powerfully not only because of the echo but because of the reminder of the opening line of the 'glad preamble', of the 'gentle breeze'. A reminder, too, of course, of the way in which that 'corresponding mild creative breeeze' has become by I.46 a 'Tempest, a redundant energy / Vexing its own creation'. There is little easy solace in his poetry.

Wordsworth draws our attention to the problem of balance because it is so hard to sustain: this reflects the problem of the poem itself. The questions, 'Why is he writing?' and 'What is he writing?' are prompted in any reading of the poem. Some of the hints of an answer are given in traditional terms, early in the poem, where he talks of the holy, prophetic nature of the poet's calling:

> To the open fields I told
> A prophecy: poetic numbers came
> Spontaneously, and clothed in priestly robe
> My spirit, thus singled out, as it might seem,
> For holy services.

But he so undercuts the tradition by emphasising his own weakness that it becomes a hindrance.

> Then, last wish –
> My last and favourite aspiration – then
> I yearn towards some philosophic song
> Of truth that cherishes our daily life,
> With meditations passionate from deep
> Recesses in man's heart, immortal verse
> Thoughfully fitted to the Orphean lyre ... (I.228–34)

If the reference to the philosophic song of truth reminds us of Coleridge's hopes for the poem, the mention of Orpheus brings him up short:

> But from this awful burden I full soon
> Take refuge and beguile myself with trust
> That mellower years will bring a riper mind
> And clearer insight. (I.235–8)

The weight is terrible because he feels unequal to it: to assume such a role is to invite the possibility of failure already confronted.

Wordsworth does not know himself, or, to use his own verb, 'trust' himself, sufficiently. In spite of his declarations to the contrary, he can indeed 'miss' his 'way'. He can embrace his declared freedom early in the poem ('enfranchised' has the very political connotations that he denies by a process of removal in *1850*), but questions immediately follow, with a Keatsian anxiety ('what dwelling shall receive me? In what vale / Shall be my harbour ...?') which seems to undermine that declaration. He can rejoice:

> It is shaken off –
> As by miraculous gift 'tis shaken off –
> That burden of my own unnatural self,
> The heavy weight of many a weary day
> Not mine, and such as were not made for me. (I.21–5)

But he does, as he and we soon learn, protest too much. He points, in these lines, to the nature of the opening breeze, 'half conscious of the joy it gives', and in doing so points to his own 'unnatural self'. We are made only too conscious of his own self-consciousness, and before long, of the implications and complications of that self – or, rather, those selves.

It is partly a stylistic matter, which is not to diminish it: on the contrary, style for Wordsworth, as for Coleridge, is a question of how to write about himself. A dramatic illustration is provided by a comparison between *1805*, I.33–54, and the *1850* version.

> Enough that I am free, for months to come
> May dedicate myself to chosen tasks –
> May quit the tiresome sea and dwell on shore,
> If not a settler on the soil, at least
> To drink wild water, and to pluck green herbs,
> And gather fruits fresh from their native tree.
> Nay more – if I may trust myself, this hour
> Hath brought a gift that consecrates my joy,
> For I, methought, while the sweet breath of heaven
> Was blowing on my body, felt within
> A corresponding mild creative breeze,
> A vital breeze which travelled gently on
> O'er things which it had made, and is become
> A tempest, a redundant energy
> Vexing its own creation. 'Tis a power

> That does not come unrecognized, a storm
> Which, breaking up a long-continued frost,
> Brings with it vernal promises, the hope
> Of active days, of dignity and thought,
> Of prowess in an honourable field,
> Pure passions, virtues, knowledge, and delight,
> The holy life of music and of verse. (*1805*)
>
> Dear Liberty! Yet what would it avail
> But for a gift that consecrates the joy?
> For I, methought, while the sweet breath of heaven
> Was blowing on my body, felt within
> A correspondent breeze, that gently moved
> With quickening virtue, but is now become
> A tempest, a redundant energy,
> Vexing its own creation. Thanks to both,
> And their congenial powers, that, while they join
> In breaking up a long-continued frost,
> Bring with them vernal promises, the hope
> Of active days urged on by flying hours, –
> Days of sweet leisure, taxed with patient thought
> Abstruse, nor wanting punctual service high,
> Matins and vespers of harmonious verse! (*1850*)

The whole drift and temper has altered, and we are presented with two very different accounts of himself. The precariousness of the moment and its significance, and therefore of the self in either version, is underlined by his *1805* comment, 'If I may trust myself' (I.39). Within each version, as the succeeding lines demonstrate, the self is itself divided:

> My own voice cheered me , and – far more – the mind's
> Internal echo of the imperfect sound.
> To both I listened ... (I.64–6)

To resort to his own imagery, the waters are becoming muddied: internal and external do not simply reflect each other; one is an 'imperfect sound', and the paradoxical suggestion is that the internal echo is closer to the sound of perfection.

When he chides himself for his apparent failure as a poet, he speaks of his 'more subtle selfishness' (I.247), at the same time 'so much wanting in myself / That I recoil and droop'. His perplexity is put in terms of that self that, it would seem, is not his:

> Thus baffled by a mind that every hour
> Turns recreant to her task. (I.269–70)

The mind in *The Prelude* is a treacherous thing, not necessarily his, nor under his control. At this very point he resorts to the verb so crucial to his ideas of balance:

> ... takes heart again
> Then feels immediately some hollow thought
> Hang like an interdict upon her hopes. (I.260–2)

But here, far from being a concrete verb, the whole phrase is curiously metaphysical. Within a hundred lines he begins to wonder that 'all the early miseries, / Regrets, vexations, lassitudes ... should ever have made up / The calm of existence that is mine when I / Am worthy of myself' (I.360). This is his problem, what it means to be worthy of himself, particularly when he seems to be so many different beings: when launching into the boat-stealing episode shortly afterwards, and describing himself as 'alone' and a 'stranger' in the vale of Patterdale, he is a stranger to himself and to us. When the whole episode is over,

> for many days my brain
> Worked with a dim and undetermined sense
> Of unknown modes of being. In my thoughts
> There was a darkness – call it solitude
> Or blank desertion. No familiar shapes
> Of hourly objects, images of trees,
> Of sea or sky, no colours of green fields,
> But huge and mighty forms that do not live
> Like living men moved slowly through my mind
> By day, and were the trouble of my dreams. (I.418–27)

It is these 'unknown modes of being' – both within and without – that he pursues in Book II. So far as his own sense of self is concerned, the gap between past and present is paramount – the self as it was then, and the remembering self. Characteristically, he first expresses this with a paradoxical notion of a peaceful weight. Even in this early stage of the poem, Wordsworth works by opposites:

> A tranquillizing spirit presses now
> On my corporeal frame, so wide appears

> The vacancy between me and those days
> Which yet have such self-presence in my mind
> That sometimes when I think of them I seem
> Two consciousnesses – conscious of myself
> And of some other being. (II.27–33)

At this point he seems to shift both focus and tone, as he lowers the pitch of the rhetoric. Neither version is entirely successful, because he cannot recreate precisely the nature of his split psyche. The bizarre strangeness to himself of what he had been is transformed into something almost humdrum.

> A grey stone
> Of native rock, left midway in the square
> Of our small market-village, was the home
> And centre of these joys; and when, returned
> After long absence, thither I repaired,
> I found that it was split, and gone to build
> A smart assembly-room that perked and flared
> With wash and rough-cast, elbowing the ground
> Which had been ours. (II.37–45)

This is one of those places where the (almost literally) concrete does not in fact lend its weight to the mighty abstractions that have preceded it: interestingly in *1850* Wordsworth emphasises the abstract element by capitalising 'Being' (line 33), removes any hint of the rock's being split ('Gone was the old grey stone'), and alters the rather puzzling 'elbowing' to the matter-of-fact 'usurped'. But these falterings are in themselves important for an understanding of his poem, his perception of himself across that 'vacancy' of years. When he digs his heels into the ice in the first book, the line of trees becomes 'feebler and feebler'; he sees more by seeing less, keeping his balance, as it were, with a gaze that borders, as in a 'dreamless sleep', on blindness.

As the poem proceeds, the problems increase. He cannot escape his sense of bewilderment, a 'strangeness in my mind, / A feeling that I was not for that hour / Nor for that place. But wherefore be cast down? Why should I grieve? I was a chosen son.' His 'holy powers' survive the transformations of *1850*, but not his sense of being thus chosen. In *1805* there are several passages which echo this line, later regarded as something like blasphemy: here the point to note is this contradiction between the lightheartedness of much of the surrounding verse, the concentration on superficiality, the sense of strangeness, and this bold recognition of his own religious election. He is, rather like the Ancient Mariner, blessed with 'holy powers / And faculties ... / To apprehend all passions and all moods / Which time and place and season do impress / Upon the visible universe, and work / Like charges there by force of my own mind'. Recalling the opening lines of the poem about freedom he says in *1805*, 'I was a freeman – in the purest sense / Was free – and to majestic ends was strong' (III.89–90). No such claim is allowed in *1850*. But in *1805* his 'mind returned / Into its former self', and he became aware of a new world, of new powers. The verse works its mighty way, and the reader is left to register the claims of *1805*, and the awkwardness with which he wrestles in *1850* as he tries to comprehend it all.

Wordsworth's claims are reminiscent of Coleridge's account of the Imagination as the 'infinite I AM':

> Unknown, unthought of, yet I was most rich,
> I had a world about me – 'twas my own,
> I made it; for it only lived to me
> And to the God who looked into my mind. (III.141–4)

This could well be regarded as the ultimate claim, provoking charges of madness: so sure is Wordsworth that he will only acknowledge this, 'If prophecy be madness'. But, as the poem reaches the first of its spiritual climaxes, he openly and honestly confronts the paradox that there are no words adequate for the task, even as he adopts the Miltonic mantle, and rejoices in his own mighty solitude and singleness, the blind seer.

> And here, o friend, have I retraced my life
> Up to an eminence, and told a tale
> Of matters which not falsely I may call
> The glory of my youth. Of genius, power,
> Creation and divinity itself
> I have been speaking, for my theme has been
> What passed within me! Not of outward things
> Done visibly for other minds – words, signs,
> Symbols or actions – but of my own heart
> Have I been speaking, and my youthful mind.
> O heavens, how awful is the might of souls,
> And what they do within themselves while yet
> The yoke of earth is new to them, the world

> Nothing but a wild field where they were sown!
> This is in truth heroic argument
> And genuine prowess, which I wished to touch
> With hand however weak, but in the main
> It lies far hidden from the reach of words.
> Points have we all of us within our souls
> Where all stand single; this I feel, and make
> Breathings for incommunicable powers. (III.168–88)

Alongside several such magnificent passages there are many lines of subfusc verse, reflecting, as he readily admits, his disillusionment with Cambridge and its obvious superficialities. The curious combination of 'grave and gay' makes for an odd effect; it is as though he is determined to convey the bemusement sparked by this period of 'submissive idleness'. The oddity is increased by his recognition, towards the end of the Book, of the complexities of memory, the relation of past to present, the problem, in a word, of truth.

> Of these and other kindred notices
> I cannot say what portion is in truth
> The naked recollection of that time,
> And what may rather have been called to life
> By after-meditation. (III.644–8)

If it is the case, as he had said earlier, that 'each man is a memory to himself' (III.189), then the implications are disturbing. Wordsworth gives several indications of his own self-awareness here: 'We see but darkly / Even when we look behind us' (III.492–3). But this Keatsian hint at dark passages and blind alleys has another aspect, again 'teasing us out of thought':

> Caverns there were within my mind which sun
> Could never penetrate, yet did there not
> Want store of leafy arbours where the light
> Might enter in at will. (III.246–9)

But he does not want to dwell on these darknesses: it is enough that he can, like Coleridge in the limetree bower, feel at least the light of the sun. If 'Imagination slept' (III.260), there were some compensations. His honesty, however, will not allow him to deceive himself for long, and the question of whether he woke or slept recurs:

I confess
That, having in my native hills given loose
To a schoolboy's dreaming, I had raised a pile
Upon the basis of the coming time,
Which now before me melted fast away –
Which could not live, scarcely had life enough
To mock the builder. (III.433–9)

To construct a poem is analogous to establishing and 'fixing' a habitation on firm foundations. Just as Michael finds that, even supported by the 'power of love', he cannot complete the sheepfold he had begun with Luke, so Wordsworth has to confront the flimsiness of what must have seemed the most substantial of materials: it can become airy nothingness. Antaeus – and Prospero – can be defeated.

One of the major paradoxes of the poem is that this possibility of defeat and loss is intertwined with such great claims. Book IV provides an instance of this. The metaphorical ascent of Book III is answered here by a much more solidified climb, as Wordsworth leaves a party and drinks in the wonders of the dawn. It is a rare moment of unity and harmony, those musical terms he had used in earlier books to express the Coleridgean spirit of the Universe:

all
The solid mountains were as bright as clouds
Grain-tinctured, drenched in empyrean light;
And in the meadows and the lower grounds
Was all the sweetness of a common dawn –
Dew, vapours, and the melody of birds,
And labourers going forth into the fields. (IV.333–9)

This is the world, in part, of *Lyrical Ballads*, the landscape in all its glory, but the more glorious because of its commonness, its representativeness, the place of humanity in this landscape given its proper weight. This weight allows him to appeal to Coleridge on his own terms, in that just as the mariner blesses the watersnakes 'unawares', so Wordsworth proclaims:

Ah, need I say, dear friend, that to the brim
My heart was full? I made no vows, but vows
Were then made for me; bond unknown to me
Was given that I should be, else sinning greatly,

> A dedicated spirit. On I walked
> In blessedness, which even yet remains. (IV.340–5)

The Coleridgean vocabulary is balanced by the Wordsworthian tone, distinctive in its sense of inescapable, religious awe.

And yet this moment has come from apparently nowhere. Wordsworth begins this passage with a verb that has its own importance for him –

> The memory of one particular hour
> Does here rise up against me! (IV.315–16)

Many things rise up to the surface of Wordsworth's mind: as he says, earlier in the same Book, 'and at once / Some fair enchanting image in my mind / Rose up full-formed like Venus from the sea ...' (IV.103–5). But even here he is determined to slip in another crucial word, 'admonishment'. Although he is only talking about the frolics of his beloved dog, he is anxious to emphasise the admonitory nature of these images, the way in which, just as 'Those walks ... come back on me again' (IV.127–8), so these remembrances can disturb him, as if in reproof. What comes out from the past, however apparently benignly, comes reproachfully. In Book IV, he moves from celebrating the fact that, as with Moses, 'Gently did my soul / Put off her veil, and self-transmuted stood / Naked as in the presence of her God' (IV.140), to the bewildering sense of his being a second Nessus:

> The very garments that I wore appeared
> To prey upon my strength, and stopped the course
> And quiet stream of self-forgetfulness.
> Something there was about me that perplexed
> The authentic sight of reason, pressed too closely
> On that religious dignity of mind
> That is the very faculty of truth. (IV.292–8)[11]

This passage leads to the epiphany in the Lakeland dawn: if Wordsworth is puzzled, then the reader is even more so. This is why the repetition of the imagery of rising and mounting ('mountings of the mind') is so important for him, in that it allows him to play on the opposition with the 'inner falling off' (IV.270). The image of himself in a boat is central to this complex network of images:

> As one who hangs down-bending from the side
> Of a slow-moving boat upon the breast
> Of a still water, solacing himself
> With such discoveries as his eye can make
> Beneath him in the bottom of the deeps,
> Sees many beauteous sights (weeds, fishes, flowers,
> Grots, pebbles, roots of trees) and fancies more,
> Yet often is perplexed and cannot part
> The shadow from the substance – rocks and sky,
> Mountains and clouds, from that which is indeed
> The region, and the things which there abide
> In their true dwelling – now is crossed by gleam
> Of his own image, by a sunbeam now,
> And motions that are sent he knows not whence,
> Impediments that make his task more sweet. (IV. 247–61)

This inability to separate substance and shadow is a recurrent theme of *The Prelude*: here it is put in terms of the image of reflection, but that becomes entangled with his own image, his sense of himself. For Wordsworth this is both pleasurable and painful: he has to convey this curious combination ('Strange rendezvous my mind was at that time' (IV.346)), making the appropriate claims for each, without cancelling out the other. If John Clare was later to cry that his life 'hath been one chain of contradictions' (a cry he then contradicts), he is anticipated by Wordsworth's agonisings.

The ambiguity surrounding that verb 'rose' (IV.316) is fleshed out in the encounter with the discharged soldier, one of the first of many such episodes in the poem. The mountainous setting is more than descriptive padding: 'a steep ascent / ... to the ridge / Of that sharp rising, glittered in the moon / And seemed before my eyes another stream / Creeping with silent lapse to join the brook / That murmured in the valley.' In this other world, in his solitude, he hears and feels a curious happiness – 'what beauteous pictures now / Rose in harmonious imagery! They rose / As from some distant region of my soul / And came along my dreams.' While these pictures are apparently 'beauteous', they come from the dream world that has already shown itself to be one of perplexity: the 'trouble of [his] dreams' in Book I had been caused by the mighty forms of the mountain stalking after him ('the huge cliff / Rose up between me and the stars'). By a similar token, the emphasis on the chance nature of this meeting is as important as it is in 'Resolution and Independence'. The old soldier is equally mysterious, an emblematic figure representing 'A desolation, a simplicity / That seemed akin to solitude'; he has that 'steadiness', that sense of being 'fixed to his place', to which, as we have seen, Wordsworth aspires for so much of the poem. But his 'voice of dead complaint' (again, the reader of *1850* has to forgo this chilling phrase), lends him the admonitory air of the leechgatherer (and later, of the blind beggar).

> Slowly from his resting-place
> He rose, and with a lean and wasted arm
> In measured gesture lifted to his head
> Returned my salutation … (IV.436–9)

Once again, the active verb recalls those other risings, and the cumulative effect is for the soldier and the poet to merge; it is the poet who is led to comment, 'we must measure back / The way which we have come.' The literal point echoes the metaphorical point of the whole poem: this is precisely what Wordsworth is doing. There is a reminder here of the 'Old Man Travelling', but whereas that is a dramatisation, brief and frustratingly incomprehensible, here Wordsworth is seeing a projection of himself in this 'ghostly figure':

> Solemn and sublime
> He might have seemed, but that in all he said
> There was a strange half-absence – and a tone
> Of weakness and indifference, as of one
> Remembering the importance of his theme
> But feeling it no longer. (IV.473–8)

This could well be a description of the poet as he has presented himself in the course of the poem up to this point.

The even more powerful encounter in Book V serves a similar function, in that Wordsworth confronts the transience, the insignificance, of human life, the frailty of the natural world and the relationship of the poet to that world:

> 'Oh, why has not the mind
> Some element to stamp her image on
> In nature somewhat nearer to her own?
> Why, gifted with such powers to send abroad
> Her spirit, must it lodge in shrines so frail?' (V.43–8)

Wordsworth's alteration to this passage in *1850* is of significance in that he shifts the subject of the experience that follows – the dream of the reader of Cervantes – from a friend to himself, thereby underlining his bafflement as to his sense of self. The framing device of the dream recalls the dream landscape of so much of the poem, and immediately before this episode the discharged soldier has been presented in a similar, if less elaborate, mode. That ominous verb recurs:

> these sore thoughts [of disquietude]
> Came to him, and to height unusual rose
> While listlessly he sat ... (V.60–2)

The vision in the dream is of an Arab, carrying a stone – Euclid's elements – and a shell – the repository of poetry. But the book of poetry – 'something of more worth' – in fact foretells the end of the world. As he holds the shell to his ear, he hears, in effect, an echo of Kubla Khan's 'ancestral voices prophesying war':

> [I] heard that instant in an unknown tongue,
> Which yet I understood, articulate sounds,
> A loud prophetic blast of harmony.
> An ode in passion uttered, which foretold
> Destruction to the children of the earth
> By deluge now at hand. (V.94–9)

The contradictions, the puzzling oppositions, cannot be gainsaid. The Arab is likened implicitly to the poet – 'he looked often backward with wild look' – and in his doubleness – both Cervantes hero and Arab of the desert – he reflects the poet himself – 'Of these was neither, and was both at once' (V.126). The whole episode is terrifying, with its culmination of the 'fleet waters of the drowning world / In chase of him': the poet is left by this revenant, and awakes in horror. In case we have missed the point, Wordsworth proceeds to make it for us, giving his double being 'a substance', believing that 'in the blind and awful lair / Of such a madness reason did lie couched', and declaring that he too 'could share that maniac's anxiousness, could go / Upon like errand' (V.160–1). Fear and terror have become madness, but only half-perceived, just as the figure itself is both everything and nothing. The echo of 'Resolution and Independence' cannot be missed; but for all the horror, there is the suggestion that out of this madness can emerge a vision: Shakespeare and Milton are possible exemplars of this train of thought. At the same time, it is hard to forget the cataclysmic sense of the world's ending, of the Biblical flood sweeping all before it. The irony of this Book is indeed that it is called 'Books' and focuses on the wasted children of his own generation:

> a dwarf man! – in knowledge, virtue, skill,
> In what he is not and in what he is,
> The noontide shadow of a man complete. (V.295–7)

All that the poet holds dear has come to nothing, in this Utilitarian age whose workmen have 'overbridged / The froward chaos of futurity.' The most he can do is to resort to his memories of the past, with the famous lines 'There was a boy'; to answer the tumult of the present and the future he plays with the boy's 'mimic hootings to the silent owls', and the landscape becomes a crazy symphony of shouts and screams, 'echoes loud / Redoubled and redoubled'. It is a magical celebration of the power of repetition, the repetition of noise not merely for its own sake, but as image of the boy's fragmented self.[12] At such a moment, there is indeed no telling the 'shadow from the substance', no separating of echo from echo, no start or finish. It is a perfect moment of what John Clare was to call 'non-identity'; in the ensuing silence the boy becomes, mysteriously, one with nature. This moving moment is the more powerful because we learn, after this epiphany, that the child is dead.

> And they would shout
> Across the watery vale, and shout again
> Responsive to his call, with quivering peals
> And long halloos and screams, and echoes loud
> Redoubled and redoubled – concourse wild
> Of mirth and jocund din. And when it chanced
> That pauses of deep silence mocked his skill
> Then sometimes in that silence while he hung
> Listening, a gentle shock of mild surprise
> Has carried far into his heart the voice
> Of mountain torrents; or the visible scene
> Would enter unawares into his mind
> With all its solemn imagery, its rocks,
> Its woods, and that uncertain heaven, received
> Into the bosom of the steady lake. (V.399–413)

The full force of these lines is impressed upon us by what follows: again, with the phrase, 'like a dream of novelty' (V.453), Wordsworth takes us into that strange 'twilight' world. He remembers how, as a boy, he had seen a pile of clothes on the shore of Esthwaite, 'left, as I supposed, / By one who there was bathing' (V.461–2). It is as though a process of Hartleian association is transformed into a moment of psychic terror: another kind of repetition is at work, taking us back by verbal echo to the now dead boy and his mimic hootings, to the shadows of the past which cast themselves continually forward:

> meanwhile the calm lake
> Grew dark with all the shadows on its breast,
> And now and then a fish up-leaping snapped
> The breathless stillness. (V.464–7)

The dreadful 'snapped' is a hint of what is to come: as the earth seems to hold its breath, the truth emerges, literally, from the water.

> At length, the dead man, mid that beauteous scene
> Of trees and hills and water, bolt upright
> Rose with his ghastly face – a spectre shape,
> Of terror even. (V.470–3)

Susan Wolfson has written eloquently about this passage, about its origins in *1799*, about the use, yet again, of the verb 'rose', and about the importance of the fact that, in *1799*, this episode is immediately followed by the first mention of the 'spots of time' (in *1805* not to emerge until Book XI, after the French Revolution, and his sense of the complete failure, or impairment, of his imagination).[13] Part of her point is that the poem demands to be read, formally, in terms of its revisions; Zachary Leader has questioned this approach, believing as he does that Wordsworth does not intend to leave the poem hanging in the air, a series of incomplete fragments.[14] His argument about intention, and Wordsworth's desire to leave, in *1850*, a finished poem, is persuasive, and certainly has important ramifications for editorial practice. Fortunately, the critic, as opposed to the editor, can appear to have it both ways: although it is at this very juncture that Wordsworth, surprisingly, makes a large gesture towards an almost Platonic idea of art and truth, we, knowing what we do, can see beneath the polished surfaces that he would like to embrace.

> Thence came a spirit hallowing what I saw
> With decoration and ideal grace,
> A dignity, a smoothness, like the works
> Of Grecian art and purest poesy. (V.478–81)

Even as the poem stands, in whatever version we read it, this apparently Keatsian celebration of 'purest poesy' is not entirely persuasive, for the simple reason that Wordsworth's mind does not usually work this way. Much truer to his bent is the culmination of Book V, with its sense, in spite of everything, of uncertainty, of flux and reflux. In lines of remarkable force Wordsworth shows how mysterious the poetic power is:

> Visionary power
> Attends upon the motions of the winds
> Embodied in the mystery of words;
> There darkness makes abode, and all the host
> Of shadowy things do work their changes there,
> As in a mansion like their proper home.
> Even forms and substances are circumfused
> By that transparent veil with light divine,
> And through the turnings intricate of verse
> Present themselves as objects recognised
> In flashes, and with a glory scarce their own. (V.619–29)

This is the world of darkness and shifting shadows, the world of 'Tintern Abbey' and Keats's 'Nightingale', rather than 'The Grecian Urn'.

The Prelude's infinite and intimate complexities are fully felt in Book VI, in which Wordsworth embraces perplexity and sublimity, deep personal friendships and the isolation of the sublime, set in a political context that takes him from the quiet purlieus of Cambridge to the torrents of Europe. He is torn inwardly:

> My inner knowledge
> (This barely will I note) was oft in depth
> And delicacy like another mind
> Sequestered from outward taste in books. (VI.113–16)

The problem of saying what he really means is again at the forefront:

Mighty is the charm
Of those abstractions to a mind beset
With images and haunted by itself.

The word 'grace' is crucial, especially when it is associated with his sister Dorothy:

blest
Between those Sunday wanderings with a joy
Above all joys, that seemed another morn
Risen on mid noon: the presence, friend, I mean
Of that sole sister, she who has been long
Thy treasure also, thy true friend and mine,
Now after separation desolate
Restored to me – such absence that she seemed
A gift then first bestowed. (VI.210–18)

A comparison between Dorothy's appearance here and that in 'Tintern Abbey' is telling, in that not only is her first appearance in *The Prelude* put in such touching Miltonic terms, thereby uniting the personal with the epic, but she is partially defined by her absence up to this point (the same is true of Mary Hutchinson, the woman who becomes his wife). So powerful is the recollection that Wordsworth, through ' a strong / Confusion', places Coleridge in that scene, which in its bleakness is a foreshadowing of the crucial spot of time in Book XI.

But thou art with us, with us in the past,
The present, with us in the times to come. (VI.251–2)

The repetition echoes the merging of tenses, the merging of selves – 'twins almost in genius and in mind' – which is central to the structure of the poem, certainly in the 1805 version. What Wordsworth is saying is that, for this move from Cambridge to France and Revolution, he needs Coleridge to have been there, even though he was not, for the simple reason that they had not yet met. But against that imagined companionship he sets the 'awful solitude' of the Chartreuse, followed by the 'solitudes sublime' of the Alps they cross (so bizarrely) unwittingly. This passage towards the end of Book VI contains his paean to the Imagination –

> the Power so called
> Through sad incompetence of human speech,
> That awful Power rose from the mind's abyss
> Like an unfathered vapour that enwraps
> At once, some lonely traveller. I was lost ... (VI.562–6)

Thus *1850*, which puts the emphasis on the linguistic problem of which we are consious in *1805*, but which he does not feel the need to spell out: the Imagination's awful power is clear enough –

> here that power
> In all the might of its endowments, came
> Athwart me! I was lost as in a cloud ... (VI.527–9)

It is impossible to paraphrase this climactic moment, in which all the opposites of the poem so far are hurled together in syntactic and linguistic contradiction:

> The immeasurable height
> Of woods decaying, never to be decayed,
> The stationary blasts of waterfalls,
> And everywhere along the hollow rent
> Winds thwarting winds, bewildered and forlorn. (VI.556–60)

It is typical of Wordsworth to answer the 'dithyrhambic fervour' of Book VI with the bafflement (his word) of Book VII, in which he tries to come to terms with the city of London. He cannot sustain the tone of Book VI, the heroic argument; but nor can he cope with the 'Babel din' of the metropolis. All the more important, then, for him to face it, in all its diversity and terror.[15] To some readers, Book VII can seem an oddity, as he deliberately divests himself of those bardic robes he had donned in the previous book. But this is the ultimate test (before his engagement with the French Revolution) of whether he can, after all, arrive at 'Composure and ennobling harmony', which is the last and perhaps surprising line of this strangely weird book. There is one passage in particular which deserves quotation: it is as though we catch Wordsworth seeing humanity through Blake's eyes; but we also get Wordsworth's obsession with balance which, when lost, causes his own sense of himself to disappear. The emblem he chooses to make his point is that of the blind beggar, a figure similar to those others, such as the discharged soldier, with which readers of Wordsworth become so familiar. The 'apt admonishment' of the leechgatherer foreshadows the final line of this section, with its reference to 'another world', of which he has been conscious since the first book of the poem. When his mind turns round 'As with the might of waters', he harks back to the torrents we have seen and heard in Book VI.The paper on the blind man's chest, 'The story of the man and who he was', takes us back to the poet himself, and his own attempt to give his own story. On one level, Wordsworth is as helpless as the blind beggar.[16] In his imaginative indigence Wordsworth petitions us as silently as the beggar does him.

> How often in the overflowing streets
> Have I gone forwards with the crowd, and said
> Unto myself, 'The face of everyone
> That passes by me is a mystery!'
> Thus have I looked, nor ceased to look, oppressed
> By thoughts of what and whither, when and how,
> Until the shapes before my eyes became
> A second-sight procession such as glides
> Over still mountains, or appears in dreams,
> And all the ballast of familiar life –
> The present and the past, hope, fear, all stays,
> All laws, of acting, thinking, speaking man –
> Went from me, neither knowing me, nor known.
> And once, far travelled in such mood, beyond
> The reach of common indications, lost
> Amid the moving pageant, 'twas my chance
> Abruptly to be smitten with the view
> Of a blind beggar, who, with upright face,
> Stood propped aginst a wall, upon his chest
> Wearing a written paper to explain
> The story of the man and who he was.
> My mind did at this spectacle turn round
> As with the might of waters, and it seemed
> To me that in this label was a type
> Or emblem of the utmost that we know
> Both of ourselves and of the universe;
> And, on the shape of this unmoving man,
> His fixèd face and sightless eyes, I looked
> As if admonished from another world. (VII.594–622)

Against such fear is the retreat provided by Book VIII, whose title spells out what he has so far failed to demonstrate, 'love of nature leading to love of mankind'. The country fair on Helvellyn is the Eden of his childhood, 'the paradise / Where I was reared' (VIII.304), the place of freedom and self-reliance, of 'simplicity, / And beauty, and inevitable grace.' This is the world of *Lyrical Ballads*, with all its work, hardship, and suffering; but Wordsworth is quite prepared to idealise the shepherd figure, resorting to Miltonic echoes. In spite of this, confusion is rife.

> As when a traveller has from open day
> With torches passed into some vault of earth,
> The grotto of Antiparos or the den
> Of Yordas among Craven's mountain tracts;
> He looks and sees the cavern spread and grow
> Widening itself on all sides, sees, or thinks
> He sees, erelong the roof above his head,
> Which instantly unsettles and recedes –
> Substance and shadow, light and darkness, all
> Commingled, making up a canopy
> Of shapes and forms and tendencies to shape
> That shift and vanish, change and interchange
> Like spectres – ferment quiet and sublime
> Which after a short space works less and less,
> Till, every effort, every motion gone,
> The scene before him lies in perfect view
> Exposed and lifeless as a written book! (VIII.711–27)

By making sense of things we kill them: the written book, like the written words in Book VII, in London, reduces things to lifelessness. Wordsworth has never put things so bleakly, as he apparently undermines his whole enterprise as an autobiographical poet. But, miraculously, as in 'Tintern Abbey', the mind revives, and the 'senseless mass' is embraced in all its contrariness, 'A spectacle to which there is no end'. Not for the first time, the poet is a Prospero-like figure, waving his magic wand.

Wordsworth knows, of course, that the wand has to be broken. Near the beginning of Book X, where he writes about the Revolution, he again relates how he sees things in terms of reading an unintelligible book.

upon these
And other sights looking as doth a man
Upon a volume whose contents he knows
Are memorable but from him locked up,
Being written in a tongue he cannot read,
So that he questions the mute leaves with pain
And half upbraids their silence. (X.48–54)

His great fear is that his own book, too, is unintelligible, just as the world seemed in 'Tintern Abbey'. Wordsworth seems deliberately to be invoking the idea of the blind seer – Milton, Homer – only to take away whatever hope might be derived from that image.

The poem goes into great detail about the French Revolution in Books IX and X: but for Dorothy and Coleridge, he would not have survived the tumult. The political upheavals parallel his own, and when he opens Book XI he acknowledges that his poem, like his life, has not gone as he had expected, seemingly ending in 'utter loss of hope itself / And things to hope for!' The essential trust in the future ('Things evermore about to be') has been betrayed. As he says, 'Thus strangely did I war against myself', a war which leads him to look for salvation to Godwinian rationalism –

And hence an emptiness
Fell on the historian's page, and even on that
Of poets, pregnant with more absolute truth.

Having reached this nadir, this absolute abyss around which he has many times skirted, Wordsworth turns back, finally, to the 'spots of time' he had first written about in the very first version of 1799.

These moments of epiphany have been held back; this is one aspect of the revisionary reading of *The Prelude* that I find wholly persuasive, in that once we have read *1799*, we cannot help but wonder where these 'spots of time' will rise, as so much does in this poem, to the surface. What this means, in terms of the act of reading *The Prelude*, is that the modern reader is conscious of the holding-back. Wordsworth in *1805* leads us to think that we are indeed left with an empty page, and it is tempting to read that emptiness back into all that has gone before. Although he resorts to several epiphanic moments throughout the poem, he deliberately avoids the notion of 'spots of time' until this point, and the effect is rather like 'Was it for this?' in reverse. That nagging question with which the enterprise begins is more than just a rhetorical device, as we discover in *1805*. A reading that takes in all stages of the poem cannot help but ask, 'was it for what?' There is that gap at the heart of the poem, and typically these 'spots' play around that idea of gap. In the first place, the revision that becomes Book XI extends the first episode, of the gibbet, in a striking way: the murderer's name has been carved on the turf, and is kept 'fresh and visible' from year to year. At the sight of the name, the poet flees, as though the knowledge is too much for him to bear, too cruel a truth. He loses his companion, 'honest James', and is alone, at one with the various solitary images of this episode. He has to admit that he cannot be precise about what he calls 'the visionary dreariness' of this moment: only by reading the whole poem can the reader begin to make sense of these lines.

> Forthwith I left the spot
> And reascending the bare common saw
> A naked pool that lay beneath the hills,
> The beacon on the summit, and more near,
> A girl who bore a pitcher on her head
> And seemed with difficult steps to force her way
> Against the blowing wind. It was in truth
> An ordinary sight, but I should need
> Colours and words that are unknown to man
> To paint the visionary dreariness
> Which, while I looked all round for my lost guide,
> Did at that time invest the naked pool,
> The beacon on the lonely eminence,
> The woman and her garments vexed and tossed
> By the strong wind. (XI.301–15)

The paradox is that out of this very bleakness, this scene not merely of remembrance but of memorial, a scene it were better had been never seen, out of this 'monumental writing', arises a paean to the powers of childhood and the Imagination. At the same time, just as this recollection grows out of something truly appalling – the perpetual, anonymous reminder, carved into the landscape, of death by violence – so he has to acknowledge that whatever he learns from this experience is a lesson that will elude him. It is a recognition of his mortality, but also of his fragility as a poet. He is lost, he admits, as he was then, and as he will be so many times in the future. The yawning gap between past and present, between childhood vision and adult blindness, mirrors the gap at the heart of the poem.

The days gone by
Come back upon me from the dawn almost
Of life; the hiding-places of my power
Seem open, I approach, and then they close;
I see by glimpses now, when age comes on
May scarcely see at all; and I would give
While yet we may (as far as words can give)
A substance and a life to what I feel –
I would enshrine the spirit of the past
For future restoration. (XI.333–42)

With the second 'spot of time' also about death, that of his father, which like the inscription of the murderer's name, seems to him a 'chastisement', we come full circle, to those early moments of guilt in the very first versions of the poem, retained in Books I and II of *1805*. As then, he is now haunted by the elements; but paradoxically out of these blank emblems – 'types and symbols of eternity', we might suppose – he draws sustenance, 'as at a fountain'.

Unfortunately, Wordsworth feels the need to conclude his poem; perhaps he had been better advised to follow the conclusion of *Rasselas*, in which nothing is concluded. If 'words find easy way', that is not the impression given by the rest of the poem. On the other hand, the celebrated account in the final book of the ascent of Mount Snowdon could be said to justify much of what he does in these final sections of the poem. The passage is rightly recognised as Wordsworth's fitting climax, in which he moves from the profoundly physical to the profoundly visionary. Within the space of 30 lines he recalls, obliquely, earlier epiphanic moments of the poem, including the turf from that spot of time, now lit and and falling like a flash, the moon in naked, glorious solitude, the 'mist at our feet', the blue chasm, 'through which / Mounted the roar of waters, torrents, stress / Innumerable, roaring with one voice!':

The universal spectacle throughout
Was shaped for admiration and delight,
Grand in itself alone, but in that breach
Through which the homeless voice of waters rose,
That dark deep thoroughfare, had nature lodged
The soul, the imagination of the whole. (XIII.60–5)

When he had crossed the Alps, in Book VI, Wordsworth had been thrown into puzzlement and confusion; here, at the end of the poem, he provides a rhetorical answer to those earlier doubts, but he also presents an emotional argument that forms a framework for the whole poem. It is here that he finally throws off his own unnatural self, as he celebrates that ability of the great:

> They from their native selves can send abroad
> Like transformation, for themselves create
> A like existence, and, whene'er it is
> Created for them, catch it by an instant. (XIII.93–6)

It is only as a result of this communion with the natural world that they reach the 'highest bliss', the 'consciousness / Of who they are.' This is what he has been working towards throughout the whole poem.

In personal terms, Wordsworth quite appropriately turns to the talismanic figures in his life – Dorothy and Coleridge (and, in *1850*, Mary Hutchinson); only Wordsworth can address a sister or a friend with such unmawkish tenderness. In urging Coleridge to 'call back to mind / The mood in which this poem was begun', he urges the reader to do so as well, to enter again that wide loop of time, to go back to the question he had asked of the 'life which I had lived, / 'Where art thou? Hear I not a voice from thee / Which 'tis reproach to hear?' 'Anon I rose / As if on wings, and saw beneath me stretched / Vast prospect of the world which I had been / And was ...' Wordsworth's life had been a world, and still is, as he ends his poem. To ask where Coleridge was, is to ask where he, Wordsworth, was, so dependent were they on each other. Now, at the poem's end, he talks of them both as 'Prophets of nature ... What we have loved / Others will love, and we may teach them how.' It is something of a major triumph that Wordsworth, who has spent so much of the poem talking about his own double self, of his solitude with that troubled psyche, of his many failures to realise his ambitions as a writer, of his consequent fear of the written word and its deadening power, should move with such generosity in these final lines towards Coleridge, in an embrace of reconciliation and recognition of Coleridge's own place in posterity: 'Thy moment of glory will be raised!' As Wordsworth has acknowledged on several occasions, the silent monument was as telling as any 'monumental words'; for the poem has, after all, been an 'offering of love' to Coleridge, just as 'Tintern Abbey' had been to Dorothy. He has, in fact, justified himself to Coleridge.

> Others too
> There are among the walks of homely life
> Still higher, men for contemplation framed,
> Shy, and unpractised in the strife of phrase,
> Meek men, whose very souls perhaps would sink
> Beneath them, summoned to such intercourse.
> Theirs is the language of the heavens, the power,
> The thought, the image, and the silent joy.
> Words are but under-agents in their souls;
> When they are grasping with their greatest strength,
> They do not breathe among them. This I speak
> In gratitude to God, who feeds our hearts
> For his own service – knoweth, loveth us,
> When we are unregarded by the world. (XII.264–77)

Wordsworth, it is not often said, is one of the humblest of the Romantic writers; here he could be writing about so many of the characters who inhabit *Lyrical Ballads*, with their meekness and humility; he could be writing about John Clare, the 'unregarded' poet whose work he did not know; he could be remembering the 'silent joy' of the stars' arrival in their domestic homes of the spheres, in the gloss to 'The Ancient Mariner'; but, bearing in mind his *Essays on Epitaphs*, with their talk of the ambiguities and dangers of language, and hearing the echoes of 'under-soul' (III.539–40) and 'under-presence' (XIII.71–3), he could be writing about himself.

4
Keats and Shelley: 'The dark idolatry of self'

When Keats received a copy of Shelley's drama *The Cenci,* he felt obliged to give a truthful verdict: it was all very well, he told the author in August 1820, but in a typically Keatsian phrase he urged him to 'curb his magnanimity'; the world might indeed deserve bettering, but an artist's task was, in the first place, to attend to the words on the page, 'to load every rift with ore'.[1] Keats did not, of course, subscribe to the belief that poetry was what 'oft was thought, but ne'er so well expressed'; but he could not allow Shelley to get away with a general desire to put the world to rights at the expense of his obligations as a poet, in the old sense of maker and creator. One of the ironies here is that Shelley himself, in his *Defence of Poetry,* invokes precisely that Greek notion, as had his model, Sidney: the poet is a creator, indeed the Godlike figure that Coleridge invokes in his attempt to describe the Imagination. But for Shelley to create is rather different from making, especially once he has taken the Platonic leap into a world of ideal forms; let mere mortals do the making, the approximating to the ideal of which he himself has knowledge.

The debate between Keats and Shelley was sadly if necessarily brief: within a year Keats was dead, to be memorialised by Shelley in his pastoral elegy *Adonais*. That poem is a strong reminder that in fact each poet, in his own way, was tackling the problem that Keats had put so starkly in his letter: in his short writing life Keats continually addressed the question of the nature of poetry and the poet, and so too did Shelley. With Keats, the constant wrestling occupies practically every poem, and many letters; he does not leave the kind of manifesto contained in Shelley's *Defence* or in the Prefaces to so many of Shelley's poems. But if we think of Shelley as the more positive writer, the one with a clearer sense of what poetry is, there is something uncanny about the fact that in the poem he was working on at his untimely death, 'The Triumph of Life', the last words he wrote were, '"Then, what is life?" I cried.' The conclusion of the *Defence* talks of the poet as a legislator of the world, but one unacknowledged; at the centre of the same piece he places the image of the poet as nightingale, singing to cheer its own solitude. In short, Shelley's questions, if less insistent, echo Keats's, whose final year is taken up with questions to which there seem to be few answers. Both attempts at *Hyperion* fail, and although he gives stylistic reasons for this ('too Miltonic'), there is also the fact that he does not know how to cope with Moneta's dismissal of him as 'of the dreamer's tribe'. And yet, against the questioning and self-undermining of these final fragments, there is the apparent certainty of 'To Autumn', where indeed every rift is loaded with ore.

The two poets are engaged, 20 years after *Lyrical Ballads*, with those large and intractable issues that had preoccupied Wordsworth and Coleridge. The climate has changed, certainly, and with it the nature of some of the questions, but the basic problem remains: what is poetry for, and what is the character of the poet? Should the poet be writing about himself, or should he be addressing the present age, whilst hoping for some future in which all manner of things shall be well? As we have seen, for both Wordsworth and Coleridge the nature of poetry becomes entangled in the nature of the poet. For Keats, there is no such thing as the poetical character: or, rather, and more subtly, the 'chief characteristic of the poetical character is that it has none'.[2] It is not just that the poet is 'chameleon-like', Shakespearian in his ability to be an Iago or an Imogen, to peck about the gravel with the sparrow, to get inside – bizarrely – a billiard ball; to be a poet is to lose oneself by not being a poet. This is, at least partially, the central crux of his poetry: just as the poet wants not to be a poet, so the poetry wants to deny its own existence. But whereas Wordsworth, in some of his ballads, arrived at something like this Keatsian self-denying ordinance, Keats, in loading every rift with ore, loads every line of his poetry with himself. It is virtually impossible not to recognise a line of poetry as by Keats, as it draws attention to itself even as it wishes to hide itself, or, even more impossible, to hide behind itself. This contradiction makes for some very odd reading, and presents Keats with problems that he finds insoluble. His emphasis on the importance of writing as a craft leads to the realisation that in *Hyperion* he has lost himself altogether in his Miltonic mantle, just as early in his career he tries on the robes of Spenser, Shakespeare, Dryden, and Chatterton. Keats is in many ways the epitome of Harold Bloom's notion of the 'anxiety of influence': he trumpets the virtues of having no character, but when he realises that he has lost his altogether he falls silent.

Shelley also is alert to the paradoxes of his own view of poetry. From very early on he resorts to Prefaces which are often more directly revealing than the poems themselves, in which the reader is often left floundering. Leavis famously spoke of Shelley's 'loose hold on the actual',[3] hoping to echo Arnold's talk of the beautiful but ineffectual angel, 'flapping its wings in the void'. Arnold's emphasis on the 'void' is actually of some critical use, whereas Leavis makes rather heavy weather of the necessary consequence of Shelley's own description of his work (*Alastor*, in this case) as 'allegorical': as early as 1815, Shelley was apparently certain of his intentions.

> [Alastor] represents a youth of uncorrupted feelings and adventurous genius led forth by an imagination inflamed and purified through familiarity with all that is excellent and majestic, to the contemplation of the universe. He drinks deep of the fountains of knowledge, and is still insatiate. The magnificence and beauty of the external world sinks profoundly into the frame of his conceptions, and affords to their modifications a variety not to be exhausted.

Eventually, the external beauties 'cease to suffice', and his 'mind is at length suddenly awakened and thirsts for intercourse with an intelligence similar to itself ... He imagines to himself the Being whom he loves.' But there is nothing to match his conceptions, and he dies in disappointment. Quite clearly this is a poem about his own ideal of the poet; but he is anxious to draw the moral for his readers. He acknowledges the poet's 'self-centred seclusion' to be the cause of his downfall; but he then goes on to affirm that his fate is preferable to that of those who refuse the lures of passion, those who are 'morally dead'. In asserting his belief in the value of those who search for the truth of existence, even when 'the vacancy of their spirit suddenly makes itself felt', he quotes Wordsworth's lines from *The Excursion* to make the point:

> The good die first,
> And those whose hearts are dry as summer dust,
> Burn to the socket!

For all his declared optimism, Shelley here embraces the notion of the doomed poet, doomed because of an impossible vision. Its very impossibility might seem to deny the poet's role, but the attempt has to be made, whatever the cost. On one level, the cost is failure and early death; on another, it is that contradiction of so much Romantic writing, the poet whose triumph is silence. The poem is presented as an elegy on himself (for the connection between the poet and the Poet is soon made, encouraged by the Preface). He is almost a Wordsworthian figure, a solitary whose tomb is the natural world:

> He lived, he died, he sung, in solitude.
> Strangers have wept to hear his passionate notes,
> And virgins, as unknown he passed, have pined
> And wasted for fond love of his wild eyes.
> The fire of those soft orbs has ceased to burn,
> And Silence, too enamoured of that voice,
> Locks its mute music in her rugged cell. (60–6)

The poem spells out in detail what the Preface had stated baldly: the hero is a paragon of virtue and 'divine philosophy', an archetypal wanderer, 'To seek strange truths in undiscovered lands.' If there are echoes here of Wordsworth, there are stronger ones, in terms of the poetic tone and structure of the quest, of Southey's *Thalaba* (1801), which helps to explain the poem's allegorical shape, far removed from Wordsworthian 'matter-of-factness'. He creates in a dream his other half, as Keats imagines the union between Porphyro and Madeleine in 'The Eve of St Agnes'; both poets are conscious, as Wordsworth appears not to have been, of the potential sexuality of the imaginative act.

> His strong heart sunk and sickened with excess
> Of love. He reared his shuddering limbs and quelled
> His gasping breath, and spread his arms to meet
> Her panting bosom:... she drew back a while,
> Then, yielding to the irresistible joy,
> With frantic gesture and short breathless cry
> Folded his frame in her dissolving arms.
> Now blackness veiled his dizzy eyes, and night
> Involved and swallowed up the vision; sleep,
> Like a dark flood suspended in its course,
> Rolled back its impulse on his vacant brain. (181–91)

Shelley's fondness for this idea of the vacant brain is telling: he has earlier in the poem spoken of the way in which 'meaning on his vacant mind / Flashed like strong inspiration'. Vacancy seems to be a necessary concomitant of the visionary moment; but it is also a consequence, and the poet is left, like Keats's knight, alone:

> Whither have fled
> The hues of heaven that canopied his bower
> Of yesternight? The sounds that soothed his sleep,
> The mystery and the majesty of Earth,
> The joy, the exultation? His wan eyes
> Gaze on the empty scene as vacantly
> As ocean's moon looks on the moon in heaven. (196–202)

If these questions echo those of Wordsworth and Coleridge in their respective Odes, Shelley cannot reinstate the 'joy, the exultation'. The bulk of the poem is given over to the poet's gradual death: the natural world reflects him wherever he goes.

> 'O Stream!
> Whose source is inaccessibly profound,
> Whither do thy mysterious waters tend?
> Thou imagest my life. Thy darksome stillness,
> Thy dazzling waves, thy loud and hollow gulfs,
> Thy searchless fountain, and invisible course
> Have each their type in me.' (502–8)

Although he uses, earlier in the poem, the phrase 'joyous madness', as he moves towards the climax he distances himself from Wordsworth's 'despondency and madness', and arrives at a puzzling amalgam which is caught well in the poet's dying moments.

> But when heaven remained
> Utterly black, the murky shades involved
> An image, silent, cold, and motionless,
> As their own voiceless earth and vacant air.
> Even as a vapour fed with golden beams
> That ministered on sunlight, ere the west
> Eclipses it, was now that wondrous frame –
> No sense, no motion, no divinity –
> A fragile lute, on whose harmonious strings
> The breath of heaven did wander – a bright stream
> Once fed with many-voicèd waves – a dream

Of youth, which night and time have quenched for ever,
Still, dark, and dry, and unremembered now. (659–71)

Shelley's insistence, at the limits of coherent syntax, that nothing can bring back the lost vision leads him to emphasise the state of non-being:

– but thou art fled –
Thou can no longer know or love the shapes
Of this phantasmal scene, who have to thee
Been purest ministers, who are, alas!
Now thou art not! (686–99)

Art's 'cold powers' are of no use.

Art and eloquence,
And all the shows o' the world are frail and vain
To weep a loss that turns their lights to shade.
It is a woe too 'deep for tears', when all
Is reft at once. (710–14)

The effect of these lines is similar to two kinds of Wordsworthian poem: on the one hand the 'Immortality Ode', in which he is determined to end on an affirmative note, in spite of the 'thoughts that do often lie too deep for tears', and on the other the elegiac poems in which he acknowledges the gap, the loss, the helplessness, a kind of poetry which would prefer, if it could, to deny itself.

Against *Alastor* should be set a poem written two years later, more ambitious, more like the 'political' Shelley to which most readers have grown accustomed. *The Revolt of Islam* is presented as an 'experiment on the temper of the public mind, as to how far a thirst for a happier condition of moral and political society survives, among the enlightened and refined, the tempests which have shaken the age in which we live.' In these circumstances the methods and virtues of poetry are more or less self-evident.

I have sought to enlist the harmony of metrical language, the etherial combinations of the fancy, the rapid and subtle transitions of human passion, all those elements which essentially compose a Poem, in the cause of a liberal and comprehensive morality; and in the view of kindling within the bosoms of my readers a virtuous

> enthusiasm for those doctrines of liberty and justice, that faith and hope in something good, which neither violence nor misrepresentation nor prejudice can ever totally extinguish from mankind.

Shelley quite rightly insists that he can only proceed episodically: 'methodical and systematic argument' have no place in his poetry. His answer to the question, 'What is a poet?', anticipates the claims he will make at much greater length in the *Defence*; 'It is the business of the Poet to communicate to others the pleasure and the enthusiasm arising out of those images and feelings in the vivid presence of which within his own mind consists at once his inspiration and his reward.' Lest this sound too self-centred, too much a reflection of the poet in *Alastor*, Shelley sets his poem in the context of world history, but also in the more recent turbulence of the French Revolution: he is not content, as was Wordsworth in his Preface to *Lyrical Ballads*, to make a fleeting allusion to 'revolutions in society'. He traces the history of the Revolution, and the ensuing despair in Britain, before what he sees as a new dawn. 'But mankind appear to me to be emerging from their trance. I am aware, methinks, of a slow, gradual, silent change. In that belief I have composed the following Poem.' He feels that he has at least the right credentials, in that he has experienced – through reading, travel, converse, communion with nature – all that is necessary for a poet to hear: he is the ideal listener. Shelley is, then, the nightingale, singing in the dark, and the person who hears him, not knowing quite where the song is coming from. In terms of the relation between poet and audience, Shelley is curiously both in the poem, and yet not; he is the poet, but stands back from the poem, wondering what it is. As he puts in in the Dedication to Mary:

> Is it, that now my inexperienced fingers
>   But strike the prelude of a loftier strain?
> Or, must the lyre on which my spirit lingers
>   Soon pause in silence, ne'er to sound again,
>   Though it might shake the Anarch Custom's reign,
> And charm the minds of men to Truth's own sway
>   Holier than was Amphion's? I would fain
> Reply in hope – but I am worn away,
> And Death and Love are yet contending for their prey.
>
> And what art thou? I know, but dare not speak:
>   Time may interpret to his silent years. (stanzas x, xi)

The Revolt of Islam announces a new kind of poetry, a deliberate challenge to the reviewers and critics, forcefully staking its claims against current trends, and written, as Shelley tells Godwin in December 1817, 'with the same feeling ... as the communications of a dying man'.[4] The poem circles around itself, one canto folding into another, allowing narrative within narrative, characters merging with each other. Just as *Alastor* had conjured up his other half, only to lose her and thus himself, so here in Canto II we get the beginnings of a relationship between Cythna and Laon which rests on similar foundations.

> 'As mine own shadow was this child to me,
> A second self, far dearer and more fair:
> Which clothed in undissolving radiancy
> All those steep paths which languor and despair
> Of human things, had made so dark and bare,
> But which I trod alone.' (II.xxiv)

Shelley's 'second self' echoes Wordsworth's in *The Prelude*; Coleridge, too, had spoken of shadow and substance, with a similar sense of puzzlement, not knowing which was which. Here is a second-generation Romantic writer pursuing the question of identity, spelling out the way in which the poet creates the object of his love, his second self.

> For, before Cythna loved it, had my song
> Peopled with thoughts the boundless universe,
> A mighty congregation, which were strong
> Where'er they trod the darkness to disperse
> The cloud of that unutterable curse
> Which clings upon mankind: – all things become
> Slaves to my holy and heroic verse,
> Earth, sea and sky, the planets, life and fame
> And fate, or whate'er else binds the world's wondrous frame. (II.xxx)

The narrative of Canto III necessitates Cythna's capture and her sale into slavery. As with Byron in *The Prisoner of Chillon,* Shelley turns the world upside down in a dreamworld that becomes nightmare, in which sense of self is lost along with sense of anything:

> A gulf, a void, a sense of senselessness –
> These things dwelt in me, even as shadows keep

Their watch in some dim charnel's loneliness,
A shoreless sea, a sky sunless and planetless!

The forms which peopled this terrific trance
I well remember – like a choir of devils,
Around me they involved a giddy dance;
Legions seemed gathering from the misty levels
Of Ocean, to supply those ceaseless revels,
Foul, ceaseless shadows: – thought could not divide
The actual world from these entangling evils,
Which so bemocked themselves, that I descried
All shapes like mine own self, hideously multiplied. (III.xxii, xxiii)

This world of chaos is also, of course, the world of madness, the madness of the sailors in 'The Ancient Mariner', of Bonnivard in Chillon, the madness of not knowing:

Was Cythna then a dream, and all my youth
And all it hopes and fears, and all its joys and ruth?

This madness came again. (IV.iv–v)

As I have suggested, this relation of madness to lack of proper knowledge is central to much Romantic poetry; but the very vision of the poet is itself a direct route to Wordsworth's 'despondency and madness'. Not to know is both a cause and a sign of madness, as John Clare discovers in his asylum poetry: but knowledge is itself equally an indication of madness.

In this particular instance, the hero's madness eases as the old man who rescues him tries to make sense of things; by the end of Canto IV the poet (Laon) sees his reflection in the lake, and in doing so, sees his youth superimposed upon it, and ere long his beloved Cythna is there too, but also not there in an extraordinarily concentrated merging of images. Shelley's finding and losing of his identity at this point is matched by writing that suggests struggle and difficulty:

And though their lustre now was spent and faded,
Yet in my hollow looks and withered mien
The likeness of a shape for which was braided
The brightest woof of genius, still was seen -
One who, methought, had gone from the world's scene,

And left it vacant – 'twas her lover's face –
It might resemble her – it once had been
The mirror of her thoughts, and still the grace
Which her mind's shadow cast, left there a lingering trace. (IV.xxx)

The first line of the next stanza is rather like an ultimate condensed form of Wordsworth's 'A Slumber did my Spirit seal'. This apparent merging of Cythna and Laon has led to a realisation of their final separation, and to the impossible question,

What then was I? She slumbered with the dead.

What Laon cannot understand is that, in spite of everything, he now has a hope that he had not had before. But he has no idea whether or why it is justified.

Was that corpse a shade
Such as self-torturing thought from madness breeds? (IV.xxxiv)

Some kind of answer is provided in Canto VI, where the two lovers are united in a marvellous moment of silence,

as might befall
Two disunited spirits when they leap
In union from this earth's obscure and fading sleep.

Was it one moment that confounded thus
All thought, all sense, all feeling, into one
Unutterable power, which shielded us
Even from our own cold looks, when we had gone
Into a wide and wild oblivion
Of tumult and of tenderness? or now
Had ages, such as make the moon and sun,
The seasons, and mankind their changes know,
Left fear and time unfelt by us alone below? (VI.xxxiv–xxxv)

Shelley contains both the metaphysics of the moment and the physicality. He seems at times to be putting Wordsworth into reverse, as at the start of Canto VII.

> I told her of my sufferings and my madness,
> And how, awakened from that dreary mood
> By Liberty's uprise, the strength of gladness
> Came to my spirit in my solitude;
> *And all that now I was.* (VII.ii [my italics])

Shelley cannot embrace this process without reference to Laon's sense of self: he has, in regarding her, to regard himself. Significantly, Cythna tells of how, in her captive madness, she created by her visionary imagination a child in the image of Laon. But the baby is snatched from her, as Wordsworth's Lucy is snatched by death. In this poem of repeated loss and renewal, Shelley provides Cythna with the ideal poetic solution, as she writes in the sand:

> Clear, elemental shapes, whose smallest change
> A subtler language within language wrought:
> The key of truths which once were dimly taught
> In old Crotona; – and sweet melodies
> Of love, in that lorn solitude I caught
> From mine own voice in dream, when thy dear eyes
> Shone through my sleep, and did that utterance harmonize.
> (VII.xxxii)

What she writes is left in the sand, to be washed away by the tides; this secret language keeps us permanently excluded. Not only do we live 'in our own world', as he puts it, we keep its secrets to ourselves. Cythna's secrets allow her to utter 'sweet melodies', which are in fact his songs: the two are united in their harmonies, but united in solitude. We as readers, and as the outside world, have no part to play in this *egoisme à deux*; the very structure of the poem keeps us out, as does the private world they create for each other.

That is one, very deliberately articulated problem of this poem: in many ways, *The Revolt of Islam* is an extended version of *Alastor*, which in the extension becomes much more elusive. The eschewal of narrative contributes to the ploy of keeping the reader out of this self-enclosed drama, this world in which the characters are urged to know themselves, but at the same time to avoid 'the dark idolatry of self.' This seems to be part of the central point, that self-knowledge cannot be attained by the kind of self-centred egotism castigated in the Preface to *Alastor*; on the contrary, it depends on self-denial, on seeing oneself as another. But the other problem of this poem is its political ambitions, and here the allegorical 'veil' might seem too much of an obscuring garment. In Canto IX, for example, we get a hint of the 'Ode to the West Wind', of revolutionary hope and fervour that grows directly out of the couple's union:

> Lo! we two are here –
> We have survived a ruin wide and deep –
> Strange thoughts are mine ...
> We know not what will come. (IX.xix–xx)

Shelley finds it difficult to explain the connection, let alone the optimism.

> I smile, though human love should make me weep.

As the couple face death they cling on to the notion of posterity's remembrance; but once again it is a matter of secrecy, as Shelley counters the Wordsworthian (and Horatian) notion of 'monumental memorials':

> what we have done
> None shall dare vouch, though it be truly known;
> That record shall remain, when they must pass
> Who built their pride on its oblivion;
> And fame, in human hope which sculptured was,
> Survive the perished scrolls of unenduring brass. (IX.xxxi)

What is virtually impossible for him is to have it both ways, any more than he can forge a convincing link between his exploration of the self and that of a turbulent society intent on self-idolatry. But for all its failings, this poem in its scope and ambition sums up much of what the Romantic poets had achieved by 1817, even as it looks ahead to the questionings of Wordsworth and Keats.

The range of *The Revolt of Islam* is matched by several of Shelley's other works, and more than matched by *Prometheus Unbound*: this 'lyrical drama' is his version of the *Paradise Lost* myth, the myth that holds such attractions for all the major Romantic writers. Keats writes his version of the fall of the gods very soon after *Prometheus*, conscious above all of the Miltonic precedent; Blake's whole mythology spins on the same axis, cavalierly mixing Christian and pagan and private imagery; writers such as Wordsworth and John Clare use the myth of the fall in a much more personal way. For Shelley the Prometheus figure is not only the Aeschylean tragic hero; in his helpless pinning to the rock he transmogrifies into the crucified figure of Christ. If this provides room for theological confusion, it allows Shelley the freedom to rework the mythology of fall and redemption, without relying on Blakean contortions. The advantage of Prometheus, as Blake had seen, is that as an image of force and creativity, he is simultaneously a political and an artistic figure, a figure of contradictory and conflicting impulses. To misuse the oft-quoted line from Blake, Shelley is of the devil's party and knows it full well: it was because of his pamphlet on atheism that he had been sent down from Oxford. Shelley's Preface makes plain his belief that poetry is itself a political act, reflecting at its best the 'peculiarity of the moral and intellectual condition of the minds among which they have been produced'. 'The sacred Milton' was, he reminds us, a republican, a 'bold inquirer into words and religion'. It is the poet's task to be adequate – as Arnold was to put it later in the century – to the age.[5]

> The great writers of our own age are, we have reason to suppose, the companions and forerunners of some unimagined change in our own social condition or the opinions which cement it. The cloud of mind is discharging its collected lightning, and the equilibrium between institutions and opinions is now restoring, or about to be restored.

His optimism is intimately related to his belief in poetry as a creative and combining force. Far from being a solitary figure, as in *Alastor,* the poet

> is the combined product of such internal powers as modify the nature of others; and of such external influences as excite and sustain these powers; he is not one, but both. Every man's mind is, in this respect, modified by all the objects of nature and art; by every word and every suggestion which he ever admitted to act upon his consciousness; it is the mirror upon which all forms are reflected, and in which they compose one form. Poets, not otherwise than philosophers, painters, sculptors, and musicians, are, in one sense, the creators, and, in another, the creations, of their age.

This double role of the poet helps to explain the inward-looking nature of so much of his poetry, whereby the poet as creator, as God-like figure, does not in fact have the freedom implied by that equation. Those images in the water, those blurrings of identity, are consequent upon this 'subjection', as he puts it, from which the 'loftiest do not escape'. Poetry has its constrictions as much as it has its freedoms: not for nothing do we come across so many images of imprisonment in these writers. At the start of *The Prelude* Wordsworth celebrates his escape from the city, 'enfranchised and at large': but that early freedom, even with its political implications, is undermined by another Miltonic reference. 'The earth lies all before me' – as indeed it did for Adam and Eve at the very point when they are driven from the Garden of Eden. To be a poet, even for Shelley in *Prometheus Unbound*, is to be aware of the poet's constraints. The central image, after all, is of the crucified hero.

But he is not simply Prometheus. We are led to ask, 'Who is this Christ-like figure? Who are Asia and Panthea? Who and what is God?' Shelley seems to be asking, in Act II Scene iv, Blake's question of the tiger: 'Did he who made the Lamb make thee?' Demogorgon's anwer sums up the poem's conundrum:

> If the abysm
> Could vomit forth its secrets ... But a voice
> Is wanting, the deep truth is imageless. (II.iv.114–16)

The only effective language in this world of apparitions is music, as the Earth says:

> Language is a perpetual Orphic song,
> Which rules with Daedal harmony a throng
> Of thoughts and forms, which else senseless and shapeless were.
> (IV.415–17)

Such music of the spheres recalls the earlier chorus of echoes: and not only are echoes unseen, they are very soon unheard. As Wordsworth learns in *The Prelude*, echoes are, like Keats's fancy, 'deceiving elfs', mocking what they echo, and those who try to listen to them. 'How the notes sink upon the dying wind!' This is the obverse of the mild, creative breeze.

It would obviously be perverse to say of this prophetic poem that it is actually about failure. As in his 'Ode to the West Wind', Shelley embraces an optimism that is essential to his 'passion for reforming the world.' But *Prometheus Unbound* is none the less something of a paradox. It is a quest ('Follow, follow, follow me!'), but a quest in which the search for political, moral and aesthetic truth is really inexplicable. The whole poem, with its immense canvas of sprawling images, is forever deferring its meaning, for the simple reason that meaning is beyond its reach. Words flow, tumbling out in profusion, but the more they come, the more they baffle. The same effect can be found in the 'Hymn to Intellectual Beauty' and 'Mont Blanc', where long sentences fall over themselves as they try to keep up with the dizzy spectacle. 'Mont Blanc' concludes with a breathtaking swerve that questions its own premises:

> Winds contend
> Silently there, and heap the snow with breath
> Rapid and strong, but silently! Its home
> The voiceless lightning in these solitudes
> Keeps innocently, and like vapour broods
> Over the snow. The secret Strength of things
> Which governs thought, and to the infinite dome
> Of Heaven is as a law, inhabits thee!
> And what were thou, and earth, and stars, and sea,
> If to the human mind's imaginings
> Silence and solitude were vacancy? (134–44)

Julian and Maddalo appears to be a very different kind of poem; but it too faces the issue of creative genius, without recourse to fantastical mythology. Maddalo – a Venetian 'of the most consummate genius ... [whose] ambition preys upon itself' – is pitted against the English Julian, who hopes for a better world, and the Maniac, of whom 'I can give no information.' It is as if Shelley had divided himself, like Gaul, into three parts. Maddalo, unpersuaded by Julian's buoyant optimism, takes him to visit the madman incarcerated nearby: perhaps if Julian listens to him, he will see the folly of optimism. The Maniac's speech is confused and fragmented: 'I am mad. I fear / My fancy is o'erwrought ... thou art not here ... / Pale art thou, 'tis most true ... but thou art gone, / Thy work is finished ... I am left alone!' Much of what he says is addressed to a lover from his past, rather like Laon and Cythna, or Alastor and his other self. Again, the poet points to the futility of poetry:

How vain
Are words! I thought never to speak again,
Not even in secret ... (472–4)

Maddalo makes a memorable observation to Julian:

'Most wretched men
Are cradled into poetry by wrong.
They learn in suffering what they teach in song.' (544–6)

Wordsworth and Keats might both have said something similar. Julian leaves Venice, to return 'after many years / And many changes'; in Maddalo's absence, his daughter tells that the Maniac's beloved returned and then left. When Julian presses her for more, she 'told me how / All happened – but the cold world shall not know.' This is Wordsworthian anti-narrative taken to its extreme: the poet refuses to intrude upon the privacy of the Maniac and his beloved, and the poem abruptly ends. It is hard not to admit the strangeness of this poem: at times it seems like Browning, a teasing monologue which leaves us in suspense. But there are enough poems by Byron to provide a precedent for this kind of psychological exploration of a particular state of mind: both poets are clearly fascinated by the idea of a fragmentary narrative technique that matches the waywardness of a maddened mind. What sets Shelley's poem apart is not so much the recognition that 'words are vain' as his refusal to finish the poem, denying his role as a communicator of any sort. The woman who knows the story warns him against knowledge:

'Let the silent years
Be closed and cered over their memory
As yon mute marble where their corpses lie.' (613–15)

This knowledge once gained is so terrible that he will not pass it on. Julian, as the narrator, the poet, has already begun to identify with the Maniac, and the reader makes the disturbing connection between poetry and madness, and between them both and love. In the Preface to *The Revolt of Islam*, Shelley had concluded, 'Love is celebrated everywhere as the sole law which should govern the moral world.' But the poems themselves suggest that it is not quite so simple, except in purely abstract terms; the kind of blurring of identities that occurs in a Shelleyan relationship does not necessarily lead to happiness, for the reason that the sense of self-identity gets lost, at which point love can lead to madness. At the end of the poem Shelley is denying Maddalo's Keatsian words about poetry and wrongs, 'learning in suffering what they teach in song.' Julian, as the poet, will teach nothing in song. Like the Maniac addressing his loved one, he is reduced to saying, 'How vain are words!' The mocking echoes of *Prometheus Unbound* seem to be saying something similar, just as the boy's 'mimic hootings' in *The Prelude* lead directly into the death of the boy poet.

Whereas *Julian and Maddalo* would satisfy Leavis with its very firm 'hold on the actual', Shelley's classic poem of love, *Epipsychidion*, makes few concessions with its Platonic forms.

> Ah me!
> I am not thine. I am a part of *thee*. (51–2)

This other is the very cause of his downfall:

> She met me, Stranger, upon life's rough way,
> And lured me towards sweet Death; as Night by Day,
> Winter by Spring, or Sorrow by swift Hope,
> Led into light, life, peace. (71–4)

For all her beauty she cannot sate him, any more than Alastor's vision could him. If she becomes all beauty, an 'Image of some bright Eternity', then she loses her individuality. Ironically, this suits the poet who wants everything:

> Love is like understanding, that grows bright,
> Gazing on many truths; 'tis like thy light,
> Imagination! which from earth and sky,
> And from the depths of human fantasy,
> As from a thousand prisms and mirrors, fills
> The Universe with glorious beams, and kills
> Error, the worm, with many a sun-like arrow
> Of its reverberated lightning. Narrow
> The heart that loves, the brain that contemplates,
> The life that wears, the spirit that creates
> One object, and one form, and builds thereby
> A sepulchre for its eternity. (162–73)

The cynic might say that here speaks a man happy to enjoy more than one relationship at a time: but even the cynic would have to acknowledge that the poet falls foul of his own Blake-like desire to kill the worm of error. He falls in love with an ideal Being, whose sudden death leaves him bereft, 'this soul out of my soul'. In losing her he loses himself, and is back in a world of chaos, as though Creation had never taken place.

> But neither prayer nor verse could dissipate
> The night which closed on her: nor uncreate
> That world within this Chaos, mine and me,
> Of which she was the veiled Divinity,
> The world I say of thoughts that worshipped her. (241–5)

After the typical Shelleyan quest for the loved one, he rises to a pitch of ecstasy, sustained far longer than seems possible, before the final deflation.

> One hope with two wills, one will beneath
> Two overshadowing minds, one life, one death,
> One Heaven, one Hell, one immortality,
> And one annihilation. Woe is me!
> The winged words on which my soul would pierce
> Into the height of Love's rare Universe,
> Are chains of lead around its flight of fire –
> I pant, I sink, I tremble, I expire! (584–91)

The effect is curious, in that so much energy has been expended on the virtues of Platonic affection, only for it to be blown away. When, in the 'Ode to the West Wind', Shelley cries, 'I fall upon the thorns of life, I bleed, I die', we can place this cry of personal despair in a classical tradition of the Ode, whereby that cry is depersonalised.[6] But here something rather different appears to be involved; not only does poetry fail him, his sense of unity and oneness is self-defeating. For the protagonists to be one is in fact to invite disaster: immortal they may be, but Shelley laments the very union he has worked towards. To be one is, in these terms, to be nothing: far from being complementary, they are identical. To merge thus is to die. There is irony in that last line, in which 'we' becomes 'I' again, insistently: as he passes into an oblivion that he had thought would be a blissful vacancy of two minds joined into one, he asserts, with each verb, the pronoun that defines him, the very sense of himself that he is losing. As with *Julian and Maddalo, Epipsychidion* ends in failure.

*

Keats juggles all his life with the questions posed in his letter to Shelley: if he is to be a poet (and he is not even sure about that) then what does this mean? Is it indeed enough to 'load every rift with ore', or should he, as he suggests as early as 'Sleep and Poetry' (1816), face the 'agony and strife of human hearts'? There are times when he thinks he would be better off as a philosopher, rather than a 'versifying pet lamb'; and yet he admits that Thomson's *Castle of Indolence* is one of his favourite poems, catching as it does something of his particular brand of idle langour. 'O for a life of Sensations rather than of thoughts!' he cries;[7] but the poet-figure of *Hyperion* cries, 'knowledge enormous makes a god of me.' This is to summarise very briefly some of the obvious conflicts that find expression in his work and his letters: he would certainly not say, with Wordsworth, that each of his poems had a purpose, let alone a 'worthy' one, any more than he would talk so committedly, as does Shelley, of his belief in change and reform, and the poet's essential role in that human drama. Critics point to the scarcity of the references in his work to the French Revolution; many have argued that it is Keats's influence that is the major one in later eighteenth-century verse, leading to the idea of 'art for art's sake' – a phrase used for critics' own convenience rather than for any particular illumination it might offer. Some have argued that the sense of a poet's obligation that emerges in 'Sleep and Poetry' is the quality that mars his 'true' work: in other words that he allows the Wordsworthian 'purpose' to become too heavy a weight. There is certainly little doubt about his influence on the Victorians, and that their debates on the function of poetry, starting with Tennyson's 1832 volume, pick up the questions that his poetry leaves behind. But, then, it could be said that this is Keats's major contribution to the arguments about poetry and the poet, in that he is above all the poet of the question mark. Many would argue that he is more interested in the questions than the answers: if answers there are, they should be 'whispered quietly', as he puts it, to one's neighbour. Not for Keats the loud blast of the prophet's trumpet.

To characterise Shelley in those prophetic terms alone is deeply misleading, and Shelley's salute to Keats in *Adonais* (to which I turn at the end of this chapter) is not quite the poem we might expect from him. None the less, there is no denying the determination of Shelley's affirmative thrust: his mind is of a different cast from Keats's. This is apparent on the stylistic level: whereas Shelley speaks as though there were one common poetic language, a spring from which every poet drinks (not the same as Wordsworth's points about language), Keats turns to specific poets, not merely for sanction and support, but initially as a way of learning his craft, and then as a means of losing himself. 'Negative capability' is a stylistic as well as a moral and aesthetic imperative.

Keats's first surviving poem is, appropriately, an 'Imitation of Spenser'. As Charles Brown recorded, 'it was the *Fairie Queene* that awakened his genius ... enamoured of the stanza, he attempted to imitate it and succeeded.'[8] Whether the poem is a 'success' is more of a moot point than Brown suggests: in fact Keats often does himself few favours by his blatant early imitations, whether they be of Spenser, Shakespeare, Milton, or even his champion, Leigh Hunt. It is also true that the Spenserian stanza, as filtered through the eighteenth century and into the nineteenth, no longer has for us the charms it even held for Wordsworth and Byron. But for Keats it was an obvious start. What is worth dwelling on here is the characteristic 'if only' tone: this penultimate stanza, for instance, with its references to Virgil, Spenser, Shakespeare, Milton and Beattie, is not just pastiche, it is an elaborate admission that he cannot match his predecessors. Ironically, the literary allusions and echoes do not offer support so much as undercut his attempt at verse:

> Ah! could I tell the wonders of an isle
> That in that fairest lake had placed been.
> I could e'en Dido of her grief beguile,
> Or rob from aged Lear his bitter tears;
> For sure so fair a place was never seen,
> Of all that ever charmed romantic eye.
> It seemed an emerald i'the silver sheen
> Of the bright waters; or as when on high,
> Through clouds of fleecy white, laughs the cerulean sky.

Keats is wishing he could do better; he is also writing about something that does not exist. The effect of these early fumblings is to make the scene itself remote beyond conjecture, in that he admits to being unable to tell us about a scene unseen. The more we ponder those references to Dido and Lear, the more puzzling they become, except in so far as they point to his concern with the 'agonies, the strife of human hearts'. It is as though Keats cannot leave them out: they have no place in this poem, but inadvertently they draw attention to what Keats would really prefer to be doing. His 'Imitation' becomes a wish to achieve something grander. Keats's letters display an ambivalent attitude towards his audience, posterity, and fame: even in this five-finger exercise he is beginning to think about such things.

Other early poems reinforce this sense not just of a literary past, on which he can draw, or models he can follow: some poets are celebrated as images of fame, of genius either recognised or ignored. Chatterton becomes a soul-mate:

> How soon the film of death obscured that eye,
> Whence genius wildly flashed, and high debate.
> How soon that voice, majestic and elate,
> Melted in dying murmurs!
>
> ('To Chatterton')

But Chatterton in death continues singing 'to the rolling spheres': as the Grecian Urn will be, he is 'Above the ingrate world and human fears.' At this stage in his career (and whether that is the right word at this point in his life is the very question Keats keeps asking himself, as the medical profession beckons), Keats is unable to work through the complex implications of this. In the meantime he continues with his imitations: 'Specimen of an Induction' (Spenser and Leigh Hunt mixed with water), 'Calidore', a self-confessed 'fragment', or the sonnet, 'Oh, how I love', something of a mishmash, in which he combines his stylistic efforts with his sense of other poets:

> There warm my breast with patriotic lore,
> Musing on Milton's fate, or Sidney's bier,
> Till their stern forms before my mind arise –
> Perhaps on the wing of poesy upsoar,
> Full often dropping a delicious tear
> When some melodious sorrow spells mine eyes.

If this is confirmation that the child is father of the man, the poem also confirms that the child is still the child. Keats is well aware of his own failings: as he writes to his brother George, there is the recurrent fear that 'I should never hear Apollo's song'. He can hope, putting his faith in the poetic 'trance', but conscious that the trance is hard to attain, let alone sustain, for the reason that, as Wordsworth put it, it comes 'unawares':

> A sudden glow comes on them, nought they see
> In water, earth, or air, but prey.

He might comfort himself in rather ridiculous fashion:

> As to my sonnets, though none else should heed them,
> I feel delighted, still, that you should read them. ('To my brother George', 117–18)

But, against that, he says to Charles Cowden Clarke,

> Just like that bird am I in loss of time
> Whene'er I venture on the stream of rhyme.
> With shattered boat, oar snapped, and canvas rent
> I slowly sail, scarce knowing my intent. ('To Charles Cowden Clarke', 15–18)

It is only in 'Sleep and Poetry' (1816) that Keats begins to spell out more fully the problems of poetry. The poem is sufficiently well-known to require little comment, especially in its opposition between the luxurious joys of 'Poesy' and the prospect of something 'nobler' whereby he will address himself to human suffering: if this is Keats the young poet mapping out a clear plan of action, we also have to register his own acknowledgement of the difficulties. On the one hand the absurdities of the 'realm ... of Flora and old Pan'; on the other the problem involved in the 'vast idea' before him.

Keats has to die many deaths in the course of this poem. As he grasps his pen for 'Poesy', he cries, already anticipating the 'Nightingale':

> Yet, to my ardent prayer,
> Yield from thy sanctuary some clear air,
> Smoothed for intoxication by the breath
> Of flowering bays, that I may die a death
> Of luxury and my young spirit follow
> The morning sunbeams to the great Apollo
> Like a fresh sacrifice. (55–61)

Just as practically every poem by Keats looks inwards to its own workings, mulling over its own existence, its role as poetry and his as a poet, so his complete oeuvre is astonishingly self-referential, with the Odes acting as the final condensation, the final oozings, of all that has gone before. The luxurious death is not just a matter of 'an excess of pleasure': it is the ecstasy of the poet losing himself in an elysian world that becomes a book,

> Whence I may copy many a lovely saying
> About the leaves and flowers, about the playing
> Of nymphs in woods and fountains, and the shade
> Keeping a silence round a sleeping maid,
> And many a verse for so strange influence
> That we must ever wonder how and whence
> It came. (65–71)

His vision of the chariot of human suffering is even more teasing.

> Most awfully intent,
> The driver of those steeds is forward bent
> And seems to listen. Oh, that I might know
> All that he writes with such a hurrying glow.
> The visions all are fled – the car is fled
> Into the light of heaven, and in their stead
> A sense of real things comes doubly strong,
> And, like a muddy stream, would bear along
> My soul to nothingness. (151–9)

This is more complex and more threatening: the poet is the charioteer, but also the observer, unable to know what is written. This loss of self is that total 'annihilation' of which Shelley speaks in *Epipsychidion*: as Keats implies, this death is a result of the loss of the imagination (attributed here to the 'rocking horse' of the heroic couplet). The personal dread of loss and failure permeates his work. 'Sleep and Poetry' is a curious combination of regret and defiance, in that although he knows what he must do, he knows that he cannot, yet, do it. Towards the end of the poem, he looks around him, and writes of some of the paintings and sculptures in Leigh Hunt's house. One of the most striking images is of Sappho:

> Sappho's meek head was there half smiling down
> At nothing; just as though the earnest frown
> Of overthinking had that moment gone
> From off her brow and left her all alone. (381–4)

This is Keats in higher mode, finding the voice by which we recognise him: there is something appropriate about his concentration on the poet who is remembered only by fragments. Sappho's importance as an icon for the Romantics lies precisely in the small amount of her work that has survived: just as Wordsworth 'sees by glimpses now' the crucial moments of his past, so we see Sappho by glimpses. Keats captures wonderfully that mystery, that Sphynx-like 'half smiling down ' – ' at nothing'; she has, as it were, 'overthought' herself, lost herself, a mere vacant stare that underlines her isolation. Sappho here is a forerunner of the Moneta/Mnemosyne figure of the two versions of *Hyperion*: Keats has already had a brief glimpse of the way he will develop, even though he has, at this stage, to admit that Poesy, 'from off her thrones / ... overlooked things that I scarce could tell'. It is left to *Endymion* to pursue matters further.

Endymion, Keats's longest and most ambitious poem, is perhaps the least read. With its form of the quest or 'Romance', its echoes and allusions, it continues the tradition of Landor's *Gebir*, of Southey's *Thalaba*, and Shelley's *Alastor*. Keats's doubts about it are fully exposed in the tortured Preface, in which he confesses his sense of failure (both imaginative and stylistic) even as he dedicates it to Chatterton. As we have seen, other poets publish their failures or near-misses; but Keats is more honest in his announcement of his lack of maturity, his confusion.

> The imagination of a boy is healthy, and the mature imagination of a man is healthy; but there is a space of life between, in which the soul is in a ferment, the character undecided, the way of life uncertain, the ambition thick-sighted: thence proceeds mawkishness, and all the thousand bitters which those men I speak of [*sc.* critics] must necessarily taste in going over the following pages.

Keats's anticipation of a critical mauling proved correct, so much so that from this distance we might wonder why he put himself in such an exposed position. In spite of his hesitations, he could be extremely stubborn, as the disagreement with his publisher over the Preface suggests. But his stubbornness derives from his own curiously compounded ambition, and from his sense of what poetry might be.

Earlier in the Preface he actually admits, 'It is just that this youngster should die away': as Shelley talks of vacancy as somehow essential to his poetry, so Keats needs to explore this 'space of life between', to present it as part of himself, for the poem is exactly that, part of himself, a reflection and a production of his life at a particular time. There is something wilfully perverse about this apparent egotism in a man who talks repeatedly of the need to leave himself behind. But it is as though the death of this poem is essential for his progress, 'a sad thought for me, if I had not some hope that while it is dwindling I may be plotting, and fitting myself for verse fit to live': publication is necessary in order to expose his failure: that 'space of life between' requires representation, it requires the answering vacancy of his longest poem, almost as the other extreme of Sappho's silent solitude.

The hymn to Pan in the first Canto spells out, in ways he had not achieved before this, the complexities of this simultaneous embrace and withdrawal.

> 'Be still the unimaginable lodge
> For solitary thinkings – such as dodge
> Conception to the very bourne of heaven,
> Then leave the naked brain; be still the leaven,
> That spreading in this dull and clodded earth
> Gives it a touch ethereal, a new birth;
> Be still a symbol of immensity,
> A firmament reflected in a sea,
> An element filling the space between,
> An unknown – but no more! We humbly screen
> With uplift hands our foreheads, lowly bending.' (I.293–303)

As so often with Keats, quest gives way ere long to sleep, and thus to dream; and, as just as often, the dream is source of both enlightenment and frustration. 'Conception' is again the important word, with all its implications of creativity and sensuality, as the later union between Endymion and Diana suggests (*pace* Miriam Allott, who glosses, 'probably clear formulation'):[9]

> Ah, can I tell
> The enchantment that afterwards befell?
> Yet it was but a dream – yet such a dream
> That never tongue, although it overteem
> With mellow utterance like a cavern spring,

Could figure out and to conception bring
All I beheld and felt. (I.572–8)

The dream, unsurprisingly but essentially, fades: 'like a spark / That needs must die ... my sweet-dream / Fell into nothing.' But the apparently trite and obvious moves towards a fine subtlety beyond paraphrase.

The Morphean fount
Of that fine element that visions, dreams,
And fitful clues of sleep are made of, streams
Into its airy channels with so subtle,
So thin a breathing, not the spidered shuttle,
Circled a million times within the space
Of a swallow's nest-door, could delay a trace,
A tinting of its quality – how light
Must dreams themselves be, seeing they're more slight
Than the mere nothing that engenders them! (I.747–55)

Nothingness, going back to Sappho's glance, is, then, essential: far from it being a case of 'nothing comes from nothing', nothingness creates the dreams which are both everything and nothing. When she finishes her plea, the irony is many-layered:

'Why pierce high-fronted heaven to the quick
For nothing but a dream?' (I.759-60)

Endymion's response contains the famous account of the 'pleasure-thermometer', the physical leading by stages to the spiritual, that 'sort of oneness', the 'fellowship with essence, till we shine / Full alchemized, and free of space'. Whilst the conclusion of the first Canto contains within itself the germs of much of the following year's poetry, it is important to note also the presencce here of Death, the talk of 'half-forgetfulness'. Like the poet of the Odes, Endymion asks 'whither are they fled?' There is also talk of the cell of Echo, 'where she sits / And babbles through silence till her wits / Are gone in tender madness, and anon / Faints into sleep, with many a dying tone / Of sadness'. As with Wordsworth and Shelley, echo is itself a contradiction, a necessary part of poetry, even as the Orphic voice repeats itself, ever more faintly.

Something of this paradox is examined in the second canto, where

Endymion confronts the very self he seeks in his restless spiritual quest, as he tries to escape it.

> There, when new wonders ceased to float before
> And thoughts of self came on, how crude and sore
> The journey homeward to habitual self!
> A mad pursuing of the fog-born elf,
> Whose flitting lantern, through rude nettle-briar,
> Cheats us into a swamp, into a fire,
> Into the bosom of a hated thing.
> What misery most drowningly doth sing
> In lone Endymion's ear, now he has sought
> The goal of consciousness? Ah, 'tis the thought,
> The deadly feel of solitude; for lo!
> He cannot see the heavens, nor the flow
> Of rivers ... (II.274–86)

Here is the painful truth, in the realisation that the search to find oneself ends in self-loathing.

The poem as a whole does not succeed because it is trying for an impossible resolution. Keats's fascination with Greek myth leads him towards the necessary narrative conclusion, and away from the exploration of the powers of Poetry and the imagination. There are many strong moments, such as the visit to the Cave of Quietude. But the poem's split character is reflected in Endymion's cry to Diana:

> What is this soul then? Whence
> Came it? It does not seem my own, and I
> Have no self-passion or identity. (IV.475–7)

Both versions of *Hyperion* address these questions, once in dramatised form, once with the poet himself at the centre. As I have pointed out, Keats attributes his failure to complete the first version to the stylistic weight of Milton, and it is possible to understand what he means, as he loses himself stylistically in the model he has adopted; there is perhaps poetic justice here for a poet who claims 'non-identity' as his goal. Rather ironically, Arnold suggests later in the century that Keats is too powerful a model for contemporary poets (the irony compounded by Arnold's own inability to escape the Keatsian cadences).[10] Certainly in his Odes, Keats arrives, through endless honing, at a style so distinctive that it becomes a cloying influence on the next generation of poets. His verdict on *Hyperion* echoes Saturn's words to Thea:

> I am gone
> Away from my own bosom; I have left
> My strong identity, my real self,
> Somewhere between the throne and where I sit
> Here on this spot of earth. (I.112–16)

The poem pursues the conflict between these old Titans who rely on their strong sense of identity, and the revolting Olympians who ideally have no character, who represent the true poetic spirit. But the fall of the old gods, the loss of their glory, is as poignantly captured as Milton's depiction of Satan and his minions. 'It is left

> Deserted, void, nor any haunt of mine.
> The blaze, the splendour and the symmetry
> I cannot see – but darkness, death and darkness. (I.240–2)

In Keatsian terms, this can be put another way: this is the Chamber of Maiden Thought, the dark world of the nightingale. For all the desire to set off the old gods against the new (Apollo, 'first in beauty shall be first in might'), Keats's sympathies are with Hyperion, the god whose name gives the poem its title. When Hyperion appears in Canto II, it is as a figure spreading radiance, which in turn makes the scene more awful.

> In pale and silver silence they remained,
> Till suddenly a splendour, like the morn,
> Pervaded all the beetling gloomy steps,
> All the sad spaces of oblivion,
> And every gulf, and every chasm old,
> And every height, and every sullen depth,
> Voiceless, or hoarse with loud tormented streams;
> And all the everlasting cataracts,
> And all the headlong torrents far and near,
> Mantled before in darkness and huge shade,
> Now saw the light and made it terrible. (II.356–66)

This is similar to the apocalyptic torrents of *The Prelude*, 'the types and symbols of eternity, of first and last, and hope forever without end';

but Keats is writing about the old order, not the new. The final irony is that Apollo is as puzzled as the Titans. As he dies into life, the poem finishes, in mid-sentence. Whatever the stylistic excuses, Keats seems unable to effect this transmogrification. Byron's Manfred cries, at his end, 'It is not so difficult to die'; but Keats, not content with such passive acceptance, cannot achieve Apollo's resurrection. Whereas *Endymion* shows Keats's falling foul of his own narrative intentions, here the myth seems to replicate his own anguish. The other narrative poems tend to present him with similar problems, almost as though he strains too hard to point the moral. *Lamia's* pessimism is portrayed as a failure of the imagination in the face of 'cold philosophy'; *Isabella* is as interesting for its goulish dwelling on loss as it is for its attempts at social comment; only *The Eve of St Agnes* captures the full ambiguity of an imaginative world built around the tenuousness of the dream. Its richness depends for its effect on this ambiguity.

The Odes provide the consummation Keats devoutly wishes: in them he captures the depths of suffering, the depths of the metaphysical darkness, feeling the full weary weight of this unintelligible world. As he listens to the nightingale, literally and metaphorically 'in the dark', he wants to match the bird's 'ecstasy' with his own literal desire to get outside the prison of his own body. But like Apollo, he too finds that, however rich it might be to die at this point, he cannot do it. In any case, it would be a futile gesture, because at the very point of ecstasy, the bird leaves him. The poet is left with his own heavy burden of self, the very thing he had wanted to avoid. The Ode presents us with a failure, and that is its paradoxical success: its questions are honest, and the refusal to answer them is the guarantee of the poem's aesthetic honesty. In the 'Grecian Urn', however, Keats clings on to a chill notion of art, an aesthetic object that only partially answers its own impossible questions. He has forgotten that he is at his best when asking questions.

*

Keats died in Rome in March 1821. For Shelley, who produced his elegiac *Adonais* in July of the same year, it was almost no surprise: '[his] genius ... was not less delicate and fragile than it was beautiful; and where the cankerworms abound, what wonder if its young flower was blighted in the bud?' As both poets knew, if beauty was truth, and truth beauty, that was no guarantee of immortality. Shelley's late lyric sums up, in Darleyan fashion, the implications of such fragility.

When the lamp is shattered
The light in the dust lies dead –
When the cloud is scattered
The rainbow's glory is shed.
When the lute is broken
Sweet tones are remembered not;
When the lips have spoken
Loved accents are soon forgot.

As music and splendour
Survive not the lamp and the lute,
The heart's echoes render
No song when the spirit is mute: –
No song but sad dirges,
Like the wind thro' a ruined cell,
Or the mournful surges
That ring the dead seaman's knell.

This is almost the perfect commentary on *Adonais*.

Shelley's tribute to Keats self-consciously places itself in the tradition that had served Milton in *Lycidas*, and which was to serve Arnold when he memorialised Clough in *Thyrsis*. As with those poems, *Adonais* demonstrates the difficulties of a poet mourning another's death: it becomes a challenge to the very idea of poetry and the poet. Within the first three stanzas, Shelley moves from the hoped-for comforts of the genre to the despair of those who remain, as though he wants to emphasise the hollowness of the very model he is using: echo's repetitions can mock those who strain to hear the dying fall.

I weep for Adonais – he is dead!
O, weep for Adonais! though our tears
Thaw not the frost which binds so dear a head!
And thou, sad Hour, selected from all years
To mourn our loss, rouse thy obscure compeers,
And teach them thine own sorrow, say: 'With me
Died Adonais; till the future dares
Forget the Past, his fate and fame shall be
An echo and a light unto eternity!' ...

Oh, weep for Adonais – he is dead!
Wake, melancholy Mother, wake and weep!
Yet wherefore? Quench within their burning bed

Thy fiery tears, and let thy loud heart keep
Like his, a mute and uncomplaining sleep;
For he is gone, where all things wise and fair
Descend; – oh, dream not that the amorous Deep
Will yet restore him to the vital air;
Death feeds on his mute voice, and laughs at our despair.
(stanzas i and iii)

Those that mourn might persuade themselves that he survives, that the tears on his face are his. Death and life become confused, and in her tears she weeps away her existence. The fragility extends beyond the poet's death:

All he had loved, and moulded into thought,
From shape, and hue, and odour, and sweet sound,
Lamented Adonais ...

Lost Echo sits amid the voiceless mountains,
And feeds her grief with his remembered lay,
And will no more reply to winds or fountains,
Or amorous bird perched on the young green spray,
Or herdsman's horn, or bell at closing day;
Since she can mimic not his lips, more dear
Than those for whose disdain she pined away
Into a shadow of all sounds: – a drear
Murmur, between their songs, is all the woodmen hear. (xiv–xv)

At this crucial juncture of the poem, there is a desperate sense of fracture, a sense of the very Chaos he had hoped God had banished. The verse, the syntax, seems to crumble under the weight of its own contradications, leading to those dreaded questions of identity that apparently cannot be avoided. Shelley speaks for all mankind, but also for himself:

The leprous corpse, touched by this spirit tender,
Exhales itself in flowers of gentle breath;
Like incarnations of the stars, when splendour
Is changed to fragrance, they illumine death
And mock the merry worm that wakes beneath;
Nought we know, dies. Shall that alone which knows
Be as a word consumed before the sheath

By sightless lightning? – the intense atom glows
A moment, then is quenched in a most cold repose.

Alas! that all we loved of him should be
But for our grief, as if it had not been,
And grief itself be mortal! Woe is me!
Whence are we, and why are we? of what scene
The actors or spectators? (xx–xxi)

As some of the echoes imply by indirection, Shelley speaks especially for all poets. He tries to effect the Miltonic turn, with the declaration that Adonais is not dead –

Tis we, who lost in stormy visions, keep
With phantoms an unprofitable strife,
And in mad trance, strike with our spirit's knife
Invulnerable nothings. – *We* decay
Like corpses in a charnel; fear and grief
Convulse us and consume us day by day,
And cold hopes swarm like worms within our living clay. (xxxix)

Adonais becomes part of the natural world, 'made one with Nature', a 'portion of the loveliness / Which once he made more lovely'. He is one with Chatterton, Sidney, and Lucan, 'by his death approved': his death is his final guarantor. Adonais is indeed dead, but in a world where the distinction between life and death is illusory.

Life, like a dome of many-coloured glass,
Stains the white radiance of Eternity,
Until Death tramples it to fragments. – Die,
If thou wouldst be with that which thou dost seek!
Follow, where all is fled! (lii)

No more let Life divide what Death can join together. (liii)

The poet, like the hero of the poem, has himself to die: he is 'borne darkly, fearfully, afar'.

The cumulative effect of *Adonais* is complex and disturbing. As with so many Romantic poems, the movement of the verse ebbs and flows with the train of thought. In terms of the claims for poetry that are made here, it picks up Keats's own challenge of being 'half in love with easeful death'. Keats, in exploring the possibilities of dying into life, had not got beyond the convulsions; whilst in *Adonais* the poet appears to become part of the Universe, to merge with it, Keats's desire to merge with the nightingale, itself a poetic icon, had been thwarted to such an extent that by the end of the poem he had not known who or where he was. The bird as poet had left him as poet; he had been both poet and audience. His attempt at self-definition had resulted in his being a solitary and deserted listener, a striking reversal of Wordsworth's highland girl. It is Shelley's image, in his *Defence*, of the poet as nightingale that is the most arresting corollary of what Keats explores in his famous 'Ode'. Keats's attempt to effect some kind of aesthetic resolution in the 'Grecian Urn' seems very much too neat a conclusion for a poet who usually mistrusts conclusions. Shelley's 'last clouds of cold mortality', in the penultimate stanza of *Adonais*, recalls Keats's 'cold Pastoral', which will survive when 'old age shall this generation waste.' Yeats, a hundred years later, was to merge Keats's two Odes, with his mechanical singing bird of Byzantium. Although only 'half in love with easeful death', Keats finds his own death by failing, in fact, to die. Shelley, in *Adonais*, in addressing himself to the recently dead Keats, makes the point that Keats both is, and is not, dead. The pastoral elegy, tuned to rescue poetry from its own demise, and therefore the poet from his, fails him. Keats has, in death, like Lucan and Chatterton, become a poet. The poet in *Adonais* can only memorialise Keats by joining him in death. The rest is, of course, silence.

5
Clare: 'This sad non-identity'

In a letter to one of his publishers, James Hessey, in April1820, John Clare says, 'I write to you & Taylor as I shoud do to a Country friend I tell you my most simple opinion of things that strike me in my own rude way as I shoud have done 3 or 4 years back'; a little later in the same letter, he continues: 'some folks tell me my letters will creep into print & that it is a serious benefit for me to try to polish I only tell them I must then make an apollagy to creep after them as a preface & all will go right – what a polishd letter this woud be if it was printed !!!' [1] The three exclamation marks suggest something of the lightness of touch of the whole letter, and of Clare's attitude to the whole business of creeping into print and becoming polished. Eight years later, in a brief note to another writer and editor, Allan Cunningham, he describes himself as a 'plain unpolished fellow'.[2] There is a direct relation between his view of himself and his writings; the very idea of his being dressed up for public consumption is one that amuses him.

Clare is less amused when he sees the extent of the polishing to which William Hilton goes in his famous portrait:

> tell him bluntly he has forcd poor J.C. from his flail & spade to strut on canvass in the town of lunon & I will take him from his 'water nymphs' to lye on the hobs of our dirty cottages to be read by every greazy thumbd wench & chubby clown in spite of his 'RAs' &c &c so tell the gentleman his doom.[3]

It is partly a matter of the simple truth: for Clare, as Thomas Pringle the Scots poet was glad to discover, a spade should always be a spade. But it is also a matter of how the 'plain unpolished fellow' should be presented to the public.

Much has been said and written about the implications, both for Clare and his audience, of marketing him as the 'Northamptonshire Peasant Poet': 'creeping into print' presents more problems for Clare than for perhaps any other poet, certainly in this period, and this in turn presents problems for us, his readers.[4] Just as, in his letters, he is engaged in a private dialogue with a friend, so in his poems he is often writing for himself, without any particular audience in mind. This is especially true of his early poems and of his asylum poems.

Given the circumstances of his life, it should be no surprise that Clare continually faces the question of his status in the literary world. When he looks back on his life from the perspective of the Northampton asylum where he spends the last 23 years of his life, he calls one of his slight and simple poems, 'The Peasant Poet.'

> He loved the brook's soft sound
> The swallows swimming by
> He loved the daisy covered ground
> The cloud bedappled sky
> To him the dismal storm appeared
> The very voice of God
> And when the Evening rock was reared
> Stood Moses with his rod
> And everything his eyes surveyed
> The insects I' the brake
> Where Creatures God almighty made
> He loved them for his sake
> A silent man in lifes affairs
> A thinker from a Boy
> A Peasant in his daily cares –
> The Poet in his joy.

Whilst much of his life is in fact a struggle against that label and its implications, Clare can be proud to be the 'peasant', if this can mean a genuine acknowledgement of where he belongs, of his roots not only in a particular place with its particular way of life, but also in a tradition that exists apart from the literary one against which, as he knows only too well, he will be judged. It is the difficulties of this complex relationship, of an existence that is so evidently self-contradictory, that concern this chapter; irrespective of any claim we want to make for him, his life as a writer, far from being tangential to that of the major figures of his day, can be seen as a reflection of theirs. This could be put another way, whereby it could be said that Clare provides, in his life and work, the most dramatic and extreme enactment of the central thesis of this book. Far from enjoying the 'spontaneous overflow of powerful feelings', the Romantics wrestle with the paradox of writing itself, in that to write is both to assert and to deny oneself. The circularity of Clare's career, as embodied in the image of the 'Peasant Poet', can be seen in the way his very earliest poems anticipate the questions he will be asking all those years later, as he languishes in the asylum, to all intents and purposes forgotten. Most people think he is already dead.

In the poem that first displays his wares to the public in 1820, 'Helpstone', Clare almost unwittingly demonstrates his dilemma: he is writing in the tradition of Goldsmith's *Deserted Village*, and yet that tradition excludes him even as it invites. The poem is a celebration of the obscurity he regrets: one of the ironies is that this place he calls home denies him the poetic existence and identity he craves. The tensions are apparent in the opening lines, where his circumstances and the literary tradition in which he writes emphasise the hopelessness of his ambitions:

> Hail humble Helpstone where thy valies spread
> And thy mean village lifts its lowly head
> Unknown to grandeur and unknown to fame
> No minstrel boasting to advance thy name
> Unletterd spot unheard in poets song
> Where bustling labour drives the hours along
> Where dawning genius never met the day
> Where useless ign'rance slumbers life away
> Unknown nor heeded where low genius trys
> Above the vulgar and the vain to rise.

All that survives is the memory of a place that has been destroyed: whatever the literary tradition, there can be little doubt about enclosure's part in all of this. The attack on wealth, later in the poem, earned Clare the rebukes of his patron, Lord Radstock, and eventually considerable editorial mangling of the poem in subsequent editions: even if it now seems rather tame, the poem had powerful political implications. The devastation wrought by the 'woodman's cruel axe' is irreversible, and looks ahead to Clare's much more forceful later poetry. 'Those scenes exist no more', which means by extension that he too exists no more, except as part of a vanished memory, both social and private. All he can hope for, coming full circle, is, like Goldsmith's poet, to 'die at home at last.' A poem in which he had, it appeared, hoped to assert himself, ends with his own anticipated death. Forty years later, his major poem 'I Am' will extend a similar hand of resigned friendship to the grave.

Clare's first volume of poetry, *Poems Descriptive of Rural Life and Scenery* (1820), was undoubtedly a commercial success, perhaps too much so for the publishers who wanted to dampen his ambition.[5] When we look at back at the book from this distance, we might find it harder to rhapsodise: although there are hints of something unusual here, there is much that is trite or second-hand, as Clare follows the obvious path of imitation. Those who saw in him a second Stephen Duck or Robert Bloomfield were not too wide of the mark, and Clare was only too happy to acknowledge his debts. His second volume, *The Village Minstrel* (1821), is rather more ambitious, especially in the title poem (originally called 'The Peasant Boy'), which will eventually lead to his first major long poem, *The Shepherd's Calendar* (1827). The very title has its literary connotations, and Clare's denials of any reference to Beattie's *Minstrel* ring a little hollow when we know of his knowledge of that seminal poem; but what marks out the title poem is his determination to spell out much more fully who he is. He is writing as a representative of the rural community, but anxious to strike a balance between his own personal experience in all its vivid detail, the mythopoeic quality he bestows on this by having a 'hero', Lubin, from whom he can keep a decent distance, and the literary tradition that reminds the reader not just of Beattie but of the whole line of eighteenth-century Spenserians. In their very different ways, Wordsworth and Keats and Byron had all seen the value of this tradition as a starting point: for Clare, the highly wrought stanza form provides him, ironically, with a more humble kind of hedge-school. The opening stanza presents more of a challenge than had 'Helpstone':

> While learned genius rush to bold extreemes
> & sun beams snatch to light the muses fires
> A humble rustic hums his lowly dreams
> Far in the swail where poverty retires
> & sings what nature & what truth inspires
> The charms that rise from rural scenery
> Which he in pastures & in woods admires
> The sports the feelings of his infancy
> & such like artless things how mean so ere they be.

If there is a hint of Crabbe there, in the appeal to nature and truth, there is at the same time a strong recognition that he does not see himself as a second Crabbe. This humble rustic becomes, in the third stanza, the peasant 'Lubin' who cannot conceal his ambition even as he enjoys his loneliness, 'listning unseen birds to hear them sing.' Neither for the first nor the last time, Clare's poem reveals the central ambiguity of the peasant who would be a poet; he might regard himself as 'far from the jocund crew', but much of the poem is devoted to those very pleasures part of him wants to deny. What impresses initially is the concealment nature provides, allowing him a ready identification with the solitaries of the natural world: if the birds are unseen, then so is he.

> Sequestered nature was his hearts delight
> Him woud she lead thro wood & lonly plain
> Searching the pooty from the rushey dyke
> & while the thrush sung her long silencd strain
> He thought it sweet & mockt it oer again
> & while he pluckt the primrose in its pride
> He ponderd oer its bloom tween joy & pain
> & a rude sonnet in its praise he tryd
> Where natures simple way the aid of art supplyd. (stanza 18)

If this imitation of the thrush (painfully elegiac, in that its song is now a thing of the past) reminds us of the mimic hootings in *The Prelude*, the difference between Clare and Wordsworth is immense: Wordsworth's experience of the natural world involves a complex interaction, whereas Clare's at this stage is a humble recognition of sameness and sweetness, relishing the dialect word 'pooty', mocking his own efforts as he mocks the thrush ('rude sonnet' should be a contradiction in terms). If the bird's song is 'long silencd', this is an unhappy augury for his own. The early part of the poem is anxious to underscore this paradox; the poet is 'unperceivd' for the simple reason that 'theres few to notice him or hear his simple tale.' In spite of his desire to sing, it is the silence of the natural world, its privacy, that attracts him, and, intriguingly, the poem blossoms as he immerses himself in this world that he regards as his alone. He can identify with the bleakness of nature as autumn fades into winter, but he can celebrate his special knowledge of what becomes a crucial word, its 'secrets'.

> A Solitair thro autumns wan decay
> He heard the tuteling robin sound her knell
> 'Serv'd the coy sun more shoy to slink away
> & lingering oak shade how it brownd & fell
> & many a way of nature he coud tell
> That still are secrets to un'scerning eyes.

The secrets of nature become his secrets; but, as with George Darley, to be so in love with secrecy carries its own dangers.

Whereas 'Helpstone' had mourned, rather conventionally, the changes 'wrought in all the neighbourhood' as Wordsworth puts it in 'Michael', 'The Village Minstrel' attacks the perceived effects of enclosure head-on. There is verse of considerable force here, but also a sense of his own poetic impotence:

> His heart wrung pains, his unavailing woes
> No words can utter & no tongue can tell
> When ploughs destroyd the green when groves of willow fell.
> (stanza 103)

When his voice is needed, he discovers that he has not yet found it. This is a poignant moment in his development, looking ahead in its espousal of memory to the partial, and therefore teasing, solution of *The Shepherd's Calendar*. The silence of nature becomes the sadder silence of what is remembered:

> How hed look for the green a green no more
> Mourning to scenes that made him no reply
> Save the strong accents they in memory bore
> 'Our scenes that charmd thy youth are dead to bloom no more.'

This is a glimpse of the terrible anguish that permeates the work of his middle years: if the landscape changes, then so does he.

> O samely naked leas so bleak so strange. (stanza 123)

As with 'Helpstone', the poem ends on a note of despair, the more powerfully sensed here because of what has gone before. As Lubin looks, as it were, beyond the end of the poem, he cannot see, he cannot unravel the 'secrets' of time: he is left to go 'thro ignorance his doubtful way'. There is something of the 'burden of the mystery' here, that sense of 'being in a mist' familiar to Wordsworth and Keats; but also a glance over the shoulder at Milton and the expulsion from Eden. That is, after all, how Clare saw the effects of enclosure on his childhood Paradise. And, as also with 'Helpstone', we are left with a dreadful anticipation of 'I Am', where the word 'strange' tolls like Keats's 'forlorn'. For Clare, the strange is the unfamiliar (and the rhyme with 'change' is relentless in its logic), and the unfamiliar is the absence of what he knows; in knowing the Helpstone of his youth, he knows himself.

> Ah as the traveller from the mountain top
> Looks down on misty kingdoms spread below
> & meditates beneath the steepey drop
> What life & lands exist & oceans flow
> How feign that hour the anxious soul woud know
> Of all his eye beholds – but its in vain
> So lubin eager views this world of woe
> & wishes time her secrets woud explain
> If he may live for joys to come or sink in welming pain
>
> Fates close kept thoughts wi in her bosom hide
> She is no gossip secrets to betray
> Times steady movements must her end descide
> & leave him painfull still to hope the day
> & group thro ignorance his doubtful way
> By wisdoms disregard & fools anoyd
> & if no worth anticipates the lay
> Then let his childish notions be destroyd
> & he his time employ as erst its been employd. (stanzas 131–2)

The third stanza of a very brief song sums up Clare's desolation:

> Alas, to me no home belongs
> But what my dreams create;
> Vain cuckoo-like, I sing my songs,
> And leave the rest to fate.

This has all the stark directness of the asylum. A more complex statement of a similar sentiment is to be found in 'Love and Solitude', in which Clare sadly yearns solipsistically for his own self-imprisonment, 'And my own shadow all my company'. He would get his wish soon enough; there is something terrible about seeing him gaze with such wide eyes at the impossible contradiction at the centre of his life as a poet. One of the most prolific poets of the nineteenth century, almost constitutionally unable to stop writing, takes his premature leave of the Muse.

> I hate the very noise of troublous man
> Who did and does me all the harm he can.
> Free from the world I would a prisoner be
> And my own shadow all my company;
> And lonely see the shooting stars appear,
> Worlds rushing into judgment all the year.
> Oh, lead me onward to the loneliest shade,
> The dearest place that quiet ever made,
> Where kingcups grow most beauteous to behold
> And shut up green and open into gold.
> Farewell to poesy – and leave the will;
> Take all the world away – and leave me still
> The mirth and music of a woman's voice,
> That bids the heart be happy and rejoice.

Against such bleakness, such awareness of his own 'strangeness' and lack of definition, can be set a poem written more or less at the same time. In 'To the Rural Muse' Clare seems happier playing what is something of a literary game, wooing the Muse in seemingly conventional style: but it is soon clear that she is no conventional figure, and that he relishes her very oddity.

> Simple enchantress, wreathd in summer blooms
> Of slender bent stalks topt wi' feathery down
> Heaths creeping fetch & glaring yellow brooms
> & ash keys wavering on thy rushey crown
> Simple enchantress how Ive wooed thy smiles
> How often sought thee far from flusht renown
> Sought thee unseen where fountain waters fell
> Touchd thy wild reed unheard, in weary toils
> & tho my heavy hand thy song defiles
> Tis hard to leave thee & to bid farewell.

Once again, Clare lends 'unseen' and 'unheard' extra force by letting them hang in ambiguity, applicable to himself and to the Muse. But whereas previously he had recognised the implications of the unseen, unheard poet, he here celebrates the paradox:

> & tho my weak song faulters sung to thee
> I cannot wild enchantress bid farwell.

Even as he acknowledges his own sense of failure, he asserts his 'ambitious pride'. Clare's personal tragedy is that he knows that he is writing poetry that demands an audience, and yet that audience is so often denied him that he is in constant danger of ceasing to have a poetic identity.

Clare was buffeted by advice from all sides to write about topics other than the countryside he knew and loved; if he insisted on sticking to the natural world, at least he might 'elevate' his thoughts and views. For editors, publishers and critics familiar with Wordsworth, Coleridge and Keats, this is understandable. What even Taylor and Hessey did not realise was that when Clare presented them with the scrawled mass of papers that made up *The Shepherd's Calendar* he was in fact obliging them, if not quite in the way they had hoped for. It is certainly wrong to think of Clare as merely the solitary figure, a real-life version, as it were, of the Wordsworthian countryman. Clare, even as early as 'Helpstone', had recognised that poetry, especially as written by a 'peasant' was a political act (and his patrons had acted accordingly). His is not just the poetry of nostalgia, the mourning for a lost Eden; it is a cry against enclosure (whether justified or not the historians can argue about), against cant and hypocrisy (for all its failings, *The Parish* is more successful as satire than we have any right to expect),[6] against the cruel, stratisfied society in which he lived. Clare never had to confront the Keatsian dilemma, of whether or not he should ever bid farewell to the joys of poesy, for the nobler life in which he would study the 'agonies, the strife' of human hearts: from the beginning he was never a poet to wallow in the luxury of art, in the loading of every rift with ore. Such an injunction would have made little sense to him. Nor was he the Keatsian or Shelleyan myth-maker, talking of the blast of prophecy or celebrating the arrival of Apollo as 'first in beauty' and 'first in might'. Nor did he, after his prentice years, find himself a victim of any Bloomian anxiety of influence – a fact all the more remarkable, given the circumstances: it would be hard to imagine any writer with more excuses to lose his individual voice amidst the clamour of competing voices. He was fully aware of his debt to Thomson, and Goldsmith, and Gray, not to mention Marvell and Milton; but he was not going to let them smother him with their delights. By the time in the early 1820s, when he starts work on *The Shepherd's Calendar*, he has, remarkably, found a distinctive voice for himself, a clear, clean-limbed, sure-footed gait that rarely leaves him. He himself uses the terms 'simplicity', but this is more than a stylistic matter: it is certainly far removed from Wordsworth's deliberate adoption of 'the language of men'.

John Taylor advises:

> If he has a Soul of native Fancies, Let him study to express what it dictates in that Language it will bring with it; then he will write like himself & no one else: if he has not that innate Poesy he may write clever Poems like many others who are called Poets, but he will have no just claim to the title.[7]

Clare does end up writing 'like himself', which is both an infuriating and frustrating tautology and at the same time a complex truth. If we seize upon his own use of 'simplicity', then we realize that it is closer to Blake than to Wordsworth. Clare is alert to the problem, in that if poetry 'speaks from its own heart', it is not necessarily true that 'all hearts reply': as a passage from 'May' suggests, this does not particularly bother him.

> My wild field catalogue of flowers
> Grows in my ryhmes as thick as showers
> Tedious and long as they may be
> To some they never weary me
> Then wood and mead and field of grain
> I coud hunt oer and oer again
> And talk to every blossom wild
> Fond as a parent to a child
> And cull them in my childish joy
> By swarms and swarms and never cloy

If the audience does not like it, that is too bad: which is another way of saying that he is often writing not only about himself, but for himself. He is rather like the trees and birds who are rudely disturbed by humankind:

> While wood men still on spring intrudes
> And thins the shadow solitudes
> Wi sharpend axes felling down
> The oak trees budding into brown

Where as they crash upon the ground
A crowd of labourers gather round
And mix among the shadows dark
To rip the crackling staining bark
From off the tree and lay when done
The rolls in lares to meet the sun
Depriving yearly where they come
The green wood pecker of its home
That early in the spring began
Far from the sight of troubling man
And bord their round holes in each tree
In fancys sweet security
Till startld wi the woodmans noise
It wakes from all its dreaming joys.

For Clare, whatever else poetry be, it is 'fancy's sweet security'. His achievement in *The Shepherd's Calendar* is to cherish this security, whilst at the same time directly confronting his rude awakening. Whichever version we read, the poem is long-sustained: it is a celebration, but a tenuous one, merging with the realisation that what is celebrated has either gone, or will soon be gone. In 'December', the final seasonal section of the poem, he cries:

Old customs O I love the sound
However simple they may be;

but by the end of that stanza he acknowledges that they will soon be driven away.

And soon the poets song will be
The only refuge they can find.

But it is a fragile refuge, as so much of the poem has demonstrated: the very poem, the last place of safety, is itself threatened. As he puts it at the end of 'September', the 'sudden strife' of nature reduces his 'mean songs' to futility: art cannot supply a stay against life's confusions.

But hollow winds and tumbling floods
And humming showers and moaning woods
All startle into sudden strife

> And wake a might lay to life
> Making amid their strains divine
> All songs in vain so mean as mine.

'October' puts the same point more forcefully, reminding us of Clare's links with the other poets of his time, and foretelling his own nothingness in the asylum.

> These pictures linger thro the shortning day
> And cheer the lone bards mellancholy way
> Till surly Winter comes with biting breath
> And strips the woods and numbs the scene with death
> Then all is still oer wood and field and plain
> As nought had been and nought would be again.

It is logical that many of Clare's poems are about privacy, secrecy even, ranging from his sonnets addressed to solitary flowers to the song, 'Secret Love', of the asylum years. This theme runs through his work from first to last. A typical poem would be 'In Hilly Wood', from *The Village Minstrel*, unpretentious, observant, attentive, and affectionate.

> How sweet to be thus nestling deep in boughs
> Upon an ashen stoven pillowing me
> Faintly are heard the ploughmen at their ploughs
> But near an eye can find its way to see
> The sunbeams scarce molest me wi a smile
> So thick the leafy armies gather round
> & where they do the breeze blows cool the while
> Their leafy shadows dancing on the ground
> – Full many a flower too wishing to be seen
> Perks up its head the hiding grass between –
> In midwood silence thus how sweet to be
> Where all the noises that on peace intrude
> Comes from the chittering cricket bird & bee
> Whose songs have charms to sweeten solitude.

What is remarkable about this sonnet, and many others like it, is the unselfconscious nature of the writing, in a form that is one of the most potentially selfconscious ever devised. Because of its history, the sonnet is a very public, highly complex form, and yet Clare hides comfortably within it, almost as though he wasn't there at all. This curious and peculiar effect reflects the merging of private and public in so much of his work.

The important emphasis for present purposes would be on those many sonnets in which Clare defines the particularities of what he sees, for it is by these that he himself can be defined. Two examples must suffice. Firstly, 'An Autumn Morning':

> The autumn morning waked by many a gun
> Throws oer the fields her many coloured light
> Wood wildly touched close tanned & stubbles dun
> A motley paradise for earths delight
> Clouds ripple as the darkness breaks to light
> & clover fields are hid with silver mist
> One shower of cobwebs oer the surface spread
> & threads of silk in strange disorder twist
> Round every leaf & blossom's bottly head
> Hares in the drowning herbage scarcely steal
> But on the battered pathway squats abed
> & by the cart-rut nips her morning meal
> Look where we may the scene is strange & new
> & every object wears a changing hue.

The more the reader grapples with this, the harder it seems to pin it down: the language and the images of lines 5–9, for example, almost defy logic. We know that for Clare what is 'strange' is disturbing, and the word appears here with two rather different if related meanings: 'threads of silk in strange disorder twist / Round every leaf & blossoms bottly head' is the kind of image that keeps us in its own web. The disorder of the silk is 'strange' in the sense of 'curious', but also possibly 'unusual', which then anticipates the penultimate line of the poem, where the 'scene is strange & new'. There is a disturbing flux about the whole sonnet, and the final couplet hints at what has up till then been hinted at: 'Hares in the drowning herbage scarcely steal' is, for example, a line that teases with its coy withdrawal of what it half suggests; as so often with Clare the reader has to ponder whether a verb is active or passive, or a curious mixture of both. Within 14 lines Clare has managed to disorientate us ('Look where we may'): we cannot get out of this poem, we cannot escape it, any more than he can. Clare loves what he knows, the familiar, and it is against that he frequently defines himself – that is why the move from Helpstone in 1832 is so catastrophic: hence the importance of 'strangeness' here.

A rather similar effect is achieved in 'The Heronry', where Clare works the word 'seems' in a way that recalls Wordsworth:

> And when the spring with joy the earth invests
> Each tree-top seems as bending down with nests;
> For there a troop of heronshaws repair
> And yearly pile a stack of dwellings there,
> Crank on the trees and their branches stand
> And the whole scene seems changed to foreign land.

'Foreign land' is bewildering and unknown, as he soon discovers to his terrible personal cost. What is so alarming for him here is that this is part of a customary, seasonal activity: in other words the familiar contains within it its opposite, the totally and frighteningly unfamiliar. 'November' dramatises this point: whatever metaphorical mists might imply for Romantic poets, a real mist can be just as disorientating. This is one of Clare's most remarkable poems: with its series of disjointed clauses, it seems to achieve the impossible, to present the familiar whilst denying familiarity ('neighbour meets with neighbour unawares' – this is a wonderful variation on the Wordsworthian / Coleridgean use of 'unawares'). Clare is precise in his imprecision: 'The place we occupy seems all the world', and yet, for all the apparent hope of this line, the truth is that we do not know where we are. Just as we stare into the mist and cannot see, so we cannot be seen. Once again, too, we are drawn into the poem by the pronoun: 'we' are part of this strange world of mist, in the middle of which the ploughman 'goes unseen'. In all its rich bleakness, this poem alone appears to embrace Clare's central problem of identity and definition.

> The shepherds almost wonder where they dwell
> And the old dog for his right journey stares
> The path leads somewhere but they cannot tell
> And neighbour meets with neighbour unawares
> The maiden passes close beside her cow
> And wanders on and thinks her far away
> The ploughman goes unseen behind his plough
> And seems to loose his horses half the day
> The lazy mist creeps on in journey slow
> The maidens shout and wonder where they go

So dull and dark are the november days
The lazy mist high up the evening curled
And now the morn quite hides in smokey haze
The place we occupy seems all the world.

More familiar examples of Clare's intimacy would be the bird poems: the firetail anxiously guarding her blue eggs, the wryneck frightening away the prying schoolboy with her snake-like hiss, the secret toils of the thrush. There is something particularly touching about 'The Nightingales Nest', which celebrates the bird's solitude and, importantly, its existence separate from the poet's. This bird is no symbolic, literary creature: the opening lines are all-encompassing as they take the reader into the poem, going back into the past, into the poet's childhood – just as a child in the present continues the tradition – emphasising the security of the setting, the delicacy of the moment, the anxiety.

Up this green woodland ride lets softly rove
And list the nightingale – she dwelleth here
Hush let the wood gate softly clap – for fear
The noise may drive her from her very home of love ...

All seemed as hidden as a thought unborn.

That final line is startling because it lifts the poem onto another plane, earned, as it were, by the carefulness of what has preceded it. There are times when Clare can remind us of Marvell (and, as we know, he did at least once pretend to be Marvell),[8] and here the bird suddenly becomes something totally mysterious, oddly so in that we already know a lot about her; she is suddenly totally unknown and unknowable, even unimaginable. This apparently casual simile suggests something entirely beyond our grasp – to use his phrase in 'To the Snipe', 'mystic indeed'.

Clare's nightingale has an ecstasy rather different from that of Keats:

But if I touched a bush or scarcely stirred
All in a moment stopt – I watched in vain
The timid bird had left the hazel bush
And at a distance hid to sing again
Lost in a wilderness of listening leaves
Rich extacy would pour its luscious strain

Till envy spurred the emulating thrush
To start less wild and scarce inferior songs.

In some ways Clare is better than Keats at 'negative capability': he can enter the bird's song, into its very existence, and rejoice in it. He, the poet, has heard a truer poet, and he is happy to withdraw, and indulge the mystery and secrecy of the bird's song.

Sing on sweet bird may no worse hap befall
Thy visions then the fear that now decieves
We will not plunder music of its dower
Nor turn this spot of happiness to thrall
For melody seems hid in every flower
That blossoms near thy home – these harebells all
Seems bowing with the beautiful in song
And gaping cuckoo with its spotted leaves
Seems blushing of the singing it has heard.

Shelley's comment about the poet as solitary nightingale seems particularly germane here: he and Clare seem to be as one in their understanding of the fine line between the private and the public sphere.

The notion of privacy soon leads to the concept of poetry above and beyond words. Just as Wordsworth had believed that all men are potentially poets, so Clare comes to believe something similar, and that, by extension, poetry is everywhere. Nature is a book which all can read. 'The Progress of Ryhme' is one of a group of poems which explore these ideas, in ways that are sometimes surprisingly theoretical. Like Blake, Wordsworth and Coleridge, Clare often reverts to the religious concept of 'joy' in order to express poetry's significance:

It wast an early joy to me
That joy was love and poesy

This is Clare's version, in miniature, of Keats's beauty and truth, and with this recognition he is able to make an imaginative as well as an ultimately political point (the force of which emerges later in 'The Flitting').

I felt that Id a right to song
And sung – but in a timid strain

> Of fondness for my native plain
> For every thing I felt a love
> The weeds below the birds above
> And weeds that bloomed in summers hours
> I thought they should be reckoned flowers
> They made a garden free for all
> And so I loved them great and small
> And sung of some that pleased my eye
> Nor could I pass the thistle by
> But paused and thought it could not be
> A weed in natures poesy. (80–92)

Clare scoffs at the scoffers – 'Poh let the idle rumour ill / Their vanity is never still' – for the simple reason that his 'harp' is his 'own'. This is not just a matter of asserting himself against the nay-sayers: he is asserting himself against the weight of the literary tradition. It is important for him that he makes it sound simpler than it actually is:

> When I was in the fields alone
> With none to help and none to hear
> To bid me either hope or fear
> The bird or bee its chords would sound
> The air hummed melodies around
> I caught with eager ear the strain
> And sung the music oer again …
>
> I whispered poesys spells till they
> Gleamed round me like a summers day. (134–62)

He is, if like Shelley, also like Keats here, 'whispering his results to his neighbour'. Once again, his song is unheard: but, in a sense, that does not matter, in that he is merely reflecting back to nature its own music, 'Twas nature listened I that loved'. He is again the boy who echoes the birds: the repetitive nature of much of this poem is almost an imitation of his own mimickry, until the whole of nature bursts into song:

> and when I pluckt the blade
> Of grass upon the woodland hill
> To mock the birds with artless skill
> No music in the world beside
> Seemd half so sweet – till mine was tried

So my boy worship poesy
Made een the muses pleased with me
Untill I even danced for joy
A happy and a lonely boy
Each object to my ear and eye
Made paradise of poesy. (214-24)

Such identification with the songs of nature allows Clare to risk what few other poets would dare, as he bursts into enraptured celebration.

– 'Chew-chew Chew-chew' – and higher still
'Cheer-cheer Cheer-cheer' – more loud and shrill
'Cheer-up Cheer-up cheer-up' – and dropt
Low 'tweet tweet tweet jug jug jug' and stopt
One moment just to drink the sound
Her music made and then a round
Of stranger witching notes was heard
As if it was a stranger bird
'Wew-wew wew-wew chur-chur chur-chur
'Woo-it woo-it' could this be her
'Tee-rew Tee-rew tee-rew tee-rew
Chew-rit chew-rit' – and ever new
'Will-will will-will grig-grig grig-grig'. (238–51)

Towards the end of the poem, his beloved Mary Joyce enters the poem, a sudden presence from which the poem never quite recovers. It leads him to hope that

I should one day be
Beloved Mary een by thee
But I mistook in early day
The world – and so our hopes decay. (341–4)

The final declaration that 'hope, love, joy, are poesy' loses its wished-for triumph: his 'unheard rhapsodies' have, most disturbingly of all, been unheard by his one true love. Clare has not managed to accommodate this complexity into his poem: by introducing Mary in this fashion, he has reminded us, as well as himself, of the biographical silence at the centre of his life, and by extension, of his poetry. If indeed hope, love and joy are poesy, and he has lost the love that Mary represents, then it is true, as he is later to say, his 'hopes are all hopeless'. If there is neither hope, nor love, there can be no joy, and no poesy.

Although 'Pastoral Poesy' has been dismissed as nothing more than an 'incoherent imitation' of Wordsworth and Coleridge, it is much more than the monstrosity Howard Mills would have us believe.[9] With its insistence on paradox, it anticipates much of the asylum poetry, the 'hopelessness of hope'. Here we get 'An easy thoughtlessness of thought', and the lovely concept of 'social loneliness'; if the 'dower / Of self-creating joy' owes something to Coleridge's 'Dejection' (and why should it not?), at the heart of the poem is Clare's nurturing of his own particular form of quietude:

> And whether it be hill or moor
>   I feel whereer I go
> A silence that discourses more
>   Than any tongue can do
>
> Unruffled quietness hath made
>   A peace in every place
> And woods are resting in their shade
>   Of social loneliness.

The storm becomes a form of music, 'a poem of the woods'; and yet, after such 'strange melody', the poem ends in something approaching silence:

> Poesys selfs a dwelling joy
>   Of humble quietness.

This presents us with a rather more complex type of humility than that heralded at the beginning of 'Helpstone', where 'humble Helpstone' proved to be the poet's undoing: against his own ambition, however misplaced, his village's extreme lack of pretension, allied to the world's indifference, proved a block to what seemed at the time a necessary escape. But now, with his hard-won recognition of the equation of joy and poesy, he can contain within this one poem claims that are both humble and far-reaching: a 'language that is evergreen' makes poetry itself, in a curious way, redundant. But just as Wordsworth, resorting to etymology, uses redundancy as a concept of abundance,[10] so Clare can rejoice in his own lack of importance: the poet becomes poetry, his self that of poetry, removed to a central core of silence. Like the humble poet, poetry itself enjoys a humility which requires no justification beyond itself. If we have in mind the Wordsworthian and Coleridgean echoes in this poem, the final paradox is that whereas they write magnificent poems about the loss of poetry, and in so doing seemingly deny the loss they declare, Clare celebrates a poetry from which the poet can be altogether removed.

Clare paves the way for his exploration of silence and poetry in poems like 'The Eternity of Nature', where 'Birds singing lone flie silent past the crowd', and 'Song's Eternity', in which his individual voice is lost in the music that stretches back to the beginning of time:

> What is song's eternity
> Come and see
> Melodys of earth and sky
> Here they be
> Songs once sung to adams ears
> Can it be
> – Ballads of six thousand years
> Thrive thrive
> Songs awakened with the spheres
> Alive.

Clare achieves here what Keats aims at in his 'Nightingale': he avoids the hungry generations' tread.

> Dreamers list the honey bee
> Mark the tree
> Where the bluecap tootle tee
> Sings a glee
> Sung to Adam and to Eve
> Here they be
> When floods covered every bough
> Noahs ark
> Heard that Ballad singing now
> Hark hark.

For Clare, it is as important to listen as it is to speak.

The idea of loss has a terrible reality for Clare. He loses Mary Joyce, and proceeds to place her at the centre of his vision; he then loses his home in 1832, and moves three miles to a cottage in Northborough. Whether or not his poetry changes radically in kind after this move, there is no doubting the force of his registering of this 'flitting'. It is certainly true that, in moving, he cannot avoid the implications for his poetry. In 'Remembrances', written before the move, he has already lost his hold on his own beloved places of childhood. There is a desperate poignancy about his realisation that he could not cling on to those places: enclosure ('like a buonaparte') is certainly part of the impulse behind the poem, but more is at stake:

> Summers pleasures they are gone like to visions every one
> And the cloudy days of autumn and of winter cometh on
> I tried to call them back but unbidden they are gone
> Far away from heart and eye and for ever far away
> Dear heart and can it be that such raptures meet decay
> I thought them all eternal when by Langley bush I lay
> I thought them joys eternal when I used to shout and play
> On its banks at 'clink and bandy' 'chock' and 'taw' and ducking stone
> Where silence sitteth now on the wild heath as her own
> Like a ruin of the past all alone.

The naming of places is essential to Clare: he is rather like a second Adam in this respect. What is happening here seems in stark contrast to the generalised songs of nature he talks about in poems like 'The Eternity of Nature' and 'Song's Eternity'. Those poems can be seen as some kind of answer to the very problem posed in these poems written around the time of removal from Helpstone. As becomes clear, even in 'Remembrances', the act of naming is related to the act of poetry, which in turn is related to the desecration of the natural world. This final couplet from the third stanza challenges the very role of poetry:

> O words are poor receipts for what time hath stole away
> The ancient pulpit trees and the play.

The vision has gone; the words that might recapture it are not of much use either. The sighs of 'Song's Eternity' are here much more bleakly evoked:

> O I never call to mind
> These pleasant names of places but I leave a sigh behind
> While I see the little mouldywharps hang sweeing to the wind
> On the only aged willow that in all the field remains

> And nature hides her face where theyre sweeing in their chains
> And in a silent murmuring complains

That this is no simple pathetic fallacy is clear enough from the complexity of the poem's tone and structure. Nature's complaint is intimately tied up with Clare's sense of his lost past – which means his lost childhood – and his sense of his corresponding loss of self. The poem's conclusion is blunt:

> But love never heeded to treasure up the may
> So it went the common road with decay

Clare's obsession with 'decay' is continued in his poem of that name, where once again the details of the landscape he had known and loved have given way to a generalised nature that is unrecognisable. This is true, certainly, when he has moved, as 'The Flitting' shows only too well; but the real awfulness of his loss of poesy is that, even in Helpstone, he is lost. This is reflected in a letter he writes to Taylor in October 1831, in which he laments the present state of poetry alongside the state of the place where he lives:

> I have nothing but drawbacks & dissapoinments I live in a land overflowing with obscurity & vulgarity far away from taste & books & friends ... I see things praised that appear to me utterly worthless & read critisisms in the periodicals when I do see them that the very puffers of Blacking and Bearsgreese would be really ashamed of ... what ever remarks I may make on the ryhmes of others they shall be done honestly & with as little vanity as possible.[11]

'All the old associations are going before me.' This is what 'Decay' explores.

> O poesy is on the waine
> For fancys visions all unfitting
> I hardly know her face again
> Nature herself seems on the flitting
> The fields grow old and common things
> The grass the sky the winds ablowing
> And spots where still a beauty clings

Are sighing 'going all a going'
O poesy is on the wain
I hardly know her face again

The Eden of his childhood has left him, just as he has left it: there is a terribly reciprocal betrayal at the heart of this poem.

These heavens are gone – the mountains grey
Turned mist – the sun a homless ranger
Pursues a naked weary way
Unnoticed like a very stranger
O poesy is on its wain
I cannot find her face again.

'Remembrances', of which there are several echoes in this poem, had at least tabulated what had been lost; here the whole of nature has lost that particularity on which he had depended. It is possible to see more precisely what he had meant about words as 'poor receipts', as things cease to have any individuality: the implication is that he, too, has lost that distinctive sense of self.

The stream it is a naked stream
Where we on sundays used to ramble
The sky hangs oer a broken dream
The brambles dwindled to a bramble
O poesy is on its wane
I cannot find her haunts again.

'The Flitting', written in Northborough soon after the move, spells out the loss: he is as much a stranger as the sun in 'Decay', homeless, as he is to say so sadly in the asylum, at home.

Alone and in a stranger scene
Far from spots my heart esteems
The closen with their ancient green
Heath woods and pastures sunny streams
The hawthorns here were hung with may
But still they seem in deader green
The sun een seems to loose its way
Nor knows the quarter it is in.

The landscape not only does not define him any more, it actually challenges his sense of being:

> Strange scenes mere shadows are to me
> Vague unpersonifying things
> I love with my old hants to be
> By quiet woods and gravel springs.

Wordsworth had spoken, in 'Tintern Abbey', of 'seeing into the life of things', as though that were the self-explanatory conclusion of his visionary poetics; 'things' for Clare are threatening because, in being so undifferentiated, they undermine him. Clare cannot cope with any notion of 'substance' and 'shadow', whereas it is almost essential for Wordsworth.

What is unusual about 'The Flitting' is that Clare presents an argument whereby, in spite of his loss, he might arrive at an understanding of that very eternity of nature of which he speaks elsewhere; in many respects this can seem unconvincing, until it is related to the poems I mentioned earlier, in which he talks at greater length about that sense of a natural world which in itself is almost an adequate replacement for poetry. But that, as I have suggested, has its own built-in contradictions, as the poet almost writes himself out of existence. When Clare was removed, first in 1837 to Dr Matthew Allen's asylum in Epping Forest, and then, in 1841, to the General Lunatic Asylum in Northampton, he had to confront a much more alarming circumstance: locked away, as he quite naturally saw it, in a prison, he had to assert himself in whatever ways he could. There was no home, no family, no familiar scenery. He was lost to himself, and lost to the world. It is a quite remarkable fact of literary history that he continued to write poetry, much of it as good as anything he had written up to that point, and some of it surpassing anything he had yet done. Most of the major poems focus on what he calls in a brief prose piece, 'Self Identity', and the biographical reasons for this are too obvious to require comment. But he still manages to make an aesthetic point out of this:

> A very good common place counsel is Self Identity to bid our own hearts not to forget our own selves & always to keep self in the first place lest all the world who always keeps us behind it should forget us all together – forget not thyself & the world will not forget thee – forget thyself & the world will willingly forget thee till thou

> art nothing but a living-dead man dwelling among shadows & falsehood.[12]

Even here there are astonishing echoes of those poems written in 1832.

Clare's major long poem of the asylum years, *Child Harold,* is discussed in the next chapter, in relation to his obsession with Byron. Just as that poem remains an extended fragment, a kind of unending set of variations on the theme of lost love – to which he eventually gives the catch-all title of 'Prison Amusements' – so the bulk of his poetry from 1842 onwards can be seen as a relentless working away at this central preoccupation of self-identity.[13] I have suggested that in his early work the problem is both personal and literary; in the asylum the urgency of the personal aspect imposes itself on poems that cannot always bear the weight. But, as the identification with Byron (amongst others) suggests, Clare continues to see his painfully intimate problem of consciousness in literary terms. Even in the confines of the asylum, he sees himself primarily as a poet – indeed, as the poem quoted at the start of this chapter underlines, as a 'Peasant Poet'. The apparent contradiction that had dogged him all those years in Helpstone, continues until the bitter end.

The most famous assertion of his identity comes in the much-anthologised 'I Am'. It might be thought that Harold Bloom is being over-fanciful in his Biblical reference when he comments on the poem, but there is certainly point to his echo of Coleridge's definition of the Imagination as the infinite 'I Am'.[14] Clare's poem explores the notion of creativity, in that to assert his essential identity is to assert his role as a poet. As so often with Clare – and, as we have seen, with many of the major Romantic writers – repetition performs a curiously ambiguous role here. The first 'I Am' can seem triumphant and affirmative, but when qualified into 'what I am' it becomes its very opposite. I have been suggesting that many of Clare's poems pursue the idea of identity, of consciousness, through knowledge: to be able to name 'swordy well', 'langley bush', and so on, is to possess them, whereas to see them subsumed under a generalising 'nature' is to acknowledge their loss, and by extension his loss. Here the process is reversed: if no one knows him, then he is in effect nothing. To be forgotten is to be as deprived of one's identity as those old places are when they lose their names, or when they disappear into an irrecoverable past. The past, to use his own phrase, is not always 'a majic word'. By the third line of 'I Am' he exists only in the solipsistic consumption of his own woes, that quasi-Byronic state on which Hazlitt was so hard, and once again there is the inherent contradiction of asserting one's identity by consuming it. As so many solitaries discover, assertion of self can involve denial of self. Hence that terrible world which Clare haunts, and which haunts him, in this and many other poems, the world of lack of differentiation. Falconer's *Shipwreck*, Cowper's 'Castaway' might be the literary props behind these lines, but they are soon thrown aside as Clare sees his whole life of poetry reduced to 'nothingness'. Just as bad is the loss of the link between himself and his loved ones: for 'the dearest' to become 'strange – nay, rather, stranger than the rest' is to be reminded all too unkindly of the loss of the known and the familiar. It is as though Clare realises here the truths he forgets, or is unaware of, in so many of those painful asylum letters, in which he is writing to, or about, children or parents who are dead. The letters are so full of devoted, innocent detail that for a moment Clare seems to resurrect them as he reaches back into the past. In 'I Am' he touches on the real gap, in which even the living might as well be dead. The final stanza provides a conclusion that is emotionallly logical: he yearns for a death that will unite him with God, and the sweet sleep of his childhood, as he becomes part of the natural world. But in his longing for escape he is in fact embracing his non-existence, the very things against which he rails in the opening lines of the poem.

> I am – yet what I am, none care or knows;
> My friends forsake me like a memory lost: –
> I am the self-consumer of my woes; –
> They rise and vanish in oblivion's host,
> Like shadows in love's frenzied stifled throes: –
> And yet I am, and live – like vapours tost
>
> Into the nothingness of scorn and noise,
> Into the living sea of waking dreams,
> Where there is neither sense of life or joys,
> But the vast shipwreck of my life's esteems;
> Even the dearest, that I love the best
> Are strange – nay, rather stranger than the rest.
>
> I long for scenes, where man hath never trod
> A place where woman never smiled or wept
> There to abide with my Creator, God,
> And sleep as I in childhood, sweetly slept,
> Untroubling, and untroubled where I lie,
> The grass below – above the vaulted sky.

Part of the complexity of this poem resides in its concluding serenity, in spite, as it were, of everything. In the brutal sonnet that he writes at about the same time, he looks back over his life, and registers the terrible destruction of what he called in 'I Am' 'life's esteems'. Whilst others have forgotten him or do not know him, he knows that he exists – but such knowledge is more terrible than the idea of lying 'untroubling and untroubled'. By this stage we are a long way from any Coleridgean affirmation of the supremacy of the imagination.

> I feel I am; – I only know I am,
> And plod upon the earth, as dull and void:
> Earth's prison chilled my body with its dram
> Of dullness, and my soaring thoughts destroyed,
> I fled to solitudes from passions dream,
> But strife persued – I only know, I am.
> I was a being created in the race
> Of men disdaining bounds of place and time: –
> A spirit that could travel o'er the space
> Of earth and heaven, – like a thought sublime,
> Tracing creation, like my maker, free, –
> A soul unshackled – like eternity,
> Spurning earth's vain and soul debasing thrall
> But now I only know I am, – that's all.

A writer of Clare's persistence cannot let matters rest there. Even when all he is allowed is a pencil and a scrap of paper, he must write. One ideal to cling on to, as throughout his life, is the image of his beloved Mary Joyce. In several poems he explores whatever relationship is possible in this 'nothingness of scorn and noise'. 'Invite to Eternity' provides a sharp knock to the comfort he had derived from the idea of eternity in some of those poems of the late 1820s and early 1830s. This poem seems to sweep up into its chill embrace practically everything he has said about utter disorientation. 'Dreadful' is a word Clares uses when it is the only one appropriate; although he does not use it here, it seems critically appropriate, as he merges the absurd upheaval of the landscape with his own 'sad non-identity'. If it is hard not to think of Coleridge's life-in-death and death-in-life here, there is no suggestion of anything other than Clare's very distinctive voice in which both he and the beloved (significantly unnamed) are so lost that they do not know each other. In their union they are mere ghosts in a 'land of shadows'. When Coleridge quoted Goethe in his epigraph to *Biographia Literaria* about the path on which he loses his way, he cannot have envisaged the implications of Clare's path that itself hath 'lost its way'.

> Wilt thou go with me sweet maid
> Say maiden wilt thou go with me
> Through the valley depths of shade
> Of night and dark obscurity
> Where the path hath lost its way
> Where the sun forgets the day
> Where there's nor life nor light to see
> Sweet maiden wilt thou go with me
>
> Where stones will turn to flooding streams
> Where plains will rise like ocean waves
> Where life will fade like visioned dreams
> And mountains darken into caves
> Say maiden wilt thou go with me
> Through this sad non-identity
> Where parents live and are forgot
> And sisters live and know us not
>
> Say maiden wilt thou go with me
> In this strange death of life to be
> To live in death and be the same
> Without this life, or home, or name
> At once to be, and not to be
> That was, and is not – yet to see
> Things pass like shadows – and the sky
> Above, below, around us lie
>
> The land of shadows wilt thou trace
> And look – nor know each others face
> The present mixed with reasons gone
> And past, and present all as one
> Say maiden can thy life be led
> To join the living with the dead
> Then trace thy footsteps on with me
> We're wed to one eternity.

Clare talks in *Child Harold* of various moments where he and Mary merge. For example:

Mary thy name loved long still keeps me free
Till my lost life becomes a part of thee

or

Mary I mourn no pleasures gone
The past hath made us both as one

or

Our lives are two – our end and aim is one.

But none of these moments prepares us for the devastation of a poem such as 'Invite to Eternity'. Another line of thought in *Child Harold*, however, is one that offers some kind of solution to his agonised circumstance. He begins to talk of Mary as a silent presence which he will nurse to himself. This raises the possibility of a paradoxically silent muse, and in so doing confirms that uneasy sense the reader can get in these poems, of having no place at all: the reader's role is denied, in return for the strangely contradictory denial of the poet's. There is, literally, no audience for a poem written in a small notebook; even the 'fair copy' is by no means a straightforward text of the poem, and is never published in his lifetime. In this respect Clare's asylum verse is similar in effect to the hermetic world of Emily Dickinson, another poet without an audience. In this 'Song', Clare plays on the theme.

No single hour can stand for nought
No moment hand can move
But calenders a aching thought
Of my first lonely love

Where silence doth the loudest call
My secrets to betray
As moonlight holds the night in thrall
As suns reveal the day

I hide it in the silent shades
Till silence finds a tongue
I make its grave where time invades
Till time becomes a song

I bid my foolish heart be still
But hopes will not be chid

My heart will beat – & burn – & chill
First love will not be hid

When summer ceases to be green
& winter bare & blea –
Death may forget what I have been
But I must cease to be

When words refuse before the crowd
My Mary's name to give
The muse in silence sings aloud
& there my love will live.

'Love is a secret' he says; in his particular poetic creed, where love and poetry so often go hand in hand, then poetry too becomes a secret. This explains the strange effect of the following stanza:

I've been gathering
The springs happy weather in
Wild meadow flowers
While fell the spring showers;
And every drop reminds me
Of the days I left behind me
Of one I loved well, and the sweet places too
But these are loves secrets I must not tell you.

'The Green Lane' ends in a similarly teasing fashion.

The breeze it wispered here she comes
I look'd and there she sat
The partrich creak'd its evening songs
And whirr'd the merry chat
But what she said, or what I did
Must not be told again
They're secrets now for ever hid
Told in the Old green Lane.

A bleaker aspect of this provides a disturbing twist to the final stanza of 'Silent Love', where we see, as George Eliot puts it, 'the other side of silence'.

Such is young love when silence speaks
Till weary with the joy it seeks
The fancy shapes supplies
'Till sick of its own heart it dies

The dew drop falls at mornings hour
When none are standing by
And noiseless fades the broken flower
So lovers in their silence die.

'Secret Love' pushes things even further.

I hid my love when young while I
Coud'nt bear the buzzing of a flye
I hid my love to my despite
Till I could not bear to look at light
I dare not gaze upon her face
But left her memory in each place
Where ere I saw a wild flower lye
I kissed and bade my love goodbye …

I hid my love in field and town
Till e'en the breeze would blow me down
The Bees seemed singing ballads oe'r
The flyes buzz turned a Lions roar
And even silence found a tongue
To haunt me all the summer long
The Riddle nature could not prove
Was nothing else but secret love.

The corollary of this line of thought is that there are several poems where he has to admit, rather like Wordsworth with Lucy, that he has lost Mary ('But where Love are you?'). He sometimes dare not tell her name, or, more disastrously, forgets it.

As a poet with his eye on posterity, Clare produces one of his most remarkable poems, 'A Vision'. Here he attains a spiritual freedom, away from human wiles, and in four brief stanzas gives us a version of his life. Having lost the earth and its putative joys, he proceeds to lose himself and becomes the 'bard of immortality', the very thing spoken of by Shelley in the Chorus of Spirits in *Prometheus Unbound* ('nurslings of immortality').

I lost the love of heaven above
I spurned the lust of earth below
I felt the sweets of fancied love
And hell itself my only foe

I lost earth's joys but felt the glow
Of heaven's flame abound in me
Till loveliness and I did grow
The bard of immortality

I loved but woman fell away
I hid me from her faded fame
I snatched the sun's eternal ray
And wrote till earth was but a name

In every language upon earth
On every shore, o'er every sea,
I gave my name immortal birth,
And kept my spirit with the free.

This hard-won conclusion can be seen as the climax of Clare's work: it celebrates as few poems do the furthest reaches of creativity. At the same time its triumph depends on the poet's escape from mortal bondage, whereby he becomes one of Shelley's spirits, recreating the great 'I AM' but in another world. He names himself, thereby giving himself identity by removing himself from this world. And against this we have to set the terrible poem in which the long-lost lovers pass each other in ignorance:

And now I pass to thee unknown
Thy eye that brightens only mine

I guess and know and own it not
We're lost as strangers as we pass.

The underlying, irresolvable contradiction at the heart of Clare's asylum poetry is perhaps best caught in a letter of the late 1840s, in which he writes to a former loved one, Mary Collingwood.[15] He had written earlier that 'nature to me seems dead & her very pulse seems frozen to an iceicle in the summer sun.' By now he is writing as though from the grave: he exists, but it is the living death of which he speaks so movingly in 'Invite to Eternity'. His assertion of self, here, consists of the famous tautology, 'I am that I am', a circular self-awareness that, whilst apparently its own justification, is essentially self-defeating. The poet remains silent because there is nothing else to do in a faithless world; and silence in turn means that nothing gets done. We are back with the 'vast shipwreck of my life's esteems':

> there is no faith here so I hold my tongue & wait the end but without attention or intention – I am that I am – & done nothing yet.

6
Byron and Clare: 'An indigestion of the mind'

A common view of Byron's development follows this pattern: he tries out various forms and styles, in a rather languid way, in his youth and early manhood, and completes *Childe Harold* by 1817, before acknowledging that he has been pursuing the wrong poetic path; inspired by a reading of John Hookham Frere's *Whistlecraft*, and by his immersion in the Italian burlesque tradition, he launches himself into the *ottava rima* of *Beppo, The Vision of Judgment,* and *Don Juan*. He has found his true voice and style, his proper role as the age's satirist. This is too neat a formulation for a process that is much more complicated: even Byron, the noble Lord of such apparently supreme self-confidence, faces doubts about his own poetry, just as he ponders the validity of poetry itself. The questions he asks, particularly around the years 1816–19, are pertinent to an understanding not only of his own rather tortured attempts at self-definition, but also of the other major Romantic writers. Running alongside Byron's questions are the questions raised by, of all people, John Clare, the poet who, more than any other, recognises the full importance of what Byron is doing. Clare's obsession with Byron runs right through his writing life, until he identifies himself with his alter ego in the asylum: it is an obsession that helps him to work through some of his most pressing sources of anxiety, especially the place he might occupy in relation to those obviously much more established writers of past and present. Clare seems to realise from an early age that his own worries as to poetry's possibilities, and the durability of the imaginative vision, are a reflection of Byron's uncertainties.

Byron's declaration of 1817 has become something of a commonplace:

> I am convinced ... that ... *all* of us – Scott, Southey, Wordsworth, Moore, Campbell, I, – are all in the wrong, one as much as another, that we are upon a wrong revolutionary poetical system, or systems, not worth a damn in itself, and from which none but Rogers and Crabbe are free; and that the present and next generations will finally be of this opinion.[1]

There is much that is remarkable about this *mea culpa*, not least Byron's readiness to bracket himself with his arch enemies, Southey and Wordsworth. But what is particularly interesting is the extent to which most of his writings of this period are in themselves echoes of this sense of going down a blind alley. Ironically, in the process he produces some of his most telling verse. Byron voices a typical range of Romantic concerns with the appropriate voice, the right form, more insistently even than his contemporaries.

The date of the letter I have just quoted is important. Byron is coming to the end of *Childe Harold*, he is on the verge of getting to grips with the Italian literary tradition which will allow him to write *Beppo* and *Don Juan*; there is even a time when he believes that Italian would be the most fitting medium for him.[2] He becomes caught up in the political implications of that tradition, and proceeds to write, within the next two years, two otherwise rather odd poems, *The Lament of Tasso* and *The Prophecy of Dante*; on the personal front he has himself become, in his self-imposed exile in Italy, analogous to the great Dante. Shortly after that wrench from England in April 1816, he writes two poems that have some bearing on the argument, 'The Dream' and 'Darkness', both poems about the nature of poetry. In addition there is *The Prisoner of Chillon*, which at about the same time pursues his obsession with the idea of imprisonment. The idea is a recurrent one, with clear political significance for a poet who believes in the freedom of nations; it has, too, personal significance for a poet caught in a literary tradition which he finds constricting, but which none the less seems to serve his peculiar purposes. If Rogers and Crabbe are the only ones to be on the right track, to be free in that sense, it is a strange kind of freedom; and it would be a curious prison that enchained Byron alongside Southey and Wordsworth. The desire for freedom, let alone the means of escape, becomes a tortured business, as the tortured verse of these years might suggest.

Many of the contemporary responses to *Childe Harold* are alert to the linguistic complexities and hesitations. Hazlitt's ambiguous response, for example, is a telling comment on Byron's own ambiguities. He talks of Byron's shutting 'himself up in the Bastile of his own ruling passions'; he

> makes man after his own image, woman after his own heart; the one is a capricious tyrant, the other a yielding slave; he gives us the misanthrope and the voluptuary by turns; and with these two characters, burning or melting in their own fires, he makes out ever-lasting centos out of himself. He hangs the cloud, the film of his existence over all outward things – sits in the centre of his thoughts, and enjoys dark night, bright day, the glitter and the gloom 'in cell monastic' – we see the mournful pall, the crucifix, the death's heads, the faded chaplet of flowers, the gleaming tapers, the agonized brow of genius, the wasted form of beauty – but we are still imprisoned in a dungeon, a curtain intercepts our view, we do not breathe freely the air of nature or of our own thoughts.[3]

But, as even this passage hints, Hazlitt has a grudging admiration for Byron. He might find a particular passage in *Child Harold* 'obscure, tortured, perplexed, and abortive'; but, he goes on, 'who can say that it is not beautiful, striking, and impassioned?' The poem might be 'a mass of discordant things, incoherent', but it still makes on Hazlitt an impression to which he succumbs. As he says, 'Lord Byron, when he pleases, defies competition and surpasses all his contemporaries.' The problem for Hazlitt, as for so many of his contemporaries, is that the reader's desire for sense and order is thwarted by an intriguing, even compelling, incoherence. If Charles Lamb and Wordsworth found it hard to understand the virtues of Byron's 'power', Matthew Arnold was quite sure about it; so too was Scott.

> His poetry is like the oratory which hurries the hearers along without permitting them to pause on its solecisims or singularities. Its general structure is bold, severe, and as it were Doric, admitting few ornaments but those immediately suggested by the glowing imagination of the author, rising and sinking with the tones of his enthusiasm, roughening into argument, or softening into the melody of feeling and sentiment, as if the language fit for either were alike at the command of the poet, and the numbers not only came uncalled, but arranged themselves with little care on his part into the varied modulation which the subject requires ... If the line 'labours and the words move slow', it is in passages where the sense is correspondent to these laborious movements. A highly finished

> strain of versification resembles a dressed pleasure ground, elegant – even beautiful – but tame and insipid compared to the majesty and interest of a woodland chase, where scenes of natural loveliness are rendered sweeter and more interesting by the contrast of irregularity and wildness.[4]

Hazlitt recognised the haunting nature of Byron's verse, and related the stylistic confusion to the poetry's dreamlike quality. Hence, *Childe Harold* gives the 'same impression as a troubled dream ... as disturbed, as confused, as disjointed, as harassing, and as unprofitable. It is an indigestion of the mind.' 'The versification and style of this poem are as perverse and capricious as the method or the sentiments.'[5] Beside these comments might be set those of John Wilson, who allows himself to be more openly and uncomplicatedly well-disposed towards the Byronic effects: 'We feel as if we had transiently met such beings in real life, or had known them in the dim and dark communion of a dream ... They are fragments of a poet's dark dream of life.'[6]

Dreams, as we have seen, haunt the consciousness of many Romantic writers – and not just the poets, as De Quincey reminds us – and it would perhaps be true to say that the closer dreams are to the sources of Romantic imagination, the more haunting and unsettling they become. This is one of the truths that Byron touches on in the poems he writes whilst still caught in that prison-house of what he calls the 'wrong poetical system'. One of the ironies of the Tasso and Dante poems is that they revert to another image of prison: both poets find a particular kind of freedom within the prison walls. In other words, freedom to some extent depends upon imprisonment. And, just as important, these poems, written after the supposed release provided by *Beppo* and the start of *Don Juan*, have that peculiar, clotted quality that we associate with his earlier work. On a linguistic level they do not display the kind of freedom which Byron might appear to be claiming. Something rather similar happens with John Clare.

*

When he was imprisoned in the asylums at Epping Forest, and then Northampton, Clare found some comfort in his self-identification with Byron. He too faced a crisis which had its literary as well as its dreadful personal dimensions; he too needed to find an appropriate voice to encompass the contradictions; he too resorted to the image of the dream ('life is to me a dream that never wakes') and the nightmare, and the full significance of his earlier poems of the 1820s, in which he had drawn inspiration from Byron's 'Dream' and 'Darkness', becomes apparent. Clare, too, needed to believe that it was possible to be 'free in a prison'. Hence the importance of the fact that, amidst all the cramped jottings of the notebooks where he works towards his own versions of *Don Juan* and *Child Harold*, we find a list of quotations, two of them from Byron's *Lament of Tasso*, just as in both poems are to be found echoes of *The Prophecy of Dante*.[7] As Clare struggles to cling on to a literary identity, his Byronic solution is a reminder of how Byron himself had set about the problem. Before discussing Byron's poems, I would like to sketch out something of Clare's relationship with Byron. Just as Wordsworth and Coleridge can hardly be separated in any exploration of their work, so Byron occupies a central place in Clare's developing idea of himself.

'Though laurel wreaths my brows did ne'er environ / I think myself as great a bard as Byron.' This is not the best couplet Clare ever wrote, but it is perhaps one of the most revealing. It comes towards the end of his version of *Don Juan*, written in the asylum in Epping Forest in 1841, in a tiny notebook alongside *Child Harold*. When, with the help of some gipsies, he escaped from the asylum and trudged back home, a three-day trek to the village of Northborough, near Peterborough, he took this notebook with him, adding bits and pieces as he rested by the roadside for the night, writing prayers for his family, for the wife he was not to recognise when she met him wandering near the woods at the end of his journey home. When he had recovered sufficiently from this dreadful ordeal, he sat down to write out, as best he could, neat fair-copy versions of both poems. After six months, he was removed to the General Lunatic Asylum in Northampton, where he was to stay until his death in 1864.

When John Clare first took some of his poems to the Stamford bookseller Edward Drury in 1818 (Drury was the cousin of Keats's publisher John Taylor), Drury in exchange gave him a copy of *The Giaour*. Clare records in his 'Autobiography' that it was the first of Byron's poems he had ever seen. But before long others came his way, including *Childe Harold*, 'The Dream', and 'Darkness'. By a strange coincidence Clare was in London on the day of Byron's funeral in 1824, and he has left a poignant account of the event as it affected him.

> I happend to see it by chance as I was wandering up Oxford street on my way to Mrs Emmersons when my eye was suddenly arested by straggling gropes of the common people collected together and

> talking about a funeral ... bye and bye the grope collected into about a hundred or more when the train of a funeral suddenly appeard on which a young girl that stood beside me gave a deep sigh and utterd poor Lord Byron ... I looked up in the young girls face ... it was dark and beautiful and I coud almost feel in love with her for the sigh she had utterd for the poet.[8]

In the privacy of this remembrance (Clare's autobiography was never published in his own lifetime), Clare touches on a crucial sense of identification with the great, dead poet; for all the pomp and splendour of the occasion, it is the quiet sadness of the common people that most impresses him, the solitary girl's plaintive sigh. A year or so later, Clare makes a rare excursion into print in prose, with an 'Essay on Popularity in Authorship', which was published in the *European Magazine*. It is a remarkably polished performance.[9] Importantly, Byron is a key figure in the argument, as Clare mulls over the ambiguities of popularity and fame. As we know, Clare had good cause to ponder the matter, both now and later: the four editions of his first volume of 1820 were a false dawn for him, and that first public rapture did not greet the publication of a much better book, *The Shepherd's Calendar* in 1827. There is every reason for Clare, early on in his career as a writer, to be fascinated by Byron as a figure, as someone who has broken all the rules, who has apparently become the uncrowned King of Rhyme; and yet Clare is astute enough to remember that fashion plays its part, that immediate popularity is a chimera, that Time will deliver its own considered verdict. His sonnet on Byron sums up the argument of his essay:

> A splendid sun hath set when shall our eyes
> Behold a morn so beautiful arise
> As that which gave his mighty genius birth
> & all eclipsed the lesser lights on earth
> His first young burst of twilight did declare
> Beyond that haze a sun was rising there
> As when the morn to usher in the day
> Speeds from the east in sober garb of grey
> At first till warming into wild delight
> She casts her mantle off & shines in light
> The labours of small minds an age may dream
> & be but shadows on times running stream
> While genius in an hour makes what shall be
> The next a portion of eternity

In the asylum in Epping Forest, Clare's mind reverts to Byron. He thinks that his own imprisonment matches Byron's exile, that his own desperate love for a woman not his wife is in some way as responsible for his plight as Byron's domestic complications had been for his leaving England, that his own cries for freedom echo Byron's championing of liberty on a wider scale. Most of all, he realises that he can use Byron as a surrogate figure: there is an extraordinary stanza in *Don Juan*, where he begins by disparaging him, but ends up denying his death, and adopting his identity.

> Lord Byron poh – the man wot rites the werses
> And is just what he is and nothing more
> Who with his pen lies like the mist disperses
> And makes all nothing as it was before
> Who wed two wives and oft the truth rehearses
> And might have had some twenty thousand more
> Who has been dead so fools their lies are giving
> And still in Allens madhouse caged and living.

As we know, Clare thought he was many different people, including Nelson, Tom Spring the boxer, Jack Randall the wrestler, Burns and Cowper. But when the worthy Cyrus Redding visited him in May 1841, he asked what he would like, and when the answer came, 'books', asked the obvious question, 'what books?' Clare's reply was immediate: 'Byron'.[10] At around this time, Clare was planning, as if in a dream, his next publication:

> In a short time will be published
> A New Vol of Poems by Lord Byron
> Not yet collected in his Works
> Containing Songs
> New Cantos of Child Harold,
> And additional Hebrew Melodies, Fragments &c.

Another journal entry reads: 'Speedily will be published / The Sale of Old Wigs & Sundries / A Poem by Lord Byron'.[11] In letters of the period he refers to new Cantos of both *Child Harold* and *Don Juan* that he is writing, apparently simultaneously. When he makes his dramatic escape, he writes a letter to the seemingly untroubled Dr Allen, asking for some books to be sent on to him: all the books are by Byron. It is as though he has taken with him his own versions of Byron, the Byron he knows to be alive; but he would like to have the other Byron too. Similarly, he refuses to believe, when he does get home, that Mary Joyce, whom he now thinks of as his wife, has been dead for three years. The personal and social implications of Clare's obsession with Byron should be clear. One general literary point needs to be made here.

For Byron, his two long poems are often seen as representing two different modes of writing: the introspective, tortured egotist of *Childe Harold's Pilgrimage*, and the brilliant satirist working lazily at full stretch within the challenging confines of *Don Juan's ottava rima*. This has been put in a more provocative way, with reference to a shift from 'Romantic' to 'Augustan', a move back away from current trends towards the old established deities; and Byron's own proclamations tend to support this view.[12] But there are already hints in *Childe Harold* of an awareness of the 'Romantic' giving way to something less lofty: that, after all, is the justification he gives, quoting Beattie, for using the Spenserian stanza in the first place; and in *Don Juan*, for all the satire, there is the most careful exploration of deep feeling. This apparent opposition, and yet mingling of genres, is mirrored in Clare's work. At the time he is working on his first long, sustained poem, *The Shepherd's Calendar*, he is also writing, in *The Parish*, an extensive satiric attack on the countryside as he knows it; celebration is matched by cynicism. There is a reminder here of Byron, but of Crabbe too, and of that earlier and stronger eighteenth-century strain which had formed such a staple part of Clare's formative literary diet. Donald Davie had something of this in mind when he spoke of the way in which Byron's special kind of 'Augustan-Romanticism' helped to make sense of Clare's.[13] As with Crabbe and Byron, so with Clare we often get caught by a twinge of anachronism: these couplets, this wit, do not seem to belong to the age of Wordsworth and Coleridge, Keats and Shelley. When it comes to Clare's own versions of *Child Harold* and *Don Juan*, he seems to be very self-consciously addressing the question head-on.

Clare's *Don Juan* is a fairly coarse poem, unsubtle, scatological, with few verbal felicities and with no sustained critique of the age or society. But however bizarre the poem, however slight in comparison with Byron's, it appeals to Byron for sanction. It is declaring that, confined within the madhouse of Epping Forest, Byron lives on. But he is much more persuasive on this score in his version of *Child Harold*, in which he recognises that Byron too was confronting the problem of identity, in a fragmented way that anticipated his own crisis. There is the famous and oft-quoted sentence in one of Byron's letters: 'To withdraw *myself* from *myself* (oh that cursed selfishness!) has ever been my sole, my entire, my sincere motive in scribbling at all.' Whenever he feels the tug of egotism, he will seek shelter in the notion that 'Nature stampt me in the Die of Indifference'.[14] This struggle permeates Byron's *Childe Harold,* made the more poignant by the biographical circumstances that lie behind the poem's composition. Clare says in his poem, 'My life hath been one chain of contradictions', and there is a terrible truth in that, a truth that Byron would have understood. His own poem circles around a similar sense of puzzlement – his own favourite word here is 'bafflement'. Clare's introduction to Byron through *The Giaour* assumes a particular significance, for that poem concerns itself with puzzlement, with things that cannot be fully grasped, with experiences that are apparently contradictory, and which require a contorted narrative framework to contain them.[15] This sense of baffled rage and pathos would have appealed to the John Clare who felt that he too had a version of *Child Harold* within him.

When Clare first looks at Byron's *Don Juan,* in 1824, he is struck by the incongruities: but when he reads more of the poem he is more disturbed by the formal aspects. Byron, he says, 'appears to have lost his intended plan on setting out & to have continued it with any purpose that came uppermost'.[16] Byron's methods of writing are analogous to Clare's own processes, certainly in his later years; so there is some irony in his rather prim strictures on the waywardness of *Don Juan.* Its waywardness is of course highly deceptive, and part of the point: we might hear an echo of Byron's defence of *Childe Harold*'s structure, that it was built according to the Ariosto plan, that is, no plan at all. There might be some disingenuousness there, but it is important to make the connection between the digressive habits of *Don Juan,* the provisional quality of *Childe Harold,* and what he called 'that snake of a poem', *The Giaour.* He was always adding on, always tinkering, not to give a sense of fixity or finality, but, on the contrary, to capture that sense of the poem as growth, as something developing without always knowing which way it might go next. As a result we get poems that challenge the notions of wholeness and completeness, even of consistency. There are very few fixed points in his poems; the restlessness that characterises *Childe Harold* and its hero is reflected by a moral relativity (both here and in the Tales), and by a formal ambiguity which is to find its apotheosis in *Don Juan,* but which is there too in *Childe Harold.* Hazlitt summed up his own view of Byron's formal waywardness like this:

> *Intensity* is the great and prominent distinction of Lord Byron's writings. He seldom gets beyond force of style, nor has he produced any regular work or masterly whole. He does not prepare any plan beforehand, nor revise and retouch what he has written with polished accuracy. His only object seems to be to stimulate himself and his readers for the moment – to keep both alive, to drive away *ennui*, to substitute a feverish and irritable state of excitement for listless indolence or even calm enjoyment.[17]

Clare's *Child Harold* is not in any sense either pastiche or parody. There is in fact no one in the poem called Child Harold; there is no pilgrimage in the literal sense initially implied by Byron's title. Whereas Byron's world encompasses the whole of Europe and Asia Minor, and with them their history, Clare's world is as circumscribed as that of the *Prisoner of Chillon*. The longest journey he can contemplate is from Epping Forest to Northborough. But Byron's hero soon learns that he cannot get beyond the horizon, that he is bound to the earth and the present, that his relentless journeying is in many respects a futile exercise. It would be hard to overemphasise the importance of the address to his friend Edleston at the end of Canto II. Harold's – or the poet's – identity depends on someone who has 'ceased to be'.

> Thou too art gone, thou lov'd and lovely one!
> Whom youth and youth's affection bound to me;
> Who did for me what none beside have done,
> Nor shrank from one albeit unworthy thee.
> What is my being? thou hast ceas'd to be!
> Nor stayed to welcome here thy wanderer home,
> Who mourns o'er hours which we no more shall see –
> Would they have never been, or were to come!
> Would he had ne'er return'd to find fresh cause to roam!
>
> What is the worst of woes that wait on age?
> What stamps the wrinkle deeper on the brow?
> To view each loved one blotted from life's page,
> And be alone on earth, as I am now.

Byron had voiced similar sentiments as early as his lines 'To Thyrza':

> It was not thus in days more dear,
> It never would have been, but thou

Hast fled, and left me lonely here;
Thou'rt nothing, all are nothing now.

This sense of present solitude is seized upon by Clare, and put at the very centre of his own poem. There had been, at the centre of many of Byron's narrative poems, including *The Giaour*, a dreadful abyss, as there is at the heart of *Childe Harold*. For Clare the abyss is the past that cannot be recaptured, the lost love of his life.

Mary Joyce, the object of his childhood affections, left his life when they were both in their teens. By the time he was incarcerated he believed that she was his wife, and the purpose of escaping from the asylum was to return home, to Mary. Hence the almost unbearable poignancy of the 'Song' he wrote as soon as he had made that trek from Epping Forest.

I've wandered many a weary mile
Love in my heart was burning
To seek a home in Mary[s] smile
But cold is loves returning
The cold ground was a feather bed
Truth never acts contrary
I had no home above my head
My home was love & Mary

I had no home in early youth
When my first love was thwarted
But if her heart still beats with truth
We'll never more be parted
& changing as her love may be
My own shall never vary
Nor night nor day I'm never free
But sigh for abscent Mary

Nor night nor day nor sun nor shade
Week month nor rolling year
Repairs the breach wronged love hath made
There madness – misery here
Lifes lease was lengthened by her smile
– Are truth & love contrary
No ray of hope my life beguiles
I've lost love home and Mary.

Clare' s poem, like Byron's, becomes amongst other things an examination of truth, and what truth actually implies. After this desolate song comes a defiant section beginning with a Byronic echo: 'Love is the main spring of existence – It / Becomes a soul wherebye I live to love.' He insists on challenging all the doubts that rise up against him, but no sooner has he challenged them than they recur: Mary's absence – and hence the breach of faith – presents itself to him with even greater force. Just as Byron's and Harold's identity depends upon people no longer there – and is therefore constantly under threat – so Clare is left in isolation:

> Brown are the flags and fadeing sedge
> And tanned the meadow plains
> Bright yellow is the osier hedge
> Beside the brimming drains
> The crows sit on the willow tree
> The lake is full below
> But still the dullest thing I see
> Is self that wanders slow
>
> The dullest scenes are not so dull
> As thoughts I cannot tell
> The brimming dykes are not so full
> As my hearts silent swell
> I leave my troubles to the winds
> With none to share a part
> The only joy my feeling finds
> Hides in an aching heart.

The asylum is Clare's prison, where he is locked away from what he thinks of as his two wives.

> Yet absence claims them both and keeps them too
> And locks me in a shop in spite of law
> Among a low lived set and dirty crew
> Here let the Muse oblivions curtain draw
> And let man think – for God hath often saw
> Things here too dirty for the light of day
> For in a madhouse there exists no law –
> Now stagnant grows my too refined clay
> I envy birds their wings to flye away.

This extraordinary stanza, which moves from doggerel to an almost Shakespearean desire for release, emphasises Clare's terror at stagnation and apathy, the very theme with which Byron engages in his poem. Harold is often described in terms of his 'guarded coldness', as Byron pursues the idea of aspiration and its denial, just as does Clare.

> Like the Chaldean, he could watch the stars,
> Till he had peopled them with beings bright
> As their own beams; and earth, and earthborn jars,
> And human frailties, were forgotten quite:
> Could he have kept his spirit to that flight
> He had been happy; but this clay will sink
> Its spark immortal, envying it the light
> To which it mounts, as if to break the link
> That keeps us from yon heaven which woos us to its brink.
>
> But in Man's dwellings he became a thing
> Restless and worn, and stern and wearisome,
> Droop'd as a wild-born falcon with clipt wing,
> To whom the boundless air alone were home:
> Then came his fit again, which to o'ercome
> As eagerly the barr'd up bird will beat
> His breast and beak against his wiry dome
> Till the blood tinge his plumage, so the heat
> Of his impeded soul would through his bosom eat. (III.xiv–xv)

Just before this passage Harold has indulged in an emotion that is central to the poem, that almost Wordsworthian belief in creativity for which Canto III is so well-known, and so often criticised because it seems to some not typical of Byron.

> 'Tis to create, and in creating live
> A being more intense, that we endow
> With form our fancy, gaining as we give
> The life we image, even as I do now.
> What am I? Nothing: but not so art thou,
> Soul of my thought ! with whom I traverse earth,
> Invisible but gazing, as I glow
> Mix'd with thy spirit, blended with thy birth,
> And feeling still with thee in my crush'd feelings' dearth. (III.vi)

However uneasy the verse, Byron continues this theme through much of this Canto, as when he sings the virtues of the natural world:

> I live not in myself, but I become
> Portion of that around me; and to me,
> High mountains are a feeling, but the hum
> Of human cities torture: I can see
> Nothing to loathe in nature, save to be
> A link reluctant in a fleshly chain,
> Class'd among creatures, when the soul can flee,
> And with the sky, the peak, the heaving plain
> Of ocean, or the stars, mingle, and not in vain ...
>
> And when, at length, the mind shall be all free
> From what it hates in this degraded form,
> Reft of its carnal life, save what shall be
> Existent happier in the fly and worm, –
> When elements to elements conform,
> And dust is as it should be, shall I not
> Feel all I see, less dazzling, but more warm?
> The bodiless thought? the Spirit of each spot?
> Of which, even now, I share at times the immortal lot?
>
> (III.lxxii–lxxiv)

There is no doubt at all that Clare has read his Byron carefully. In the song, 'Written in a Thunder storm', he begins with apathy, but ends in Byronic defiance, shaking his fist at the elements, as does Byron ('Then let the winds howl on!').

> My soul is apathy – a ruin vast
> Time cannot clear the ruined mass away
> My life is hell – the hopeless die is cast
> & manhoods prime is premature decay
>
> Roll on ye wrath of thunders – peal on peal
> Till worlds are ruins & myself alone
> Melt heart & soul cased in obdurate steel
> Till I can feel that nature is my throne
>
> Smile on ye elements of earth & sky
> Or frown in thunders as ye frown on me
> Bid earth & its delusions pass away
> But leave the mind as its creator free.

But just as Byron finds it hard to sustain his defiance, so Clare goes on, 'Tie all my cares up in thy arms O sleep / & give my weary spirits peace & rest.' Finally, when Clare says, 'I sigh a poet and a lover still', he reminds us that this is how Byron defines himself in his poem. To be the poet and the lover is to deny yourself a conclusion. One of the ultimate ironies of Byron's poem is that the past, on which it depends, ceases to exist; his poem is no more than 'the spell of a protracted dream'. And Clare, whose poem has been about a love that had defined him, about a past that has made some sense of the present, does not finish his poem: it is left, suspended in the present, denying itself:

> The present hour is all my lot alows
> An age of sorrow springs from lovers vows.

*

It is in *Childe Harold's Pilgrimage* Canto IV that Byron confronts his particular linguistic concerns, and significantly these come to the surface in Venice, where he wants to put his dreams ('Overweening phantasies') behind him:

> I've taught me other tongues – and in strange eyes
> Have made me not a stranger. (IV.viii)

On one level this is clearly a reference to his recently acquired knowledge of Italian; but the plural hints at something rather more mysterious. The fragments in the mirror, spoken of in Canto III, have become a chorus of different voices which assist towards a sense of himself as 'not a stranger'. As the poem has proceeded, Byron has given up the pretence that there is a distinction between the poet and his hero: the letter to Hobhouse, which prefaces Canto IV, admits that he speaks here in his own voice, and the paradox is that he then goes on to say that he talks in many voices. The parallel paradox is that it is in Italy, as he contemplates his exile, that he declares his own aspirations. 'I twine / My hopes of being remembered in my line / With my land's language.' We are brought up sharply against one of the major purposes of the poem, which is precisely to establish himself in the literary tradition as a poet on a par with the great Italians. Such aspirations are soon dismissed with an oddly Shelleyan gesture:

Meantime I seek no sympathies, nor need;
The thorns which I have reap'd are of the tree
I planted: they have torn me, and I bleed:
I should have known what fruit would spring from such a seed.
(IV.x)

But recollection of the Italian poets revives his spirits:

There is a tomb in Arqua; – rear'd in air,
Pillar'd in their sarcophagus, repose
The bones of Laura's lover: here repair
Many familiar with his well-sung woes,
The pilgrims of his genius. He arose
To raise a language, and his land reclaim
From the dull yoke of her barbaric foes. (IV.xxx)

Petrarch is important because he intertwines political and poetical achievements, and the same is true of Dante, Tasso and Ariosto. But history offers its own ironic comment on this tradition, for these writers all suffered exile, imprisonment, or oblivion. That is Byron's peculiar predicament, that he aligns himself with an apparently failed tradition, which he, in all his painful truthfulness, has to acknowledge. To 'twine' his hopes of 'being remember'd in my line / With my land's language' is a curiously tenuous ambition, given the precedent. Just how tenuous is hinted at in the very word 'twine', which anticipates the final couplet of the *Lament of Tasso*:

Yes, Leonora! it shall be our fate
To be entwined for ever – but too late!

Byron is too alert to the partings of life for him to set too much store by their denial. The resulting tension imbues the whole of *Childe Harold*, but also the other poems in which he allows himself to explore more concisely the basic contradiction of his position.

The Lament of Tasso is not a particularly good poem: what interests me here are the connections that are invited with *Childe Harold*. The opening of the second section, for example:

But this is o'er – my pleasant task is done: –
My long-sustaining friend of many years!
If I do blot thy final page with tears,

Know, that my sorrows have wrung from me none.
But thou, my young creation! my soul's child!
Which ever playing round me came and smiled,
And woo'd me from myself with thy sweet sight,
Thou too art gone – and so is my delight.

This is reminiscent of the conclusion of *Childe Harold*, Canto II, where he mourns Edleston's death; but also of the very end of the poem:

My task is done, my song hath ceased, my theme
Has died into an echo; it is fit
The spell should break of this protracted dream. (IV.clxxxv)

Hazlitt was right to say that Byron 'scorns all things, even himself.'[18] *The Lament of Tasso* is a love poem, in much the same way as Clare's *Child Harold*, in which the loved one, the Muse figure, is absent. In the case of Byron's poem on Tasso, the contradiction extends to the implications of Tasso himself, in that Byron understands his plight only too well. Alongside the idea of love go two other ideas central to Byron when working on the last two Cantos of *Childe Harold*: the emphasis on madness, and with it the destruction of meaning.

I have been patient, let me be so yet;
I had forgotten half I would forget,
But it revives – Oh! would it were my lot
To be forgetful as I am forgot!
Feel I not wroth with those who bade me dwell
In this vast lasar-house of many woes?
Where laughter is not mirth, nor thought the mind,
Nor words a language, nor ev'n men mankind;
Where cries reply to curses, shrieks to blows;
And each is tortured in his separate hell –
For we are crowded in our solitudes –
Many, but each divided by the wall,
Which echoes Madness in her babbling moods.

His love for Leonora had meant a loss of himself, a loss both desirable but an eerie parallel to his lost self in the prison:

I found the thing I sought – and that was thee:
And then I lost my being, all to be

> Absorb'd in thine; the world was past away;
> *Thou* didst annihilate the earth to me!
>
> I loved all Solitude, but little thought
> To spend I know not what of life, remote
> From all communion with existence, save
> The maniac and his tyrant; had I been
> Their fellow, many years ere this had seen
> My mind like theirs corrupted to its grave.
> But who hath seen me writhe, or heard me rave?
> Perchance in such a cell we suffer more
> Than the wrecked sailor on his desert shore;
> The world is all before him – *mine* is *here,*
> Scarce twice the space they must accord my bier.
> What though *he* perish, he may lift his eye,
> And with a dying glance upbraid the sky;
> I will not raise my own in such reproof,
> Although 'tis clouded by my dungeon roof.

His only hope is to cling on to his sense of himself as a poet, so that his cell shall become a shrine, 'which nations yet shall visit for my sake'. One of the quotations from this poem to be found in Clare's manuscript notebook of 1841 has particular poignancy: 'Imputed madness prison'd solitude / & the mind's canker in its savage mood'. Clare is in a limbo between one asylum and another; he understands only too closely and painfully the agonies of solitude and madness.

Some of the implications of *The Lament of Tasso* are worked out in the more ambitious, but equally ambiguous, *Prophecy of Dante*. The hero is a diminished figure, similar to the prisoner of Chillon, stripped of any power; his aspirations to eternity must be tamed in what amounts to a 'bitter lesson'. But there is, again, that curious sense of freedom in exile, in that he has at least avoided slavery. This spiritual freedom enables him to relive the days of old, 'When words were things which came to pass.' There is another echo of *Childe Harold* here, this time of Canto II:

> I do believe,
> Though I have found them not, that there may be
> Words which are things, hopes which will not deceive.

The poet becomes the prophet, able to foretell the future and thereby make sense of things. It had been Tasso's complaint that for him the world did not lie ahead, in any Miltonic or Wordsworthian sense: his world was here, in the dreadfully eternal present, just as for the prisoner at Chillon, there is no sense of time, but 'a sea of stagnant idleness / Blind, and boundless, mute, and motionless'. The difference between the two later poems is that here, if briefly, there can be hope, because the poet can create meaning from chaos. Whereas Tasso had spoken to Leonora in terms of desperate, doomed love, Dante addresses his country in words that recall Tasso's ardour but also Byron's poetic aspirations in *Childe Harold*. He lives both in the past and in the future:

> We can have but one country, and even yet
> Thou'rt mine – my bones shall be within thy breast
> My soul within thy language, which once set
> With our old Roman sway in the wide West;
> But I will make another tongue arise
> As lofty and more sweet, in which express'd
> The hero's ardour, or the lover's sighs,
> Shall find alike such sounds for every theme
> That every word, as brilliant as the skies,
> Shall realise a poet's proudest dream,
> And make thee Europe's nightingale of song.

But there is a darker side to all this. Byron, in his Dantesque pose, is all too conscious of the difficulties, of the ways in which language can lose its hold on the truth, as political concerns outweigh the poetical:

> how many a phrase
> Sublime shall lavish'd be on some small prince
> In all the prodigality of praise!
> And language, eloquently false, evince
> The harlotry of genius, which, like beauty,
> Too oft forgets its own self-reverence,
> And looks on prostitution as a duty.

How distressed must Byron have been had he known of Hazlitt's jibe: 'The Noble Lord is almost the only writer who has prostituted his talents in this way ... Our enthusiasm for genius or virtue is thus turned into a jest by the very person who has kindled it, and who thus fatally quenches the sparks of both.'[19] Once Byron has reached this point in his poem, he moves to the possibility, canvassed both by

Wordsworth and Clare, that the best poets might be those who have never written anything: only by preserving their silence can they keep their integrity. He resorts to that Promethean image that is to form such an ambiguous and yet central part of the structure of *Don Juan*: poetry, quite suddenly, seems to offer little solace.

> Many are poets who have never penn'd
> Their inspiration and perchance the best:
> They felt, and loved, and died, but would not lend
> Their thoughts to meaner beings; they compress'd
> The gods within them, and rejoin'd the stars
> Unlaurell'd upon earth, but far more bless'd
> Than those who are degraded by the jars
> Of passion, and their frailties link'd to fame,
> Conquerors of high renown, but full of scars.
> Many are poets but without the name,
> For what is poesy but to create
> From overfeeling good or ill; and aim
> At an external life beyond our fate,
> And be the new Prometheus of new men,
> Bestowing fire from heaven, and then, too late,
> Finding the pleasure given repaid with pain.
>
> ... the kindled marble's bust may wear
> More poesy upon its speaking brow
> Than aught less than the Homeric page may bear.

In another apparently Wordsworthian echo, he declares that 'Despair and Genius are too oft connected'. Other forms of art, such as sculpture or painting, seem preferable to poetry because, as Keats realises, they get beyond the ambiguity of words. Byron appears to be celebrating the *image* of Dante the artist, culminating, as had Coleridge in his poem to Chatterton, with the 'Prophet in his tomb.' The poet has become voiceless. The silent emblems at the end of each of these poems recall Byron's other emblematic moments in his major poems. Byron, the great talker in verse, recognises the virtue and the necessity of silence. But there is also fear: after all, the voiceless poet is a contradiction in terms. This fear had found expression in the two dream poems of 1816.

The psychological interest of 'The Dream' derives from the turmoil of the domestic circumstances in which it is written. The dream recounted in the body of the poem has its autobiographical import, but that is less compelling than his exploration of the complexities of the dreamworld, the possible truths contained in it, and the relationship between such dreams and the world of the poet. Byron touches immediately on the dual nature of our existence (incidentally picking up a hint in *Lara*, and anticipating parts of *Don Juan*):

> Our life is two-fold: Sleep hath its own world,
> A boundary between the things misnamed
> Death and existence: Sleep hath its own world,
> And a wide realm of wild reality.

But the precise nature of that 'wild reality' is itself double-natured, in that dreams 'divide our being' because of their ability to weigh upon us even as they lighten life's burden; they speak for present, past and future, and they have power, 'The tyranny of pleasure and of pain.' Dreams have a hold upon us, to the extent of altering what we are: 'they become / A portion of ourselves as of our time'; 'They make us what we were not.' Such power is indeed awesome. Byron is not interested so much in the equation of dream with poetic inspiration (as is Keats), as with the questions that dreams raise about consciousness, and therefore about identity: 'What are they? / Creations of the mind?' On a narrative level, the dream's ambiguities are an extension of what Byron explores in *The Giaour, Lara,* and *The Corsair*, where experiences are left suspended and mysterious. The power of the relationship between Lara and Kaled, for example, lies in its wordless, whispered appeal, so that it remains a mystery sealed forever from our prying ears and eyes (rather like Shelley's *Julian and Maddalo*); the same could be said of *The Giaour,* whose very fragmentariness seems to be an image of a dreamworld without temporal logic. But Byron does not go as far in these narrative poems as he does here to make the extended point about poetry.

In the third section of 'The Dream' there is a description of the doomed Boy in love (clearly to a large extent a self-portrait): he is a poetic figure.

> he was alone,
> And pale, and pacing to and fro: anon
> He sate him down, and seized a pen, and traced
> Words which I could not guess of; then he lean'd
> His bow'd head on his hands, and shook as 'twere
> With a convulsion – then arose again,

And with his teeth and quivering hands did tear
What he had written.

The 'Lady of his love' enters, and he takes her hand. Once again Byron uses the verb 'trace', which seems to have distinctive connotations for him:

a moment o'er his face
A tablet of unutterable thoughts
Was traced, and then it faded, as it came.

These lines are repeated in the sixth section of the poem, where he marries another; the poet cannot speak, and the world revolves around him with a sort of giddy madness, similar to that in *Manfred*. The Lady too sinks into a frenzy: 'her thoughts / Were combinations of disjointed things'. The poet's vision parallels hers, in that his misery mirrors her madness, and his only reward is to read 'the book of Night', to hear 'the voice from the deep abyss reveal'd / A marvel and a secret'. He not only confronts a repeated sense of absence and emptiness, he becomes 'a mark / For blight and desolation'. The poet has become a Cain-like figure.

If there can be any doubt about the plight of such a figure, then 'Darkness' spells it out for us. Like Clare's 'Dream', 'Darkness' is an apocalyptic poem about the end of the world, about the way in which nothing has any value anymore, as all the customary meanings have been lost. This is the world of 'The Ancient Mariner', where 'Ships sailorless lay rotting on the sea, / And their masts fell down piecemeal: as they dropp'd / They slept on the abyss without a surge.' The desolation of the first poem has been taken to its logical conclusion: not only are there no words for things, but the natural order is inverted. The nightmare world of *The Prisoner of Chillon* is expressed here in terms of a return to the original chaos:

The world was void,
The populous and the powerful was a lump,
Seasonless, herbless, treeless, manless, lifeless,
A lump of death – a chaos of hard clay.

Clare's 'The Dream', first published in 1822 in the *London Magazine*, plumbs similar depths. It is fascinating to see him engaging with such a world, one with which we do not normally associate him: it is only retrospectively, from the vantage point of the asylum poems, that we can see how integral this world is to his vision.

> While earth in motion like a troubld sea
> Opend in gulphs of dread imensity
> Amid the wild confusions of despair
> & buried deep the howling & the prayer
> Of countless multitudes then closd – and then
> Opend & swallowd multitudes agen
>
> Stars drunk with terror staggerd from the heaven
> & worlds on worlds like wrecks in storms were driven
> & the pale moon hung fluttering on the sight
> As startld bird whose wings are stretchd for flight …
>
> Black night resumd its uncreated vest
> & chaos came agen but not its rest
> The melting glooms that spread perpetual stains
> Kept wirring still in endless hurricanes
> & tearing noises like a troubld sea
> Broke up that silence that no more woud be
> The reeling earth sunk loosend from its stay
> & natures wrecks all felt their last decay …
>
> That soul of fire, like to its souls entombd
> That still consumes & never is consumd
> Seemd nigh at hand – were oft the sulphry damps
> Oerawd that light as glimmers dying lamps
> Spreading a horrid gloom from side to side
> A twilight scene of horrors half descryd.

'The Nightmare' is in some ways even more unsettling, for it contains a vision of his beloved Mary. But she deserts him, leaving him desolate: the source of his inspiration is the cause of his everlasting woe. Clare seems already to have found the voice that we know from his terrible asylum poems, in which the world is turned upside down.

> The gathering crowds that seemd to make one spot
> I seemd to know some & then knew them not
> Some more familiar seemd I turnd agen
> & they were strange & left a lonly pain
> & other eyes on my enquirys came
> & seemd they knew me but to feel the same

> As birds seek nests which idle boys have got
> They sought what had been & they found it not
> What memorys shadow dimly might display
> Friends loves & kin – found none and turnd away.

The apparition of Mary is heart-breaking:

> She seemd at first as living beauty seems
> Then changd more lovly in the shade of dreams
> Then faded dim confusd & hurrying bye
> Like memory wearing into vacancy.

What is so disturbing about these poems, purely from a biographical point of view, is that Clare's nightmare is to come true: he finds himself in an asylum without friends or family, without Mary, left alone as the 'self-consumer' of his woes. What Hazlitt says of Byron has a dreadful application for Clare: 'his verse glows like a flame, consuming everything in its way.'[20] Clare's verse consumes himself.

In the poems that Byron writes between 1816 and 1819, he insists on returning to one of the central problems not just for himself, but for the Romantic poets in general: the value of the poetic experience is questioned, as the protracted dream becomes an apocalyptic nightmare, and words themselves become images, in their inversions, of the madness of poetic vision; become, in fact, instruments of torture. Byron is perhaps more honest than most of his contemporaries in his exploration of this state of mind and its consequences for the poet. The combination of bewilderment, revulsion and respect from so many of his reviewers is some indication of what he achieves. That a poet such as Clare, himself obsessed with the difficulties of self-identity and self-expression, should follow much the same path as Byron is an index of both poets' centrality to the Romantic debate on the nature and value of poetry. Both had good cause to question their existence, as individuals and as poets. Clare's most famous poem faces squarely the absurdity of his own existence; 'I am; yet what I am none cares or knows.' Byron is equally courageous when he admits: 'If I had to live over again – I do not know what I would change in my life – unless it were *for – not to have lived at all.*'[21]

Postscript

> I have done nothing in the Literary way – want of funds, of introductions, of speech and address, of worldly knowledge & dexterity – of (last but not least) *brains*, has kept me & will keep me, a *poor* author – in faculties, appearance, & life. I am the living personification of those ridiculous characters which people the works of the novelist & satyrist, those ludicrous yet melancholy pictures of literary obscurity which you have so often contemplated with an alternate inclination to pity, laughter & contempt. 'Tell it not in Gath', I have found out a secret here, which would astonish the echoes of the family mansion were it noised in their vicinity – I am not a *genius*. No; nor a poet, which is a lower step in the ladder of intellectuality ... Keep my secret ... as close as you would a sigh for the youth of your heart – lock it up, as you'd put his love-letter under your boddice – for if it once gets abroad into the atmosphere, tho I sing like a dying swan no one would hear me.[1]

That letter sums up well enough the poignancy of the poet George Darley, one of that band of pale ghosts that flit noiselessly through the pages of unopened books, keeping their secrets and their sorrows to themselves. Darley's gloomy prophecy was fulfilled, in that he ended up singing like a dying swan, and no one listened. It seems apposite that he should speak in the same breath of secrecy and poetry: anyone who thinks as obsessively as does Darley about secrecy ends up with all the isolation and insecurity that goes with it. He provides something of a suitable footnote, as it were, to this study of poets who so often seem to be writing themselves out of existence.

There are some important biographical facts. George Darley was born in Dublin in 1795, and, after graduating at Trinity College, left for London, to pursue a literary career. He reviewed for the *London Magazine*, he produced volumes of poetry, he wrote textbooks on mathematics and astronomy, he wrote plays, he travelled around Europe in his role as art-critic. He was in his own day, in spite of that letter, a considerable figure. John Taylor, the publisher and editor of the *London Magazine*, thought as highly of him as did Keats, Charles Lamb, and John Clare. Taylor's partner, James Hessey, wrote on Darley's death that 'he was one of the real worthies of the earth.' But these external details do not remove the fact of his solitariness, of his lack of self-confidence: he said, rather oddly, that his whole life had been an abstraction, and such must be his works.

In leaving Ireland, Darley acknowledged that he already had no roots.

> What should I do in Ireland? Why, degenerate into one of those nameless characters, one of those useless appendages to the living world, who walk about in a threadbare coat & slouched hat, with nothing but their insignificance to secure them from the attempts of malice & nothing but their silence to recommend them to the toleration of society ... The profession of an author is somewhat less disreputable than the empty vocation of a 'Walking Shadow' such as I have described – & this explains why I am in London, tho I fear my pursuit of literary reputation has been more anxious than successful.[2]

As he was to say in a letter four months later, when he was so desperate he contemplated a return to an Ireland he did not belong to: 'I can make nothing of Authorship, and really my poetical establishment is too slender to compensate for almost total solitude.'[3]

Darley's rootlessness is in many ways typical of his time. When he reached London in 1821 the major English Romantic poets had already impressed their stamp indelibly on the progress of literature. If Darley poured such scorn on Wordsworth, Keats, Byron and Shelley, it was because the poetic cupboard seemed bare: there was nothing left to pick up but a few scraps. Much of his work, ironically, consists of pale imitations of Keats and Shelley, especially in the narrative poems *Sylvia* and *Nepenthe*, in which he demonstrates how uneasy is his relationship to the major poets of his day. I have explored some of the problems these poets themselves faced in their search for what Byron calls, in another context, a 'fitting medium': those uncertain of their own abilities were in that much more of a quandary. This is one of the reasons for Clare's importance, that he cuts his way through these tangled thickets and finds his own true voice, even when he is as reliant on Byron as he is in some of his asylum poems. Darley cannot get beyond vitriol when he contemplates Byron:

> You are a man of genius, my Lord, and as such an honour to your country: – but, Sir, it were better for our fame that you never had been born amongst us ... A renegade from your country, you

> cultivate a continental distaste for the simple energy of her language. A denizen of another clime, you endeavour to corrupt our poetry with the effeminate manner of a voluptuous latitude ... I say that you, my Lord Lucifer, have not only gone astray yourself, but have led the whole train of poetical seraphim after you.[4]

While this is quite an interesting view of Byron's effect on the literature of the time, it has its personal repercussions for Darley, who seems quite unable to find a way out from under the prevailing influences, having, as he says, 'to pick up my food, like a city sparrow, from the kennels of highway literature'.

Leslie Brisman, in his book *Romantic Origins*, has shed some light on the problem, starting with the Preface to Rousseau's Second Discourse:[5]

> It is no light undertaking to separate what is original from what is artificial in the great nature of man, and to know correctly a state which no longer exists, which perhaps never existed, which probably never will exist, and about which it is nevertheless necessary to have precise notions in order to judge our present state correctly.

If we think at this point of some of Coleridge's agonisings over existence, that is to be expected. Brisman argues, quite persuasively, that 'this state which no longer exists' finds various manifestations in the Romantics' resort to medievalism, primitivism and accounts of creativity. It seems significant that Darley, in his Preface to *The Errors of Ecstasie* (in itself a revealing title), refers to Rousseau and the 'tendency of imaginative writers to embody their own history in their works'. The point is that it is 'mythic' rather than 'factual autobiography' which interest them all. This emphasis is particularly important for a writer so conscious of his own inferior relation to the great writers of past and present. The value of Brisman's chapter on Darley lies in the fact that he rescues the long narrative poems from their own encumbrances and demonstrates how they enact Darley's concern with a poetry that, for all its stumblings and falterings towards the sublime, recognises that this is not really the way for him. *Nepenthe*, like Keats's *Hyperion*, is left unfinished. Brisman argues that Darley's 'smallness' is a '*seminal* theme – a major aspect of the search for generative origins. Underlying Darley's best work is what we might call a myth of weakness'. A study of *Sylvia* shows Darley squaring up to Miltonic precedent, only to retreat, to 'bury his identity under the cloak of plurality' and in so doing to derive his 'originality from this posture of weakness.' To do this is of course to risk everything; the abyss can assume a complacent pleasantness when emptied of its fears and terrors. As Brisman puts it, 'explosive vacancy' (as in Wordsworth's 'Lucy' poems) gives way to 'insipidity'. *Nepenthe*, as it survives, consists of two Cantos, one on Aspiration, the second on Dejection: a third was to settle for happiness with our lot on this earth. As it stands, then, the poem offers us Romantic yearnings and disappointments. The poet can seem like a child, fresh and new:

> Light! for the ardour of the clime
> Made rare my spirit, that sublime
> Bore me as buoyant as young Time
> Over the green Earth's grassy prime,
> Ere his slouch'd wing caught up her slime;
> And sprang I not from clay and crime,
> Had from those humming beds of thyme
> Lifted me near the starry chime
> To learn an empyrean rhyme.

But against that (none too happily expressed, it has to be admitted) is the struggle in Canto II between Antiquity, 'Strong Son of Chaos', and the unprotected poet in his assumed and necessary innocence: the poet settles for an 'escape from greatness', as the final lines of the poem make all too clear:

> Alas! why leave I not this toil
> Thro' stranger lands, for mine own soil?
> Far from ambition's worthless coil,
> From all this wide world's wearying moil, -
> Why leave I not this busy broil,
> For mine own clime, for mine own soil,
> My calm, dear, humble, native soil!
> There to lay me down at peace
> In my own first nothingness?

Brisman's comment on this has repercussions beyond Darley: we might remember that Byron in *Childe Harold's Pilgrimage* looks into the abyss, and has, too, to confront the problem of limitations and definitions. So too, as we have seen, does John Clare. 'Spiritually as well as physically, the poet's "first nothingness" is his "original" state, from which his buoyancy carries him as far as it will and toward which his new sense of limitation draws him home again.'

In his lyrics, Darley succeeds in finding a distinctive voice. Rather like Beddoes and Hood, he reworks the Gothic gloom of the age into something personal. 'The Mermaidens' Vesper-hymn', with slight echoes of Keats and Shelley, takes us into the strange underwater world where Darley seems at home:

> Troop home to silent grots and caves!
> Troop home, and mimic as you go
> The mournful winding of the waves
> Which to their dark abysses flow!
>
> At this sweet hour, all things beside
> In amorous pairs to covert creep;
> The swans that brush the evening tide
> Homeward in snowy couples keep.
>
> In his green den the murmuring seal
> Close by his sleek companion lies;
> While singly we to bedward steal
> And close in fruitless sleep our eyes.
>
> In bowers of love men take their rest,
> In loveless bowers we sigh alone,
> With bosom-friends are others blest, –
> But we have none! but we have none!
>
> After brief joys, so heaven dooms!
> Ta'en out in our tumultuous caves,
> With men; – we sleep in gelid rooms,
> They in their graves! they in their graves!

Whatever the embarrassments of this poem, the point to make here is that, far from being a poem about Romantic fountains upspringing, it is the reverse – a poem about a return to the deep, to nothingness. Two very different analogues come to mind: Wordsworth, whose *Prelude* is in many of its most powerful moments to do with drowning, with the poet caught unawares as the waters of the deep thunder over him; and Byron, both in *Don Juan*, where the shipwreck serves more than merely a narrative purpose, and *Childe Harold's Pilgrimage*, where he explores with his cumulative images of sea, river and lake the notion of gazing into, and also sinking into, the abyss, what Clare calls in 'I Am' the 'nothingness of scorn and noise', the 'vast shipwreck of my life's esteems.' Darley has a poem in *The Labours of Idleness* which provides a comment on that 'Syren Song': it is presented as 'Her own Epitaph'.

> Here in a little cave,
> the prettiest nook of this most grassy vale,
> all amid lilies pale,
> that turn
> their heads into my little vault and mourn –
> Stranger! I have made my grave ...
>
> Fresh is my mossy bed:
> the frequent pity of the rock falls here,
> a sweet, cold, silent tear!
> I've heard,
> sometimes, a wild and melancholy bird
> warble at my grave-head.
>
> Read this small tablet o'er,
> that holds mine epitaph on its cheek of pearl:
> 'Here lies a simple girl,
> who died,
> like a pale flower nipt in its sweet spring-tide,
> ere it had bloomed.' – No more!

This is much more reminiscent of the complexities of Wordsworth's epitaphic poems, with their embrace of a silence which mocks the poet's efforts. Darley seems compelled to write poems of this sort, to transform his personal agonies into song that is at one remove from himself. His most famous lyric says much about the problems of the isolated poet in an unlistening world:

> Wherefore, unlaurelled Boy!
> Whom the contemptuous Muse will not inspire,
> With a sad kind of joy,
> Still sing'st thou to thy solitary lyre?
>
> The melancholy winds
> Pour through unnumber'd reeds their idle woes:
> And every Naiad finds
> A stream to weep her sorrow as it flows.
>
> Her sighs unto the air
> The wood-maid's native oak doth broadly tell:

And Echo's fond despair
Intelligible rocks re-syllable.

Wherefore then should not I,
Albeit no haughty Muse my breast inspire
Fated of grief to die,
Impart it to a solitary lyre?

The lyre, alas, is not a reliable source of comfort, as another poem concludes:

in the desert hours,
Lyrist of thy visions! all my woes repeating,
With my tears for jewels do I fill the flowers,
While the stars are fleeting,
Stars are fleeting!

Thou wilt doubt the tale:
Wilt not still believe my words: Thy harp bear token! –
See! Its very bosom-strings with this deep wail, –
All – like mine – are broken!
Mine are broken!

('Listen to the Lyre')

The repetition to which Wordsworth had had recourse is for Darley a reinforcement of his loss.

The solitary poet is, as so often for Romantic writers, likened to a bird. In 'The Dove's Loneliness' there are echoes of Keats and Coleridge, but with an added sense of futility:

Break not my loneliness, O Wanderer!
There's nothing sweet but Melancholy, here. –
'Mid these dim walks and grassy wynds are seen
No gaudy flowers, undarkening the green:
No wanton bird chirrups from tree to tree,
Not a disturber of the woods but me!
Scarce in a summer doth a wild bee come
To wake my sylvan echo with his hum;
But for my weeping lullaby I have
The everlasting cadence of the wave
That falls in little breakers on the shore,
And rather seems to strive to roar – than roar;

Light Zephyr, too, spreads out his silver wings
On each green leaf, and in a whisper sings
His love to every blossom in her ear,
Too low, too soft, too sweet, for me to hear!
The soul of Peace breathes a wide calm around,
And hallows for her shrine this sacred spot of ground.

All this is more than mere posturing. Darley's letters are full of a remarkably candid awareness of his limitations, and of the potential absurdities of some of his attitudes. In a letter he writes to Richard Milnes in 1834, when on his travels across Europe he indulges in some typical self-deflation:

> My life is in its current such a canal, that an account of it would be as wearisome to you as Dutch travelling ... I am merely rotting myself to death on this sluggish ooze, longing for the last Great Fall but dreading that it will not suffocate the spirit as well as crush the body ... How am I rambling? – rambling, rambling, yet never leaving the one centre, myself. This is one of the beautiful results deriving from a life of solitude so recommended by philosophers – we become profound egotists – each the centre, & the circumference too, of his own narrow circle.[6]

As he puts it in *Errors of Ecstasie*, 'How deep this total falling off from life!' It is no surprise to find him, later in the same poem, declaring in all honesty:

I seem like one lost in a deep blue sea,
Down, down beneath the billows many a mile,
Where nought of their loud eloquence is heard,
Save a dead murmur of the rushing waves
Fleeting above, more silent than no sound.
Over my head, as high as to the moon,
The tall, insuperable waters rise,
Pure and translucent; through whose total depth
The imminent stars shoot unrefracted rays,
And whiten all the bottom of the flood.
The sea-bed hath a scenery of its own,
And nought less wondrous than the realms of air:
Hills, dells, rocks, groves, sea-flow'rs, and sedgy caves,
In crystal armour lock'd – scatter'd around!

> Here, like a mortal tenant of the sea,
> Or fabulous merman, hermit of the wave,
> I stand, the sad surveyor of the scene,
> Alone amid the deserts of the deep.

Darley is less enamoured than his contemporaries of the imagination, if only because it has been too much like a will-o'-the-wisp for him. In a letter to a young relative, late in his life, he writes:

> I quite agree with you that [the imagination], if it soar beyond bounds, leaves the mind in clouds, or brings it back to earth mystified. O dear little wretch, how have I metaphysicked you to death – forgive me for having killed you this once, & I'll never do it again if I can help it![7]

To write is not only to die, it is to be the cause of the reader's death. This is the logical extension of what other Romantic poets had suggested. For Darley it is a reflection of his personal need to hide away, in the knowledge that he can never inspire love:

> I never kept much of any person's society without in the end feeling and knowing myself far less liked than when I entered it first. I must bury myself alive to be loved at all – this was the reason I left you so soon, that I might *secure* whatever affection you had towards me.[8]

This most terrible truth helps to explain all those poems in which he buries himself, in an obviously hopeless effort to survive. In his role as a forlorn and ultimately forgotten figure, Darley reminds us of the difficulties of a literary life that never quite consolidates itself. He is an exemplum of the strains of the professional writer in the early decades of the nineteenth century. But he is also a reminder of song's tenuousness, of that very fragility of the Muse that has been the subject of this book. In a sonnet called appropriately 'Departing Music', he captures that sense of infinite loss. It can stand as his most poignant epitaph, and, in turn, as a fitting comment on those poets from under whose shadow he felt he could not escape. They too were only too conscious of poetry's tendency to undermine and vitiate, to desert them, to leave them alone with their shrivelled selves.

Its sweetness fell away
Into the calm of Night, like the last wave
That, as the westling wind blows smoothly o'er,
Spreads wide and wider, – till it lose itself
Upon the heaveless bosom of the sea.

I listened – it was gone! And yet methought
Its echoes, by the ether still undrowned,
Made some far ocean-music in mine ear:
But no! – 'twas Memory, so fond to raise
Vain semblance of joys now sepulchred
In the great gloomy Past! the gorge of Time! –
Then came one sound, one lost, forgotten sound,
That vanished by me, as a midnight bird
Fleeting upon its dark wing fast away!

Notes

Unless otherwise indicated, place of publication is London.

Chapter 1 Lyrical Ballads: 'The burden of the mystery'

In this chapter I have used the Oxford Authors edition of Wordsworth, ed. Stephen Gill (Oxford, 1984).

1. See especially Thomas MacFarland, *Romanticism and the Forms of Ruin* (Princeton, 1981).
2. Charles Burney in the *Monthly Review*, xxix (June 1799); Robert Southey in the *Critical Review*, xxiv (October 1798).
3. 'Mr Wordsworth', in *The Spirit of the Age* (1825).
4. See, amongst other books, Olivia Smith, *The Politics of Language, 1791–1819* (Oxford, 1984), which addresses the theories rather than the poetry.
5. See Richard Holmes, *Coleridge: Early Visions* (1989), and Mark Storey, *Robert Southey: A Life* (Oxford, 1997).
6. See John Jordan, *Why the Lyrical Ballads?* (Berkeley, Los Angeles and London, 1976).
7. See Coleridge and Southey, *The Fall of Robespierre* (Cambridge, 1794).
8. See D.D. Devlin, *Wordsworth and the Poetry of Epitaphs* (1980), p. 65.
9. Wordsworth, *Prose Works*, ed. W.J.B. Owen and Jane Worthington Smyser, 3 vols (Oxford, 1974), ii. 85. See Frances Ferguson, *Wordsworth: Language as Counter-Spirit* (New Haven and London, 1977).
10. See E.P. Thompson, *Witness against the Beast* (Cambridge, 1993).
11. See Mark Storey, *Poetry and Humour from Cowper to Clough* (1979).
12. D.D. Devlin is particularly useful here: see n. 8 above.
13. See Marjorie Levinson, *Wordsworth's Great Period Poems* (Cambridge, 1986).
14. See Stephen Gill, *William Wordsworth: A Life* (Oxford, 1989).
15. Keats to John Hamilton Reynolds, 3 May 1818.
16. John Stuart Mill, 'What is Poetry?', *Monthly Repository*, January 1833, in *Early Essays*, ed. J.M.W. Gibbs (1897), 201–14.

Chapter 2 Coleridge: 'The self-consuming breast'

In this chapter I have used the Oxford Authors edition of Coleridge, ed. H.J. Jackson (Oxford, 1985), and Coleridge, *Complete Poetical Works*, ed. E.H. Coleridge, 2 vols (Oxford, 1912).

1. Patrick Parrinder, *Authors and Authority* (rev. edn. 1991), p.77.
2. 'Mr Coleridge', in *The Spirit of the Age* (1825).
3. See *Complete Poetical Works* for the details.
4. Horace's 'sermoni propriora' [fitter for discourse] is also used as an epigraph for 'Reflections on Having Left a Place of Retirement'.

5. Max Schulz, *The Poetic Voices of Coleridge* (Detroit, 1963).
6. See Tim Chilcott, *A Publisher and His Circle* (1972).
7. See Paul Hamilton, *Coleridge's Poetics* (Oxford, 1983).
8. Hazlitt, 'My First Acquaintance with Poets', *The Liberal*, 1823.
9. See D.D. Devlin, *Wordsworth and the Poetry of Epitaphs* (1980), p. 22.
10. Coleridge to Thelwall, 31 December 1796, in Oxford Authors edition.
11. Coleridge to Godwin, 25 March 1801, in Oxford Authors edition.
12. Oxford Authors edition, p. 552.
13. See Devlin, *Poetry of Epitaphs*, p. 53.
14. Hazlitt, 'My First Acquaintance with Poets', 1823.
15. See Kelvin Everest, *Coleridge's Secret Ministry* (Sussex, 1979).

Chapter 3 *The Prelude*: 'The wavering balance of my mind'

In this chapter I have used the Penguin edition of the four texts of *The Prelude*, ed. Jonathan Wordsworth (Harmondsworth, 1995).

1. Stephen Gill, *William Wordsworth: A Life* (Oxford, 1989).
2. Hazlitt, 'Mr Wordsworth', *The Spirit of the Age* (1825).
3. See Stephen Gill, *Wordsworth and the Victorians* (Oxford, 1998).
4. See Mark Storey, *Poetry and Humour from Cowper to Clough* (1979).
5. See Herbert Lindenberger, *On Wordsworth's Prelude* (Princeton, 1963).
6. Stuart Curran, *Poetic Form and British Romantic Poetry* (Oxford, 1986).
7. De Quincey, *Recollections of the Lakes and the Lake Poets*, ed. David Wright (Harmondsworth, 1970).
8. See Seamus Heaney on the idea of verse as 'turning' in *Preoccupations* (1980).
9. Heaney's poem 'Antaeus' is instructive here.
10. See Christopher Ricks, 'Wordsworth: "A Pure Organic Pleasure from the Lines"', in *William Wordsworth: A Critical Anthology*, ed. Graham McMaster (Harmondsworth, 1972), pp. 505–34.
11. On this passage, see Cynthia Chase, 'The Ring of Gyges and the Coat of Darkness: Reading Rousseau with Wordsworth', in *Romanticism and Language*, ed. Arden Reed (1984), pp. 50–85.
12. See Susan Wolfson, *Formal Charges: The Shaping of Poetry in British Romanticism* (Stanford, 1997); John Hollander, *Visions and Resonances* (New York, 1975).
13. See especially ch. 4 of Wolfson's book, cited in n. 12 above.
14. Zachary Leader, *Revision and Romantic Authorship* (Oxford, 1996).
15. See David Simpson, *Irony and Authority in Romantic Poetry* (1979). I am conscious of a considerable debt to this book.
16. Jonathan Wordsworth's note to *The Prelude,* VI.620–2, in the Penguin edition.

Chapter 4 Keats and Shelley: 'The dark idolatry of self'

In this chapter I have used, for Keats, *The Poems of John Keats*, ed. Miriam Allott (1970) and, for Shelley, *The Complete Poetical Works*, ed. Thomas Hutchinson (Oxford, 1923).

1. Keats to Shelley, 16 August 1820.
2. Keats to Richard Woodhouse, 27 October 1818.
3. F.R. Leavis, *Revaluation* (1936).
4. Shelley's letter to Godwin is quoted by Mary Shelley in her note to the poem.
5. For Arnold on 'adequacy', see 'On the Modern Element in Literature', 1857.
6. See Timothy Webb, *Shelley: A Voice Not Understood* (Manchester, 1977).
7. Keats to Benjamin Bailey, 22 November 1817.
8. Charles Brown is quoted by Miriam Allott in her edition.
9. For Miriam Allott's gloss, see her note to I.577.
10. See Arnold's Preface to his first edition of *Poems* (1853).

Chapter 5 Clare: 'This sad non-identity'

In this chapter I have used the Oxford Authors edition of Clare, ed. Eric Robinson and David Powell (Oxford, 1984), and, where necessary, the same editors' Oxford English Texts Edition (Oxford, 1984–). For Clare's letters I have used my own edition (Oxford, 1985).

1. Clare to J.A. Hessey, 2 April 1820.
2. Clare to Allan Cunningham, ?April 1828.
3. Clare to John Taylor, 20 May 1820.
4. See Johanne Clare, *John Clare and the Bounds of Circumstance* (Kingston and Montreal, 1987).
5. For the reception, see *Clare: The Critical Heritage*, ed. Mark Storey (1973).
6. See R.K.R. Thornton, 'The Nature of *The Parish*', *John Clare Society Journal*, 5 (July 1986), 30–35.
7. Taylor to Clare, 1 January 1821, British Library MS. Egerton, 2245, fos. 267–8.
8. See Clare to William Hone, 23 June 1825.
9. See Howard Mills (ed.), *George Crabbe, Tales 1812* (Cambridge, 1967), p. xxxiv.
10. See *The Prelude*, I.46.
11. Clare to Taylor, October 1831.
12. *John Clare by Himself*, ed. Eric Robinson and David Powell (Ashington and Manchester, 1996), p.271.
13. See Clare to Mary Howitt, ?1848–49.
14. Harold Bloom,*The Visionary Company* (Ithaca, 1962).
15. Not Mary Joyce, as I thought in 1974: *The Poetry of John Clare: A Critical Introduction*, p. 195.

Chapter 6 Byron and Clare: 'An indigestion of the mind'

In this chapter I have used the Oxford Authors edition of Byron, ed. Jerome McGann (Oxford and New York, 1986).

1. *Byron's Letters and Journals*, ed. Leslie Marchand, V (1976), p. 265.
2. See Peter Vassallo, *Byron: The Italian Literary Influence* (1984).
3. Hazlitt, 'Lord Byron', *The Spirit of the Age* (1825).

4. Quoted in *Byron: The Critical Heritage*, ed. Andrew Rutherford (1970), pp.143–4.
5. Hazlitt, 'Lord Byron'.
6. *Byron: The Critical Heritage*, pp. 147–54.
7. See Lynne Pearce, 'John Clare and Mikhail Bakhtin: The Dialogic Imagination', doctoral thesis, University of Birmingham, 1987.
8. *John Clare by Himself*, ed. Eric Robinson and David Powell (Ashington and Manchester, 1996), pp. 156–7.
9. See J.W. Tibble and Anne Tibble (eds.), *The Prose of John Clare* (1951), pp. 206–10.
10. *Clare: The Critical Heritage*, ed. Mark Storey (1973), p. 248.
11. See *The Later Poems of John Clare*, ed. Eric Robinson and Geoffrey Summerfield (Manchester, 1964), p. 3.
12. See W.W. Robson, 'Byron and Sincerity', in M.H. Abrams (ed.), *English Romantic Poets* (London, Oxford and New York, 1975), pp. 275–302.
13. *New Statesman*, 19 June 1964, p. 964.
14. *Letters and Journals* ed. R.E. Prothero, II (1904), p. 351.
15. I have discussed Byron's narrative poems in *Byron and the Eye of Appetite* (1986).
16. *The Natural History Prose Writings of John Clare*, ed. Margaret Grainger (Oxford, 1983), p. 192.
17. Hazlitt, 'Lord Byron'.
18. Ibid.
19. Ibid.
20. Ibid.
21. *Detached Thoughts*, no. 95, quoted in the Oxford Authors edition, p. 1015.

Postscript

I have used Claude Colleer Abbott, *The Life and Letters of George Darley* (1928), and *Selected Poems of George Darley*, ed. Anne Ridler (1979).

1. *Life and Letters*,p. 20.
2. Ibid. 18.
3. Ibid. 26.
4. Ibid. 43–4.
5. Leslie Brisman, 'George Darley: Buoyant as Young Time', in *Romantic Origins* (Ithaca and London, 1978).
6. *Life and Letters*, pp.115-16; see also David Simpson, *Irony and Authority in Romantic Poetry* (1979).
7. *Life and Letters*, pp. 257–8.
8. Ibid. 262.

Index